Once Upon a Time
in Los Angeles

EARL ROGERS
Courtesy, Los Angeles Public Library

Once Upon a Time in Los Angeles

The Trials of EARL ROGERS

by
Michael Lance Trope

THE ARTHUR H. CLARK COMPANY
Spokane, Washington
2001

Library of Congress Catalog Card Number 2001017355
ISBN-0-87062-305-2

Library of Congress Cataloging-in-Publication Data
Trope, Michael Lance.
Once upon a time in Los Angeles: the trials of Earl Rogers / by
Michael Lance Trope.
    p. cm.
Includes index.
ISBN 0-87062-305-2 (alk. paper)
    1. Rogers, Earl, 1870-1922 2. Lawyers—California—Los Angeles—
Biography. I. Title.

KF373.R57 T76 2001
340'.092—dc21
[B]
                                                        2001017355

For my Grandmother Jane Trope,
for my parents,
and my daughters
Cristina, Alana and Felicia.

Contents

Illustrations

Introduction

Earl Andrus Rogers was born on November 18, 1869, in upstate New York, in the rustic town of Perry. The son of a Methodist minister and preacher who expected and prepared him to follow in his footsteps, Earl would grow up, however, to dislike the church. He would eventually discover that he did have the power to mesmerize an audience, to hold them in rapt attention, hanging on his every word. Indeed, one day he would speak in crowded rooms, but it wouldn't be in pews that his audience would clamor for seats; it would be in a courtroom. And Earl's discourse would not endeavor to save souls. Judgment day before the Lord would come for his clients some other day. If he succeeded, that day would come later and not sooner. Earl Rogers would save many a man from an appointment with the executioner.

Earl's father, Lowell Rogers, was an evangelist with the heart of an adventurer who traveled west to spread the good word, first in Oregon and northern California in the 1880s. Coming to southern California, the minister was soon carried away by the then current fad of real estate speculation. He invested in a development in Riverside County, near Colton, and permanently planted roots in the Southland, with his wife, his son, Earl, and Earl's two sisters.

Young Earl was taught music by his mother, and his knowledge and proficiency outshined most professional musicians. He was schooled at home, becoming fluent in Latin and Greek, along with several modern languages. Eventually he matriculated at Syracuse University, his father's alma mater.

Unfortunately, a downturn in his father's real estate holdings forced Earl to drop out of Syracuse before earning his degree.

His father didn't understand the nature of the water rights of land, and through the economic manipulation of these rights by shrewder men, bunko artists, he lost much of his real property holdings. Some would later surmise that Rogers took interest in the law because he wanted to help others from being taken advantage of in this way; unfortunately, his legal career would come too late to prevent his father from being fleeced out of his property.

Earl may have had to leave Syracuse before graduating, but he didn't quite leave with nothing to show for his time spent there. It was while a student at Syracuse that Earl found his first true love, Hazel Belle Green, whom he married in 1893 and took back to California. Together they would have four children; a daughter, Adela, born in 1894, and three sons, Bogart, Bryson and Thornwell. After he had achieved fame and fortune as a lawyer, his marriage grew stormy, as he and his wife frequently argued over his growing problem with alcohol. Belle would sue Earl for divorce in 1914. He would later get married to Edna Landers, whose premature death in 1919 brought on a deep depression and rapid decline in Earl. He died three years later in 1922.

Of his children it was first born Adela—named after his beloved mother—with whom he would have the closest relationship. His devotion to Adela, the apple of his eye, bordered on fanatical. It was Adela who would often accompany her father in the courtroom. He even brought Adela with him to the Los Angeles county jail to visit with Alfred Boyd when he was deciding whether or not to take on Boyd's murder case. When her parents were divorced, Adela, sharing a mutual dislike of her mother, would choose to live with her father, whom she idolized. When Adela was older she would be the one whom Earl's law partners would send to retrieve the errant

Adela Rogers St. Johns
"Courtesy of University
of Southern California, on
behalf of the USC Library
Department of Special
Collections."

Rogers. She would more than likely find her father at his favorite tavern, or at the madam Pearl Morton's parlor house, (the polite term for a brothel), bring Rogers to the Turkish baths to sober him up, get him into a newly pressed suit and deliver him to the courthouse.

Earl Rogers advised his daughter "a woman must be trained to earn a living for herself and her children, or she will be a slave." Adela Rogers St. Johns (her married name), took her father's advice, and went on to a distinguished career as a writer. Earl introduced Adela to newspaper publisher William Randolph Hearst, and she began an award-winning career in journalism, one of the first woman reporters.

She would go on to work for many of the Hearst syndicate of newspapers. Starting out as a cub reporter for the *San Fran-*

cisco Examiner when she was barely eighteen years old, Adela soon developed a very distinctive, emotional writing style. She was later assigned by Hearst to his new *Los Angeles Herald,* covering everything from the police beat to celebrity gossip, politics to sports, and many of the exciting events of her day, from the Lindbergh baby kidnapping, to the infamous Leopold and Loeb murder trial. Hearst, her employer and friend for many years, (she was one of his favorite reporters and a frequent guest at his fabled San Simeon castle, the "ranch"), billed her as "The World's Greatest Girl Reporter."

Adela was an amazing woman, well ahead of her time in terms of her ambitions, and lived a life as unusual, exciting and historic as many of the people she reported about. During the depression, she took to the streets with just a dime in her pocket, and wearing a dreary dress borrowed from MGM's costume department, to masquerade as an unemployed and homeless person. Using an alias to hide her well-known name, for weeks she sought jobs at the employment agencies, and sought aid from the city's organized charities, sleeping on park benches and in flea-bag hotels. She then wrote a sixteen-part expose of the city's cruel indifference to the plight of its poor after experiencing it firsthand. She was the very first female reporter allowed into the male bastion of the press box when she covered sporting events. Her many Hollywood friends whom she wrote about while covering celebrity news for *Photoplay* magazine called her "Mother Confessor of Hollywood." No doubt her father's tenacious ability to succeed in the face of outrageous odds rubbed off on the impressionable young Adela, leading her to many great achievements.

Adela also wrote fiction, scores of short stories published in many magazines, and novels, including *A Free Soul.* The lead character of Steven Ash, a talented, alcoholic attorney loosely based on her father, was portrayed by Lionel Barrymore in an Academy Award-winning performance, in the

1931 motion picture adapted from the novel. Adela would also have a successful career writing for Hollywood, completing thirteen screenplays. Gabrielle Dardley, indicted in January, 1914, for killing her lover, was represented during her murder trial by Earl Rogers, and inspired Adela's screenplay "The Red Kimono," produced in the late 1920s.

In 1970, Adela was awarded the Medal of Freedom by President Richard Nixon, (who had delivered her groceries as a boy in Whittier, California). She retired from newspaper work in 1948, but was lured out of retirement in 1976 at the age of 82 to cover the bank robbery trial of her old boss's grand-daughter, Patricia Hearst, for the Hearst Headline Service. Leaving behind two sons, a daughter, nine grand-children, nineteen great-grand-children, and eight great-great-grand-children, Adela Rogers St. Johns passed away in California in 1988 at the age of 94.

Adela's hugely successful career as a newspaper reporter was most likely inspired by her father's first vocation of newspaperman. Earl started out in San Diego, then wrote for one of the seven daily newspapers that flourished in Los Angeles in his day, before the competition of radio and television would thin their ranks. It was as a reporter that Rogers would first come into contact with the denizens of the court house in downtown Los Angeles, making friends with attorneys, police officers and judges. He was drawn into this world by the drama and excitement that he witnessed, as well as the respect, money and adulation that attorneys were afforded. He had a wife and children to support, and there was little money and a dim future for a newspaperman.

In 1893, Rogers started out in the office of Judge W.P. Gardiner, where he studied the law, like everything else he had set his mind to, with a vengeance. Making up for lost time, he lived night and day in the law library, devouring principles and decisions, capturing reams of information with his incredible memory. In that day and age it was not necessary to attend law school to become an attorney; one could become an apprentice to a lawyer in order to gain admittance to the bar. Rogers did just that, not setting his sights on just any lawyer, but perhaps the foremost lawyer in the State of California, and its greatest statesman, United States Senator Stephen M. White. With Earl's facile wit and easy charm, he won the highly coveted apprenticeship over many competitors with more impressive credentials. He would go on to become Senator White's favorite pupil. By the year 1897, when Earl Rogers was sworn into the California bar, he had come to emulate the Senator in many ways. He had made friends with the Senator's friends, had mastered many of the Senator's skills as a lawyer; and he had acquired the Senator's prodigious thirst for imbibing alcohol, which would one day bring his downfall. Perhaps the defining moment at the beginning of Rogers' brilliant career would be when he, at the age of 30, and his mentor, Senator White, would be pitted against each other on opposite sides of the courtroom in the murder trial of William Alford, accused of murdering Jay E. Hunter.

Los Angeles at the dawn of the 1900s was a far cry from its present incarnation. Virtually a provincial little town of a city when Earl Rogers first hung out his shingle to practice law, it was poised for a great many changes that would soon transform it. From its inception as a Spanish pueblo in 1781, Los Angeles was isolated for well over a century by the quirks of its geography. The city of L.A. was cut off from the rest of the United States by surrounding mountains and a desert. It would take the arrival of the Southern Pacific Railroad and the opening of the Panama Canal, in the late nineteenth and early twentieth century respectively, to open up the city to easy access from the rest of the country. These developments, as soon prophesied by men of vision, would bring Los Angeles through a metamorphosis into a major port city. Add to this the ingenuity of the Wright Brothers in Kittyhawk, and Los Angeles would no longer be condemned to isolation. Its balmy year-round climate lured farmers trying to escape the dust-bowl states during the depression, and film makers trying to get as far away as possible from Edison's patent-protecting thugs. With the growing popularity of the horseless carriage, as the automobile was first known, came another factor in the forces of progress that would shape Los Angeles into the sprawling megalopolis it is today; the entertainment capitol of the modern world, with its labyrinthine system of highways. Census records show that 50,000 people inhabited Los Angeles in the year 1890, shortly before Earl Rogers began his career. By the year 1930, only several years after his death, 1,200,000 people would call Los Angeles their home.

Before this transformation, the Los Angeles of the 1890s was the stomping ground of cattlemen and miners from Arizona, Nevada, and the California towns that bordered upon these states. Violence was not a newcomer to California, it predated the hordes of people that would later flock to L.A. Murder and suicides, reported in all their lurid, gruesome detail by the newspapers vying for circulation, were common occurrences. Usually the popular pastimes of gambling and prostitution were involved. However, there was no "underworld" comprised of the organized criminals and street gangs of the modern era.

The social pecking order had the proudest families of wealth and privilege at the upper echelons, including descendants of Spanish landed wealth who were the early settlers, and the many aristocratic Southerners who rode manifest destiny to "go West" as young men of adventure. Working down the social ladder one would come across the better-bred gamblers, the saloon-keeping politicians, right on down to the red-light district devotees of both sexes.

Prostitution was so widely entrenched and accepted a way of social life in early Los Angeles as to have its very own caste system. The well-heeled frequented the "parlor houses," so named for the finely appointed waiting-room parlors where clients would meet and mingle with their prospective professional paramours. Those with less disposable income would visit the "cribs," or row houses strung along Alemeda Street, with rooms barely wider than the front door.

Those at the top of the social hierarchy did not look down their noses at and crusade against vice. The pioneer spirit of the frontier engendered a "laissez faire," easy going attitude. The social stigma that today would, for example, be attached to being an ex-convict did not yet exist. In those care free, halcyon days, a candidate for chief of police actually came within one vote of winning the election, only to end up in the state penitentiary soon thereafter for a previous criminal transgression. One of Rogers' grateful clients was Charles Sebastian, who did win the election for chief of police in Los Angeles, and who would later win the mayoral race, after making his humble beginning in public life as a saloon keeper.

Politics were an open game, with no single, organized political entity having a strangle-hold on power. Los Angeles was devoid of the graft that would grip San Francisco's political machinery, and would provide Rogers with several pivotal cases that would bring him fame and fortune. Los Angelinos played the game of politics for the thrill of victory; being content, perhaps, to secure for a friend a job in the public sector. Bribery and kickbacks were not the standard, corrupt way of public life that they were in Los Angeles' neighbor to the north, San Francisco.

In these early days even the lowliest of the gamblers, called "tin homs," the pimps, and free agent hold-up men, were respectable in comparison to their modern counterparts, living as they did by their own code of honor and the pioneer spirit for risk taking. One must comprehend this "pioneer" spirit, which was so admired and which defined the city of Los Angeles, in order to understand the man behind the myth that was Earl Rogers.

Earl used a variety of courtroom antics to win his juries over. In Los Angeles, it seems, the sky was the limit. And Earl Rogers always aimed for that sky, not being grounded by the conventions of more timid men who came before him. Earl Rogers invented many of the tactics that have become common criminal law stratagem. He was a true pioneer, and his "frontier" was the legal system. Rogers was the first American lawyer to make use of the science of ballistics, and was at the cutting edge of medical forensic science as used in criminal defense. Indeed, he was more knowledgeable in the field of anatomy than many of the coroners he cross-examined, and was at one time a professor of medical jurisprudence and insanity in the old college of physicians and surgeons and he had a degree from the College of Osteopathic Physicians and Surgeons. He was one of the first attorneys to popularize the then innovative use of blackboards and charts in the courtroom, along with some more exotic props, (he would sometimes re-enact entire crime scenes in the courtroom), to get his point across to a jury. He became a Professor of Advocacy at the University of Southern California Law School. He amassed a truly extraordinary winning percentage, a statistic that will make or break a criminal attorney, handling seventy-seven important murder cases and losing only three!

Earl Rogers based all of his courtroom strategies upon the ultimate effect that they would make upon a jury. To this end, Rogers began with his own appearance. From very early on in his career, Rogers cultivated a public reputation for sartorial splendor. It is said that he had the most elaborate wardrobe, and the most expensive tailoring bill to match, in all of the city. In his own words, Rogers is reputed to have said, "true, the clothes do not make the man nor the woman, but they are the first thing you see." Mr. Rogers was quite aware that you do not get a second chance to make a first impression, and dressed, accordingly, in the height of the fashion of his day, believing that it was just good business to do so. At the Clarence Darrow bribery trial in 1912, one of his most glorious cases, he was called upon to defend the most noted attorney of his day. Earl Rogers appeared in "cutaway coat with braided edges, fawn waistcoat, spats, boutonniere, lavish cravat and bat-winged collar." Indeed, Rogers left no detail unattended to.

Rogers had another accouterment, his use of a lorgnette—a pair of eyeglasses with a short handle which at the time was used primarily by women. Rogers would use his lorgnette as a prop, with which he would emphasize for the jury his scrutiny of a piece of evidence or a witness, and perhaps get the jury to subconsciously question that evidence or witness all the more. The quintessential thespian, Rogers realized that the practice of law was, in part, the quest of an actor on a stage.

Earl Rogers' illustrious career followed the trajectory of a shooting star. He burst upon the scene from out of nowhere; and climbed to meteoric heights by improbably winning case after case, against magnificent odds. It is said that a star's life span is determined by its brilliance; the hotter a star burns, the sooner it burns out. And Earl Rogers was no exception. He would burn out at an early age, at a time in his life when other men are enjoying the material comforts bought by their hard-earned success.

Near the end of his life, his daughter, Adela, would bring her own father into a courtroom, in an attempt to have him declared *non compes mentes*, or without sound mind, in a futile attempt to save her father from himself. She would fail in this effort, not having the heart to follow through with this legal process. Earl Rogers would die a broken-down alcoholic, living in the squalor of the dingy New Broadway hotel. During the peak of his career, Earl Rogers earned over $100,000 per annum for a five or six year stretch, a king's ransom at the time. When Rogers defended Clarence Darrow in 1912, one could purchase a newly constructed home in Beverly Hills from the Los Angeles Development Company for less than $3,000. He spent it as quickly as he earned it. Earl Rogers would die penniless, having to borrow the money to pay for his last drink.

He was only fifty-two.

The following pages, however, tell the story of Earl Rogers when he was at the top of his game. As you read the chapters, try to imagine the Earl Rogers that stood before a jury, impeccably dressed in the height of fashion. As you read the cross-examinations of Earl Rogers while he was grilling witnesses, picture Earl's matinee-idol good looks as he would sneer scornfully at the poor fellow he was putting through the wringer. In your mind's eye, visualize Rogers as he would pull out his lorgnette, to peer "through its magnifying lenses, as if he (the witness) were some ridiculous insect." Imagine the audience packed to standing-room-only capacity, eager spectators spilling out into the hallways, hanging on his every word, as Rogers' mellifluous voice would carry throughout the courtroom with more emotion than an actor trained at the Royal Academy. This was a man who, during closing arguments, moved his audience from tears to laughter at will. Indeed, actors of his day would sit in his courtroom to learn a thing or two from his vocal delivery. This is the Earl Rogers who deserves to be remembered. This is the man who was larger than life, a legend in his own time, and the foremost criminal attorney in the West.

CHAPTER 1

The Case of the
Catalina Cardsharp

THE PARTICIPANTS

DEFENDANT:	Alfred Boyd
PROSECUTORS:	James Rives, D.A.
	C.C. McComas, A.D.A.
DEFENSE ATTORNEYS:	Earl Rogers; Chief Trial Counsel
	Oscar Lawler; Co-Counsel
	Luther Brown; Co-Counsel
CHARGE:	Murder

In 1891, the Banning family bought Catalina Island for several hundred thousand dollars; an astronomical sum at that time. The island became what was tantamount to the personal fiefdom of the Banning family. In the early 1900s gambling was illegal in California, but at the beautiful resort of Avalon, gambling was never interfered with. The island was operated by a set of rules established by the powerful Banning family. Frequent brass band concerts were held on the island in the Avalon Plaza. The punishment for speaking out loud during a concert was a yellow ticket from a Banning employee, dictating deportation from the island on the next boat leaving Avalon.

Not far from where the concerts took place stood Avalon's

swanky Metropole Hotel, where gambling was omnipresent. W.A. Yeager, a professional gambler also known as the Louisville Sport, was shot twice in the head and killed after a card game that had begun around midnight at the Metropole Hotel on August 12th, 1902. Alfred Boyd, a young man from Atlanta, was charged with the murder of the Louisville Sport.

Alfred Boyd was from prominent and wealthy Atlanta lineage and came to California with family money to start up a small business. Once in California he met and quickly became best friends with a fellow from the Northwest named Harry Johnson. Boyd and Johnson were both 20 years old at the time. The two men planned to open a cigar store in Los Angeles on Spring Street with the capital to be provided by Boyd. By at least one account, the cigar store was also most likely to be a front for a small gambling operation as Boyd was apparently a compulsive gambler.

Just prior to the planned opening of their business enterprise, the two took off for Catalina Island in search of women, wine and cards. Harry Johnson was to enter into a secret deal with the Louisville Sport. The deal was quite simple; Johnson would steer Boyd into a card game with the Sport at the Metropole Hotel; the Sport would fleece Boyd of all his money, and the Sport and Johnson would then divide the ill-gotten loot between them. A beautiful temptress also in complicity with the schemers enticed Boyd to the Metropole Hotel for drinks and kept him occupied while Johnson worked out the details of his deal with the Sport. A deal having been struck, Johnson then suggested that he and Boyd check out the card game action. The existence of this secret deal between Johnson and the Sport was something not known to Earl Rogers until it was sprung upon him by the prosecution at the time of trial; it was never testified to by Johnson at Boyd's preliminary hearing which took place on Catalina Island prior to the murder trial which was held in Los Angeles.

The card game began somewhere between 11:00 p.m. and midnight on the evening of August 12, 1902. By the wee hours of the morning (around 5:00 a.m.), a pile of five and ten dollar gold coins and a diamond stud that were the former property of Alfred Boyd were sitting on the green felt table in front of the Louisville Sport, who was stacking and counting his winnings. His stake completely lost in the card game, Boyd apparently asked the Louisville Sport for a loan of $50 against a family heirloom gold pocket watch that he pulled from his coat and was holding in his hand. According to Harry Johnson, the Sport looked at the gold watch held in Boyd's hand, told Boyd he wasn't interested, the watch wasn't worth "two bits," and that the card game was over. The Sport was right, for that was to be his last card game.

According to Johnson's initial account of what happened, after the Sport rejected his request for a loan on the watch, Boyd then drew out his revolver and shot the Louisville Sport twice, piercing the derby hat which he wore on his head. The body was still convulsing. Blood was streaming from the Sport's head onto the card table. At that point, Boyd pointed the muzzle of the gun directly at Johnson, smoke flowing from the barrel. A moment later he threw the gun under Johnson's chair. Johnson grabbed the gun and ran into the bar area of the hotel, yelling to bartender Jim Davin, "Oh my god he shot him!" "Oh my god he shot him!" Johnson handed the gun to a man named R.S.S. Knowles, who in turn handed the gun to a porter who was sweeping the barroom. The porter then gave the gun to John Davin, the barkeeper.

Boyd was arrested, and based upon Johnson's account of the events, he was subsequently charged with the murder of W.A. Yeager, a.k.a. the Louisville Sport. Fearful that their son would hang for the commission of a capital crime, Boyd's family sought the advice of their friend, the young but big-time corporate attorney, Oscar Lawler, who would in later years

Oscar Lawler
"Courtesy of University of
Southern California, on
behalf of the USC Library
Department of Special
Collections."

become the Assistant Attorney General of the United States. Lawler sought out and requested Earl Rogers to act as chief trial counsel in the defense of the murder case brought against Alfred Boyd.

Rogers and his eight-year-old daughter, Adela, went to the county jail so that Rogers could interview Boyd and determine if he wanted to take on his case. It was Adela's first visit to the county jail; a visit which was, according to the account in Adela's book, *"Final Verdict,"* (written when she was Adela Rogers St. Johns), *partly* the result of a domestic argument that had taken place earlier that evening between Earl and his wife. After the quarrel, Earl decided to take Adela with him to the jail while he would interview Boyd. Young Adela was convinced of Boyd's innocence and pleaded with her father that he defend Boyd. Be it the thrill of the fight, or his daughter's plea, Rogers agreed to defend young Boyd. Earl Rogers, who was only thirty-two years old at the time, took on a case that would become higher in profile than the Alford case; a case which would become an integral part of the development of his legend and reputation as the greatest criminal defense lawyer in the West.

An autopsy conducted by Drs. Claire Murphy and Edward Garret on August 14, 1902, confirmed that Yeager had been shot twice in the head. The first bullet entered just above Yeager's left eye and lodged above and behind the left ear. The second bullet entered the top of the head, three and one half inches above the root of Yeager's nose. There were extensive gun powder marks all over the upper part of Yeager's face. A preliminary hearing took place on Catalina Island and Alfred Boyd was held over for trial on the charge of murder. The District Attorney's office considered the Boyd case to be of great importance, and as a consequence the prosecution of Boyd was to be handled by the District Attorney himself, James Rives. Rives had a reputation as an attorney of solid legal training, tremendous experience, and was considered to be an excellent trial lawyer. However, it was Rives' flamboyant and colorful assistant, attorney C.C. McComas, who would handle most of the prosecution's work in the Boyd trial. McComas, Earl's adversary as the prosecutor in the Mootry murder trial and others, was known as a brilliant attorney who had a dominant courtroom demeanor. He wore his hair long over his collar, sported a drooping mustache, and was a tough, bullying prosecutor who chewed tobacco during trials. He was rarely known to miss the spittoon. It was the team of the technical and proficient District Attorney James Rives, and his cowboy assistant C.C. McComas, matched against Earl Rogers, which set the stage, and added to the buzz in the case of the People of the State of California vs. Alfred Boyd.

McComas told reporters just prior to trial that the prosecution had strong corroborative evidence and therefore the D.A.'s office was confident of securing Boyd's conviction. By all accounts it looked as though the prosecution had a virtual lock on obtaining Boyd's conviction for the murder of Yeager and that Boyd would wind up at the end of the hangman's noose. Reporter Harry Carr of the *Los Angeles Times* wrote that the District Attorney could hardly fail to obtain a conviction and death sentence. It was against this backdrop that jury selection took place. The jury was finally selected, and the showdown was set to begin on October 25, 1902. The courtroom was filled to capacity with the crowd flowing out into the hall; the atmosphere was "suffocatingly crowded." Young Boyd sat between Earl Rogers and his mother, who was present at every trial session. Over objections from the prosecution, the Court granted Rogers permission to re-enact the murder scene from the Metropole Hotel. In the space between the witness stand and the jury box stood the blood-stained green felt card table, Yeager's derby hat, and the blood-stained deck of cards.

The trial began with the prosecution putting on witnesses to lay foundation. The identification of the decedent's body, the location of the Metropole Hotel, the exact location where the Louisville Sport was found dead, were all testified to by various witnesses. The prosecution then called Harry Johnson to the witness stand. Johnson, tall and dapper, was wearing a new pressed blue suit. He had the outward appearance of everyone's All American boy as he took the stand to testify against Boyd.

C.C. McComas took Johnson through a crisp direct examination during which Johnson testified that the card game began at the Metropole between 11:00 p.m. and midnight and lasted until about five in the morning; that Boyd had lost all of his money, including $50 staked out against his diamond stud, at which time Boyd pulled out his gold watch and requested a second loan of $50 against his gold watch. Johnson went on to testify that when the Sport refused to make the $50 loan against the watch, Boyd pulled his pistol, shot the Sport twice through the head, pointed the muzzle of the smoking murder weapon directly at him for a moment, then tossed the gun beneath Johnson's chair. Johnson then explained how he picked the murder weapon up from the floor and took it into the adjoining room.

After going through this narrative of events with Johnson on direct examination, everyone anticipated that McComas would end his examination and turn Johnson over to Earl Rogers for cross-examination. However, McComas took a brief pause, turned to Johnson, and dropped a bombshell on the defense:

> Question (By McComas): Did you have any arrangement with Yeager about the game?
>
> Answer (By Johnson): Yes.
>
> Q: Tell us about that, Mr. Johnson.
>
> A: Well, I had arranged with The Sport, Mr. Yeager, that I'd get back a cut of whatever Boyd lost because I had steered Boyd into the game.
>
> Q: You stood to win no matter who lost, was that it?
>
> A: Sure.
>
> Q: So you were partners with Yeager against Boyd?
>
> A: Yes.
>
> Q: So you were giving them the double cross?
>
> A: No, I was only giving Boyd the double cross.

McComas knew that Rogers was going to try and paint a picture to the jury that Johnson was the real killer of Yeager, upset that Boyd's money and the needed capital to open their business had been lost in the card game. McComas exhibited a triumphant attitude. He had eliminated what he knew would be Rogers' strategy to create reasonable doubt. Now that any possible motive for Johnson to be suggested as the real killer of Yeager had quickly vanished into thin air, McComas ended his direct examination of Johnson and turned the witness over to Rogers for cross-examination.

It was a desperate moment for Alfred Boyd and Earl Rogers. A new defense theory was needed and needed immediately. Earl began his cross-examination of Harry Johnson, as Boyd's mother nervously looked on.

> Question (By Rogers): Why did you pick up Boyd's pistol when, according to your testimony, he threw it under your chair?
>
> Answer (By Johnson): I was concerned that Boyd might go back for the gun.
>
> Q: But you have already testified that Boyd pointed his gun at you after he had shot Yeager, yet you were not afraid.
>
> A: That's correct, I was not afraid.
>
> Q: When Boyd pointed the gun at you did you jump or at least flinch?
>
> A: No I didn't; I wasn't afraid at that time.
>
> Q: I have a copy here, Mr. Johnson, of the transcript of your testimony taken on Catalina Island during the preliminary hearing. Do you remember testifying at that hearing?
>
> A: Yes Sir, I do.
>
> Q: Now do you remember that you testified at the preliminary that you and Boyd were partners in the card game with Mr. Yeager and that you and Mr. Boyd were to split your winnings and losses—do you remember your testimony concerning that, Mr. Johnson?
>
> A: I suppose so.
>
> Q: At the preliminary hearing, you didn't testify that you and Yeager were partners, did you?
>
> A: No Sir, I did not.
>
> Q: Did you mention at the preliminary hearing that you and Yeager had any type of arrangement?
>
> A: No sir.
>
> Q: Why not?
>
> A: Well, I didn't care to.
>
> Q: I don't blame you.
>
> A: Well, I wasn't asked that.

Rogers didn't say anything for a moment, he simply looked

scornfully at Johnson who was sitting squirmishly on the witness stand.

Answer (Cont'd by Johnson): Well, I just wasn't asked that question—I wasn't asked that.

Question (By Rogers): Mr. Johnson, didn't you testify as to this new story about your arrangement with Mr. Yeager in order to make this jury think you had no motive for killing Yeager yourself? Isn't that the reason you are springing this new story about the double cross now for the first time?

A: Well—I just didn't really give it much thought, really.

Q: Were you drunk that night when Yeager was shot?

A: No.

Q: Was Yeager?

A: No.

Q: How about Mr. Boyd, was he drunk?

A: Yes, Boyd was pretty drunk.

Q: What was Boyd drinking that evening?

A: We drank apricot brandy in the daytime and straight whiskey at night.

Q: And you didn't budge at all when Boyd pointed the gun at you?

A: No, I did not.

Q: What did you do immediately after you took Boyd's gun into the barroom.

A: I'm not quite sure.

Q: Didn't you step into a wash room to wash the powder stains off your hands?

A: Why no (Johnson stammered), I don't think I did.

Q: Oh, I see, you don't think you washed them off. Not quite sure about that; I see. When Boyd shot Yeager, he held the gun in his right hand, correct?

A: Yes, that's correct.

Q: Now yesterday you testified that Boyd shot Yeager immediately after Yeager refused to loan him money on his gold watch—do you recall that?

A: Yes.

Q: Boyd asked for $50 against the watch?

A: Yes.

Q: Yeager turned him down?

A: Yes.

Q: And Boyd then shot Yeager. How much time passed between the time Yeager turned down Boyd's request and the time he shot him?

A: No time at all, it was quick as a flash.

Q: Quick as a flash?

A: Yes, quick as a flash.

Q: And Boyd held the gun in his right hand?

A: Yes.

Q: I have your testimony here from the preliminary hearing, Mr. Johnson, and you testified at the preliminary hearing that when Mr. Boyd asked for the $50 loan, that he was holding his large gold watch in his right hand. What did Mr. Boyd do with the gold watch when he used his right hand to reach for his gun and shoot Yeager?

Johnson was speechless and began to look towards the floor. Rogers took out his watch and stated,

Mr. Johnson, let's see how long it takes you to make up a response.

Judge Smith: Are you through, Mr. Johnson?

Johnson: No response.

Judge Smith: Are we to understand that you are thinking of a reply or that you are through?

Johnson: Well, your honor, I don't know what to say.

Earl Rogers: No, I guess you don't!

On redirect examination, McComas attempted to rehabilitate Johnson with some overly leading questions to which Rogers, playing completely to the jury, made loud objections in the form of speeches; all used to emphasize the equivocal nature of Johnson's answer regarding the powder burns. Well, did Johnson know or not know whether he had washed those powder burns off in the washroom?

During his resumption of Johnson's cross-examination a few minutes later, Rogers took the bullet-holed derby hat which had belonged to Yeager and placed it upon his own head while sitting at the bloodstained poker table where Yeager had been shot to death. He began to ask questions of Johnson in a soft voice regarding how Yeager was positioned when he was shot. McComas, who was having trouble hearing what Rogers was asking of Johnson, rose from his seat and walked over to the card table at which point Rogers looked at Johnson and blurted out,

"Oh, here's Mac; He'll tell you what to say!" Before McComas could interpose an objection, Rogers continued with his cross-examination of Johnson.

> Question (By Rogers): And you say you were not at all alarmed when Boyd pointed his pistol at you after he had just killed Yeager?
>
> Answer (By Johnson): That's correct,

Rogers continued to ask Johnson over and over again, while he was poking his finger through the bullet hole in the derby hat: Was he frightened when Boyd pointed the pistol at him? Did he flinch? Did he scream? Did he move a muscle? To each of these inquiries Johnson stood by his testimony that he had not screamed, he had not moved, he was not afraid; notwithstanding the fact that Boyd pointed the smoking revolver at him instantly after he had shot Yeager twice in the head.

At one point, while Rogers was poking his finger through the bullet hole in the derby hat, after he had asked the same questions for the umpteenth time, the exasperated District Attorney Rives objected to the court:

> (By Rives): Why waste the court's time with silly, useless repetition? You have already asked the witness that same question at least twenty times and he has always given you the same answer.

Rogers looked at the jury during the remarks of Mr. Rives, and once again immediately proceeded to ask Johnson if he was alarmed when Boyd pointed the smoking pistol at him. Satisfied that every juror on the panel and that all of the spectators in the courtroom were completely and absolutely aware of Johnson's contention and testimony that he was never alarmed when Boyd pointed the gun which had just been used to put two holes in Yeager's head, Rogers terminated his cross-examination of Harry Johnson.

Earl Rogers called the defendant, Alfred Boyd to the stand, who approached the witness stand with a noticed limp; the result of an injury sustained by Boyd while in school. As Boyd took the witness stand, his mother, who had been sitting next to her son during the entire trial, looked extremely nervous.

Boyd testified that he was twenty years old, that he and Johnson had gone on a vacation to Catalina, and that he had taken his pistol with him on the trip. He had taken the **pis**tol on the trip because he and Johnson were planning on shooting a seal. He subsequently learned that it was a criminal offense to shoot seals and he left his gun in the hotel room before going to the bar at the Metropole. Boyd testified that he had about twenty drinks on the day in question and was drunk at the time of Yeager's shooting. He and Johnson went and began to play cards with Yeager.

Question (By Rogers): When did you begin to lose?

Answer (By Boyd): I remember to have lost one big pot; I had already lost my diamond stud and watch.

Q: Who won the last hand?

A: Yeager.

Q: What did you do then?

A: I shoved all the money over to Yeager, it was a big pot.

Q: What happened next?

A: Well, I called for a drink of whiskey and told the bartender to bring me a good one. I was the only one drinking at the time. I leaned back in my chair and lit a cigarette. I asked Yeager if he wanted to buy me some breakfast.

The courtroom crowd laughed.

Question: What happened next?

Answer: I thought I heard Johnson say "You won't." Then I heard the shots and put my chair down and I saw Johnson walk past me out of the room. I tried to find my cane, but I couldn't because there was too much smoke in the room. I got up and walked out of the room.

Q: Did you fire those shots, Mr. Boyd?

A: No, I didn't.

Q: Did Mr. Johnson fire the shots?

A: Well, he must have, there wasn't anyone else in the room.

Q: Did you kill William Yeager?

A: No sir, I did not.

Q: Did you actually see Harry Johnson shoot Yeager?

A: No, I had quite a lot to drink and I was sleepy. I didn't see anything until after I heard the shots.

The cross-examination of Boyd by the prosecution was uneventful, and now it was time to present closing arguments and send the case out to the jury. The only opportunity left for Earl Rogers to try and save young Boyd from hanging was his impending closing argument to the jury, which was set to take place the next day.

Earl Rogers was known in those days as a fastidious dresser, a real Beau Brummel, and he appeared for his closing argument in the Boyd case wearing a frock coat and white waistband.

Rogers proceeded to calmly review the evidence that had been put on during the trial. He spoke of the good family that Boyd had come from and of how youthful he was. He spoke of the fact that Boyd had the misfortune to take up with someone of such poor character as Harry Johnson. He told the jury that Boyd's story was more credible than that of Johnson. He reminded the jury that Johnson had never testified during the preliminary hearing about the deal he supposedly had with Yeager, and that Johnson had just as much motivation to kill Yeager as Boyd, perhaps even more.

Maybe Johnson learned that Yeager wasn't going to honor their partnership pact to divide the loot cheated from Boyd.

His argument seemed low key and without much emotion. Rogers spoke with emphasis of Johnson's testimony that he didn't flinch a muscle, didn't move at all, and didn't jump or scream when he was facing down the barrel of the smoking gun which Boyd had just used to blow out Yeager's brains. He spoke again of Johnson's testimony that he wasn't frightened or alarmed when he looked down the smoking barrel of that gun; the murder weapon that had just sent Yeager to his death.

In the middle of this low key but smooth flow of argument, with the emphasis on Johnson's testimony regarding his reaction to the gun, Rogers backed to a position alongside counsel's table. He stooped over and without warning he rose straight up with a loud cry, brandishing a huge Colt .45 in his hand. Rogers waived the gun at the jury, then at the spectators in the audience, then directly at District Attorney Rives and at McComas.

Spectators rushed for the exits in the moment of panic, jurors hit the deck, the D.A. Rives and his assistant McComas were on the floor under the counsel table. Rives yelled at Earl, "Hey Earl, is it loaded?"

"Sure it's loaded," responded Rogers.

"Well then don't point it this way!" yelled Rives.

"Put it up, Mr. Rogers! Put it up!" yelled Judge Smith who was crouched behind the bench.

As the Bailiffs rushed towards Rogers he was laughing out loud and put the gun down on the counsel table. Then Rogers turned and glanced laughingly towards Rives and McComas as they were getting up from under the counsel table as he asked the jury if it was possible for them to believe one word of Johnson's testimony after having heard him state from the witness stand twenty or thirty times that he was unafraid; that he had not even so much as flinched when Boyd pointed a smoking revolver at him after just having shot a man twice in the head. The coverage in the *Los Angeles Times* described the scene:

Buffalo Bill's hottest show was a tame performance com-
pared with Earl Rogers in the Boyd trial yesterday. It was so
effective that he drove the jury under the table and the audience out the fire escapes.

After everyone's nerves had calmed down, District Attorney Rives gave a masterful closing for the prosecution in which
he condemned the "dangerous" gunplay demonstration con-
cocted by Rogers. However, Rogers had totally destroyed the
credibility of Johnson's testimony. Yeager had been shot twice
in the head by Boyd. The smell and sound of death was present in the room. Blood was dripping from Yeager's head onto
the green felt card table. The barrel of the gun was still smoking as it was pointed directly by Boyd at Johnson. The testimony of Johnson, that he had remained perfectly still during
all of this, was no longer to be believed. With the reaction of
sudden fear that had befallen everyone present when Earl
Rogers pulled out that Colt .45 in the courtroom that day, it
is little wonder that the jury rejected the testimony of Harry
Johnson and acquitted the defendant, Alfred Boyd, on the first
ballot.

This was one of just several high profile murder cases in all
of which Rogers achieved victory and freedom for his clients.
Not bad for the young Earl Rogers, who had only been a lawyer
for several years. The word was now out: If you're in trouble,
you'd better hire Earl Rogers to defend you.

CHAPTER TWO

The Case of the Dead Man's Intestines

THE PARTICIPANTS

DEFENDANT:	William Alford
PROSECUTORS:	Senator Stephen M. White
	Johnstone Jones
DEFENSE ATTORNEYS:	Earl Rogers, Chief Trial Counsel
	Paul Burke, Co-Counsel
	W.A. Harris, Co-Counsel
CHARGE:	Murder

Before the Boyd case was Rogers' defense of William Alford on the charge that he murdered Jay E. Hunter. Mr. Hunter was a prominent attorney, real estate and mining investor and an extablished member of the upper strata of Los Angeles society in the late 1890s. The privileged scion of a prominent and distinguished family hailing from Austin, Texas, he was well-educated (University of Virginia), handsome, exceedingly wealthy, and considered perhaps the city's most eligible bachelor. Hunter was a member of the exclusive California Club, was involved in numerous social and philanthropic civic activities, and was regarded as someone of immense popularity. He had lived in Los Angeles since 1887. Hunter also had an aversion to making good on his debts, a habit that would prove to be his undoing.

In 1899, at the age of 34, Hunter was killed by William Alford. In an uproar, a shocked citizenry took on a vigilante, "lynch mob" mentality. Alford was a mechanic; a man of very modest means. He had obtained a $102 judgment the previous August against Hunter and Hunter's killing revolved around a dispute concerning this debt.

The alleged debt of Hunter resulted from a real estate transaction in which Alford had sold a lot to a Mr. Frank Snow for $100 and took a promissory note from Hunter in the amount of $102 as payment. As a result of the transaction, Hunter received $300 when the lot was sold on January 7, 1899. Despite having received the $300, however, Hunter did not pay Alford the $102 he owed. After some negotiations, Hunter paid Alford $6 for a 60 day extension to pay on the note. After the 60 days had lapsed, Hunter refused to pay any more money. Alford offered to settle his claim with Hunter by having the note paid in $5 or $10 installments, even though he knew that Hunter could easily afford to pay the note in full. Hunter continued to ignore the obligation. Alford brought suit against Hunter for payment of the obligation and obtained the judgment against Hunter.

Alford then struck upon an idea. He proceeded to insert an advertisement in the local newspapers in which he offered to sell his claim against Hunter to any willing purchaser. In addition to the advertisement, Alford had little circulars printed up offering to sell his claim against Hunter, which he intended on passing out to the general public.

According to the prosecution's theory of the case, Alford went to Hunter's offices armed with copies of the circular which he intended to distribute and with a gun. In a froth, and having made remarks to numerous individuals regarding his hostile intentions towards Hunter, Alford went to Hunter's office on the fifth floor of the Stimson Building at the corner of Third and Spring Street on February 18, 1899, intent on collecting his money. An argument ensued, Alford pulled out his gun and shot Hunter to death in cold blood.

Civic activists, social and business leaders in the community and the public at large were outraged by Hunter's death and demanded that Alford be brought to justice. Although the District Attorney's office had a staff of prosecutors on the public payroll, a group of Hunter's friends arranged for the retention of perhaps the most prominent attorney in the state of California, former United States Senator Stephen M. White, to act as special prosecutor in the murder trial of Alford. Assisting White would be General Johnstone Jones, a senior prosecutor with the D.A.'s office. At that time it was possible for any citizen to hire a private prosecutor to assist the District Attorney.

And White was no lightweight.

Stephen M. White was elected to and served a term in the United States Senate, enjoying a fine reputation. He was regarded by his peers as one of the best constitutional lawyers of his time. He had a record and reputation of integrity beyond repute. A brilliant orator, White was known as an exalted criminal defense lawyer and was greatly respected by the bar in general.

When White was serving his term in the Senate, wealthy Californian Collis P. Huntington owned the powerful Southern Pacific Railroad. Huntington was a powerful man whose lobbying efforts allowed him to exert influence and control over city councils, county boards and the state legislature.

Senator White believed that California's San Pedro harbor was a natural port and supported its development as such by the government. However, Huntington owned thousands of acres of land in the Santa Monica Bay district. Because of the impact that it would have on his expansive land holdings, Huntington wanted Santa Monica to be made the official seaport of Los Angeles. Despite the efforts and desires of Huntington, Senator White insisted that San Pedro was the appropriate location for the seaport. According to White's memoirs, Huntington offered him $500,000 worth of real property if he would simply go away on vacation until Congress could pass a bill in his absence to spend millions to make Santa Monica a seaport. White refused and used all of his efforts to defeat the bill in Congress that would have made Santa Monica a seaport.

Adding further drama to the case, Senator White also happened to have been the mentor of the young Earl Rogers, lead counsel for Alford's defense, who had received his legal education and training as a law student in the Senator's office. Senator White had considered Rogers one of his favorite and most accomplished students. No more formidable attorney could have been retained in California to act as the special prosecutor in Alford's murder trial to face off against the still unproven Rogers in his first big murder trial.

A preliminary hearing took place on February 24, 1899, before Justice Morgan. Alford's head was still swathed with bandages as a result of injuries sustained on the day he shot Hunter. On February 27, 1899, Earl Rogers convinced Judge Smith to set bail at $8,000, which was posted and Alford was free on bail, pending trial. At the preliminary hearing, Alford was held to answer on the charge of first degree murder—the penalty for which was a quick trip to the gallows. A trial date was set. Testimony in Alford's murder trial commenced on May 29, 1899, in the Superior Court before Judge Smith, with several hundred people crowding into the courtroom to observe the proceedings.

The murder trial that followed attracted intense attention and the courtroom was jam-packed with lawyers, spectators and reporters on a daily basis. People fought for space in the courtroom and many would-be spectators were turned away daily.

The defense theory was simply that Alford was laying prone on his back on the floor being beaten by Hunter, who was standing over Alford and hitting him with his heavy cane. Alford pulled his gun in self-defense, and shot Hunter to death.

The prosecution put on testimony that Alford demanded his money and threatened to expose Hunter's penchant for cheating people out of their hard-earned money by posting fliers all around town. When Hunter refused to pay him, the prosecution contended that Alford in premeditated retribution pulled out his gun and shot Hunter in cold blood.

An attorney by the name of F.A. Stephenson was a tenant who occupied the office adjacent to Hunter's. He took the witness stand for the prosecution and testified that he was present when a bleeding Hunter ran into his office, with Alford chasing close behind. According to Stephenson, Alford had a gun in his hand and was attempting to aim it at Hunter so as to shoot him again. At that point Stephenson intervened, disarming Alford. Stephenson averred that there was no question but that Alford was the aggressor.

Hunter was eventually taken to the California Hospital where resident physician, Dr. C.W. Pierce assisted Dr. Carl Kurtz in several operations, trying to save Hunter's life. Their attempts were futile. Jay Hunter died on February 19, 1899, shortly before 1:00 p.m., of the bullet wounds inflicted by Alford.

Senator White put the chief autopsy surgeon, Dr. Carl Kurtz, on the witness stand and established through his direct testimony that Hunter had only used his cane defensively to ward off the attack of the aggressor, Alford. Both Dr. Kurtz and Coroner Holland testified that the path of the fatal bullet fired from Alford's gun traveled in a downward direction through the intestines of Hunter, bolstering the prosecution's claim that Alford had shot his gun while a defenseless Hunter lay on the ground beneath him. On direct examination, Dr. Kurtz identified the two bullets taken from Hunter's body and they were marked as exhibits.

Question (By White): Would you describe the path of that bullet please, Doctor.

Answer (By Kurtz): Why yes. That bullet passed through the abdominal cavity of the decedent on a downward course which in the process severed the verniform appendix.

Q: What is the appendix for?

A: Probably for the benefit of surgeons.

Dr. Kurtz who drew some laughter from the audience with that response.

Under cross-examination, Rogers had Dr. Kurtz describe in detail Alford's head wounds as they had been diagrammed on the day of the killing.

Question (By Rogers): Could these wounds be inflicted by the end of this cane?

Answer (By Kurtz): Most of them are too long for that,

Q: By what part of this cane were Mr. Alford's scalp wounds likely made, Doctor Kurtz?

A: By this part, lengthwise, (pointing to the side of the cane).

Rogers had now established that Alford's head wounds were inflicted by a blow from the side, and not the tip, of Hunter's cane. Rogers asked and received the court's permission to allow the jurors to inspect the cane. The impressive, beautiful and heavy cane, silver knob and all, was passed from one juror to the next.

Upon further cross-examination by Rogers, Dr. Kurtz testified as to the course of the bullet which passed through the abdominal cavity. He testified that a line from the point four inches below the navel to a point two and a half inches below the crest of the ileum (lower intestine) would be horizontal. These were said to be the points at which one bullet entered and came out of the abdomen, supporting the defense's contention that the shot could have been fired from the floor. However, Dr. Kurtz still maintained that the bullet traveled in the downward path.

Next, the prosecution called Dr. C.W. Pierce, the resident physician who, together with Dr. Kurtz, performed the operations on Hunter at the California Hospital when he expired. Pierce testified that, in his opinion, the bullet that killed Hunter had traveled downward through the body and not upward.

On cross-examination of Dr. Pierce, Rogers simply established that, based on the powder marks on Hunter's trousers, the bullet entered from the front and exited through the back of Hunter.

> Question (By Rogers): But you do know from examination of these two holes that the bullet entered from the front and passed out at the rear of the trousers, do you not?
>
> Answer (By Pierce): Yes.

Thus ended Rogers' cross-examination of Dr. Pierce. The doctor's opinion remained that the fatal bullet traveled downward and into the front of Hunter's body through his intestines. This testimony continued to support the prosecution's assertion that Alford stood over Hunter when he fired that fatal shot. At this point, it seemed to be an "open and shut" case; that Alford was guilty of the murder of one of Los Angeles' most popular figures.

Dr. Ralph Hagan was next called to the witness stand by the prosecution and Johnstone Jones took him through what should have been a routine and simple direct examination.

> Question (By Jones): Dr. Hagan, can you describe the spot where the fatal bullet entered Mr. Hunter's body?
>
> Answer (By Hagan): Do you want the exact measurements?
>
> Q: Yes, the exact measurement.
>
> A: On a level with, and four inches from, the anterior superior spinous process of the ileum.

Q: If you can find that long thing on me, I wish you would point it out.

As Johnstone Jones began to approach Dr. Hagan so that he could identify the location, Rogers leaned over and jabbed his finger onto a spot of Jones' stomach at which point the startled prosecutor barked out, "I didn't ask you—what do you know about anatomy?"

Answer (By Hagan): He indicated the spot exactly.

By Rogers: Aren't you going to thank me General?

The jurors and others laughed.

Question (By Jones): Do you have an opinion as to whether the course traveled by the fatal bullet was upward or downward.

Answer (By Hagan): Yes; the bullets traveled a downward course through Mr. Hunter's body.

Rogers had brought a life-size dummy into the courtroom for demonstration purposes. On cross-examination, he had Dr. Hagan show the jury how the bullets traveled in Hunter's body. The doctor did as requested and from the demonstration it was made apparent that a bullet could have been fired upward and still have taken a horizontal course in passing through the dead man's abdomen.

Dr. Hagan also testified that he dressed Alford's wounds at the Receiving Hospital, that he had found a contusion on Alford's left wrist and that Alford had been bleeding profusely from two head wounds; one of which was on the right side of the top of the head, three and one half inches in length, the other head wound one and a half inches in length.

The prosecution put on a good number of witnesses who testified as to Mr. Hunter's fine and respectable character. The testimony of Stephenson had established that Alford was the aggressor in the altercation. Drs. Pierce, Hagan and Kurtz established the cause of death and downward path of the bullets, and Mr. Hunter's good character had been established. The prosecution then rested.

To begin the defense Rogers put on an array of character witnesses to attest to the good and decent nature and character of the defendant. When it came time to put on a medical witness Rogers stated:

"Your honor, I am requesting that the Court order the Coroner to bring into this courtroom the intestines of the late Jay Hunter."

There was a commotion in the courtroom from the spectators. The judge appeared astonished. Senator White jumped to his feet and interposed objections.

"This is a ghoulish and unprecedented request, one for which there has been no foundation laid," complained the prosecutor. Just what was Rogers up to?

Earl Rogers spoke:

"The prosecution laid such a foundation, your honor. The coroner has already been called as a prosecution witness and has testified that the fatal bullet traveled downward through the intestines. The testimony was that the gun must have been fired from above and penetrated the intestines. I propose to prove that the bullet entered the intestines ranging upwards and not downwards. I need the intestines to put on this defense."

"You've really lost your mind Rogers!" retorted White.

Despite the protestations, Judge Smith ruled that it was legal to have the bowels of the decedent produced and ordered the coroner to bring them to the courtroom forthwith. The decedent's intestines were wheeled into the courtroom, contained in a large glass jar preserved by alcohol. In order to overcome additional foundation objections put forth by the prosecution, Rogers placed Coroner Holland on the stand and had him testify that the contents were, indeed, the bowels of Jay Hunter, that there was the unbroken seal on the jar placed thereon by him, and that the jar had been continuously in his possession since the time of the placement of the seal.

Rogers then called Dr. Edward M. Pallette to the stand. The doctor testified that the course of the fatal bullet would have been with the projectile traveling upwards.

With the aid of a large colored picture of the human viscera, (Rogers was one of the first attorneys to popularize the use of charts, blackboards, and other visual aids in the courtroom, such practice considered an innovation in his day), Dr. Pallette told the jury that although the bullet had entered above the navel and lodged in Hunter's posterior, it had actually been traveling upward. At the moment of the bullet's impact Mr. Hunter's shoulders were lower than his hips—as he struck Alford, who was on the ground beneath him, with his cane. In that position, and with Hunter's bowels folded over and in a doubled up posture, the bullet would have traveled up with the initial appearance of the intestines being that the bullet had traveled downward, even though the bullet had traveled upward through the folded over intestines.

> Question (By Rogers): So it was due to the stooping position of Mr. Hunter where the bowels were folded over upon themselves that the bullet could have punctured the bowels in the manner that they were?
>
> Answer (By Pallette): That's perfectly obvious to the naked eye.
>
> Q: So, in your opinion, Dr. Pallette, did Alford shoot from the floor?
>
> A: Yes. No other position could account for the travel of the bullet through the intestines.
>
> Q: At the moment the shot was fired, Hunter's shoulders must have been lower than his hips, as he bent over and struck down at the man on the floor below him?
>
> A: That's exactly what would have happened. You can see for yourself.

The prosecution's cross-examination of Dr. Pallette did nothing to impact on the credibility of his testimony on direct, other than establish that he was only twenty-five years of age and just out of medical school.

Rogers called P.J. Kennedy, a former county jailer who was

the tenant of a Mr. McKay, to the witness stand. Kennedy testified that he was present when Mr. Hunter paid a visit to Mr. McKay when the following conversation took place:

Hunter: "What do you know of my debts?"

McKay: "I have read that advertisement of a judgment against you being for sale."

Hunter: "God Damn that son of a bitch. When I meet him I will break his head."

McKay: "You had better be careful. He lives only three doors from here."

Hunter: "I don't care."

Mr. White then cross-examined Mr. Kennedy, bringing to light that his expenses were being paid by the defense.

Deputy Constable Fred H. Brakesuhler was called by the defense and testified that he had informed Mr. Hunter that Alford intended on attaching Hunter's stock in a mining venture in order to collect on the debt and that Hunter replied, "If he does, I will get even. I will do him up and fix him."

On the day of the shooting, the constable informed Hunter of the garnishment obtained against him by Alford and to which Hunter responded, "I'll be damned if I pay any amount on that judgment and if he attaches my mining stock, I'll fix him."

H.H. Edmunds, a tenant in the building where the shooting took place, testified that when he heard the shots he rushed to the corridor outside his office and saw Alford coming down the hall bleeding profusely from his head and face. He assisted Alford to a basin so that he could wash the blood from his face, and Alford tottered and fell to the floor, with the blood still gushing from his wounds.

E.E. Crandall was called to the stand and testified that Hunter had a reputation for the use of, and threats of violence. He further stated that Hunter freely called other men names and was also known to use his cane as a weapon, adding, "I once had a difficulty with him."

Question (By Rogers): Did you yourself know what the character of Mr. Hunter's temper was?

Answer (By Crandall): Mr. Hunter was quick tempered and on many occasions I heard him yelling and screaming from across the hall. He was very quick and high tempered, just the kind of man who would strike a person down if he was presented with a card which did not please him.

H.O. Collins, another tenant in Hunter's building, testified that Mr. Hunter possessed a very "irascible temper." The defense then called Sue White (no relation to Senator White) to the witness stand, where she testified that she had been acquainted with Mr. Hunter for about seven years. She had spoken to Mr. Hunter shortly before the shooting regarding the advertisement taken out by Alford in the local paper regarding Hunter's debt. As she recalled, Hunter's words were:

You are the fourth one of my friends that has called my attention to this advertisement; it is a very galling thing. Alford is a pure scoundrel. Do you see this cane? Alford means to come to my office this Saturday, and when he does I mean to take my cane and split his head right open. This thing is galling me to death; I cannot stand for it any longer."

Rogers called W.S. Mundy, who testified under oath concerning a conversation he had with attorney Stephenson the previous week while the two were in the witness waiting room. Mundy asserted that Stephenson told him that Alford had made no resistance at all when Stephensen took possession of the revolver and that Alford at that time, was too weak to make any resistance.

This testimony was in direct contradiction to Stephenson's prior testimony that Alford had chased Hunter shortly after the initial shooting, and trying to get in one more shot for good measure.

Upon cross-examination, Mr. White made sure to bring to the jury's attention the fact that Mr. Mundy and the defendant had been friends for several years, had been in business together, and had originally met when they lived in Chattanooga, Tennessee.

At the court session on June 5, 1899, Rogers requested that a bench warrant be issued for Mr. Stephenson so that he could further cross-examine him. The clerk was instructed to issue the warrant. When Stephenson appeared for further testimony, it was revealed that he was not exactly an unbiased witness. Mr. Hunter had previously given Mr. Stephenson an assignment of his 49,000 shares of mining stock in order to avoid the payment of Alford's judgment. Stephenson had previously testified that he and Mr. Hunter were "not particular friends." Thus the jury was left to decide for themselves whether the Alford that Mr. Stephenson saw right after the shooting was a madman chasing Hunter, trying to get in one more shot; or a weakened man, profusely bleeding from the head wounds that had been inflicted upon him with Hunter's heavy cane.

Rogers went on to question Stephenson about Hunter's reputation for being violent:

> Question (By Rogers): You knew Hunter carried a heavy cane, didn't you?
>
> Answer (By: Stephenson): I guess it was heavy. I think he always carried one.
>
> Q: Do you know anything about Mr. Hunter hitting people over the head with his heavy walking stick?
>
> A: I never heard of it before he struck Alford.
>
> Q: But have you heard since then about his striking people with it?
>
> A: Yes.

Mrs. Hilda Alford, the defendant's wife, then testified that she and Mr. Alford had four children and had been married for eleven years. She revealed that she had always urged her husband to carry a gun with him at all times during the course of their marriage and that to her knowledge he had always done so. It was not unusual or for any special purpose that her husband was armed on the day that Hunter was shot.

Senator White was known to be hard drinker. He was to later die at the young age of 47, afflicted with alcoholism. According to published accounts, Earl Rogers saw the Senator during a lunch break and joined him while the good Senator was drinking his bourbon. The Senator offered Earl a drink but he declined. On a couple of occasions earlier in the trial, White had been ten to thirty minutes late coming back to court after lunch; but notwithstanding, Judge Smith started those sessions at 2:00 p.m. sharp. Sometimes White would take a brief nap after lunch knowing that Assistant D.A. Jones would take up the slack for the short time period before he would return to court.

On this particular occasion, when the lunch break was over and Judge Smith resumed the trial at 2:00 p.m. sharp, Earl Rogers and General Jones were present in court. Senator White was taking a brief nap and was not yet present.

Thinking on his feet, Rogers made his move, "The defense calls William Alford."

According to first-hand accounts of what happened, Rogers felt that he had to put the defendant on the witness stand to testify as to what happened; yet he was extremely worried that White would shred Alford during cross-examination. When Rogers began his direct examination of Alford after the lunch break on June 7, 1899, the specially retained prosecutor, California's foremost attorney at that time, was not present in the courtroom, literally having been caught napping by the keen-minded Rogers.

In a detailed, yet concise and well-rehearsed direct examination administered by Rogers, Alford gave his version of the events that transpired. Jay Hunter had struck him with his heavy cane while Alford was prone on the floor in the hall outside Hunter's office, that Alford was in fear of his own death when he drew his weapon, and that he shot upwards into Hunter's body.

With the exception of several direct examinations by Jones of the many prosecution witnesses who had appeared in the trial, Senator White had conducted every witness examination deemed of importance. There was no doubt that Jones was an able and competent trial attorney; however Earl Rogers knew that it was his mentor, White who could deliver the knockout punch on cross-examination if a knockout punch were to be delivered. There was no question in Rogers mind that he would far prefer Jones to cross-examine Alford and to avoid White. Anybody but White.

Alford testified that Hunter owed him money, and although Hunter obviously had the ability to pay, he had refused to honor his debt. He testified that he took an ad out in the local paper offering to sell Hunter's obligation to him. His intent was to "shame" Hunter into paying his debt.

Alford maintained that he had no intention of assaulting Hunter or causing him any bodily harm when he went to his office with a copy of the circular he had printed regarding the debt. He told of seeing Hunter in the hallway outside of his office on the day of the shooting and requesting a meeting with him. He showed Hunter the circular. After reading the circular, Hunter called Alford some vile names, dropped the circular and his overcoat on the floor, grabbed his cane by the small end with his right hand, and struck Alford over the head with it.

At this point, Alford came down from the witness stand, and with a pointer in his hand displayed for the jury the manner in which Hunter had attacked him. As Hunter raised his cane a second time, Alford attempted to leave the area, but as he was in the process of so doing he was struck again solidly on the head and fell to the ground. It was at this point, according to Alford, that he pulled out his gun and began shooting. He swore under oath that he had not reached for his gun until after he was struck on the head by Alford and had fallen to the floor. Alford testified further:

(By Alford): "After I got up, the first man I saw was in the doorway to a room. I held my left hand in front of my face to keep the blood from dripping on the office carpet and handed the gun to him with my right hand. Just as I was handing the gun to Mr. Stephenson I fell to my knees and felt another blow to my head. I was faint for a moment or two and then I went into the hall and started to walk towards the elevator. A man helped me into the office of the City Directory Company. The next thing I remember I was in the Patrol Wagon on the way to the hospital."

During cross-examination by Jones, Alford testified that he had tried to speak to Hunter about a compromise settlement of the amount of the debt prior to his posting the circulars, telling Hunter that he would even be receptive to installment payments of $5 or $10 per month. During the cross-examination, Alford, once again, left the witness stand and got down on the floor and demonstrated for the jury the exact position in which he lay while he shot Hunter. The cross-examination of Alford was then concluded before Senator White had returned to court from his nap.

"No redirect examination, your honor," quipped Rogers after Jones had completed his uneventful cross-examination of Alford.

"You may step down, Mr. Alford," Judge Smith stated.

The defense had dodged a major bullet; Alford had avoided what would have been an exhaustive and grueling cross-examination by Senator White. At the same time the defendant had testified in a very convincing manner that he had shot Hunter in self-defense.

There was then the testimony of a Miss Shutt. She was present in the building when the shooting took place. Ms. Shutt testified that she had seen the gleam of a revolver, two men fighting on the floor, and then she heard the gun shots. This testimony, according to Rogers, was "proof positive" that when Alford fired the shots from his revolver, he was already on the floor—having been struck in the head by Hunter's cane.

The time had come for closing arguments to begin. Earl Rogers detested the fact that the prosecution in a criminal case had the final word before the jury, and firmly believed that in criminal cases it was only fair that the defense should have the last word when a client's life or liberty was at stake. At the time of the Alford trial courtrooms did not have blackboards.

When Rogers gave his closing argument in the Alford case, he had a school blackboard set up by the side of the jury box. Just before concluding, Rogers wrote out three questions and answers on the blackboard. These questions and answers were the testimony of Miss Shutt, the witness who testified that she saw the gleam of Alford's gun on the floor as the two men scuffled before the first shot was fired. Rogers looked at the jury and told them that the testimony of Miss Shutt was "proof positive" that Alford had shot in self defense after he was knocked to the floor by Hunter.

Rogers stated, "I request that the prosecution explain these questions and answers to you during their closing arguments. They must explain Miss Shutt's testimony."

Senator White gave a detailed and passionate closing argument before the jury. As he was delivering his concluding statements, Rogers blackboard and the three questions and answers of Miss Shutt's testimony remained in full view of the jurors. Senator White never did provide an explanation to the jury regarding those three questions and answers.

On June 9, 1899, the jury deliberated for only eleven minutes and reached a verdict of not guilty on the first ballot. Alford was a free man.

Former Senator Stephen White had suffered his first courtroom defeat—at the hands of his young former student and protege, a virtual beginner. The verdict was big news. And the young Earl Rogers instantly shot into notoriety and stardom in the Los Angeles community at the expense of his former mentor.

CHAPTER THREE

The Case of the Slimy Pimp

THE PARTICIPANTS

DEFENDANT:	Charles Mootry
PROSECUTOR:	C.C. McComas
DEFENSE ATTORNEYS:	Earl Rogers, Chief Trial Counsel
	Attorney Adcock, Co-Counsel
	Attorney Reymert, Co-Counsel
CHARGE:	Murder

For the year or so after the Alford case, Earl's office was deluged with cases from the underbelly of Los Angeles: gamblers, prostitutes, pimps, second-story men and thieves. In Los Angeles, most murders during the period from 1890s into the early 1900s were in some way associated with gambling and prostitution.

Earl had an employee in his office at that time by the name of Bill Jory. Jory, a large and imposing character, was loyal to a fault when it came to Earl Rogers. He was Earl's investigator, baby-sitter, and protector. Jory was familiar with many of the denizens of the Los Angeles underworld and was responsible, in part, for the huge influx of criminal cases which found their way into Earl's office. Rogers became known for taking and winning cases which had been turned down by virtually every other criminal attorney in town because they were considered to be certain convictions.

Around this time, a young woman named Martha Huff worked as a chorus girl in a seedy Los Angeles establishment called the Club Theater located on Main Street. She became Martha Mootry after she met and married Charles Mootry. On September 15, 1899, Mrs. Mootry died under peculiar circumstances. At first it appeared that she had committed suicide. Circumstances developed which led to her husband being charged with her murder. On December 4, 1899, the murder trial began.

The murder attracted much attention in the press in Los Angeles. It appeared to be an open and shut case. On the evening of the shooting, Mootry rushed into the home of A. Kempfert, a neighbor, with one of his hands covered in blood. Mootry asked that a doctor be summoned immediately, for his wife was dying. Several neighbors hurried to the Mootry residence, on the corner of Twelfth and San Jilian Street, where they found Mrs. Mootry lying on the floor in the parlor. Although her bullet wound was in her breast, she was bleeding from the mouth. They observed that there was a trail of blood leading from the parlor to the kitchen. She had been shot with a .22 caliber pistol. A physician arrived at the scene, but Mrs. Mootry died shortly thereafter. Her husband claimed that Martha had been despondent for some time over the progressive loss of her hearing and had shot herself. On a table near the chair where Mrs. Mootry was sitting when she was shot was her Dutch family bible, which had apparently been at the bottom of a trunk owned by her for many months and only taken out on the very day of her death.

Mr. Mootry claimed that when he heard the sound of the gunshot he ran to where his wife was and immediately saw that her dress was on fire, apparently having been ignited due to the close proximity of the gun to her body when she supposedly fired the self-inflicted shot. According to Mootry, he put out the fire; his hands were covered in blood due to his using a towel as he attempted to stop his wife's bleeding.

A witness supported the suicide motive. She was a young woman named Bessie Hall Valentine, a former actress and acquaintance of Mrs. Mootry. Ms. Valentine's testimony was that:

> She (Mrs. Mootry) said repeatedly, in fact, many times, that she would prefer death to being deaf completely or afflicted as she seemed to be from the loss of her faculties. She was very despondent and melancholy. She repeatedly expressed herself to the effect that she was tired of life."

Miss Valentine's testimony confirmed that she had not spoken to Mrs. Mootry for two years.

The physical and circumstantial evidence of Mr. Mootry's motive and guilt was overwhelming. Several weeks before the shooting, Mrs. Mootry had checked into a nearby rooming house on Court Street. She told the landlady that her husband was prone to violent fits and had threatened to kill her. A housekeeper had seen Mr. Mootry physically batter his wife. Various witnesses at the rooming house were present when Mootry came by and was verbally abusive to his wife. A policeman who resided at the boarding house testified that he had to intercede on one occasion to prevent Mootry from physically battering his wife. Mrs. Mootry owned the house in which the couple had lived and there was testimony of arguments instigated by Mr. Mootry over his wife's refusal to accede to his demand that she deed over the house to him. And, finally, evidence arose that Mootry was in love with another woman.

The coroner and doctor who examined Mrs. Mootry testified that there was no evidence that any portion of her dress had ever been burned and further that there were no powder burns on Mrs. Mootry's breast in the vicinity of the bullet hole.

To make matters even worse was the conduct of Mootry himself during the initial stages of the trial. According to the coverage in the *Los Angeles Times:*

> In the morning as two women entered the court-room
> dressed in infinite tawdry, he apparently recognized them,
> threw back his head with a puerile sort of glee, hurried a hand
> to his mouth, and blurted out loudly enough to attract atten-
> tion, "Oh, Mama!"

With overwhelming physical and circumstantial evidence
supporting his client's guilt, Rogers decided to put Mootry
on the stand to testify on his own behalf. On December 8,
1899, Mootry took the witness stand.

> Question (By Rogers): Were you at home on the day of the shoot-
>   ing?
>
> Answer (By Mootry): Yes sir.
>
> Q: Did you and your wife sleep together the preceding night?
>
> A: Yes sir.
>
> Q: What time did you get up?
>
> A: About 8 o'clock.
>
> Q: Which got up first?
>
> A: My wife, she got up first and tried to get breakfast, or started to.
>
> Q: After breakfast what did you do?
>
> A: She and I wiped the dishes.
>
> Q: What was your wife's condition?
>
> A: She was sick and nervous.
>
> Q: What was she doing around noon?
>
> A: She was sitting in the parlor in a rocking chair reading a bible.
>
> Q: What happened then?
>
> A: I soon heard a sound like a bursting firecracker.
>
> Q: Why did you think of a firecracker?
>
> A: We had some in the house—some red heads—left over from the
>   fourth of July.
>
> Q: What did you do?
>
> A: I ran into the parlor at once.
>
> Q: What did you see?
>
> A: That she had shot herself. I was terrified, because I had never
>   seen her with a weapon before.
>
> Q: Well, go on.

A: I saw a flame about the size of a match.

Q: What did you do?

A: I put it out, and laid her down on the floor.

Q: Did she say anything?

A: Yes, she said "I'm tired of living, I'm always sick. Good bye Charlie, I love you still."

At this point, the coverage in the *Los Angeles Times* stated that the defendant "burst into copious tears," and that after a couple of moments in an attempt to console him, Earl Rogers said "Wipe your eyes Charlie, we've got to go through with this some way." As Mootry continued to weep Rogers put the next question to him:

Question (By Rogers): Take your hand down, what happened then?

Answer (By Mootry): I put a pillow under her head. When I went to speak with her further the blood rushed into her mouth.

Q: Did you do anything else?

A: Yes, I ran into the kitchen, got a towel, wiped her face and took it back to the kitchen, dripping with blood.

Q: Did you see anything of the revolver?

A: Yes, right after the shot was fired and I rushed in I saw it on the floor by her side.

Q: Did you do anything with it?

A: I picked it up to examine it what size caliber it was. I then put the gun either on the commode or the machine, I don't know which.

Q: After the neighbors and doctor left the house what did you do next?

A: I put on my coat and went out to buy a coffin at the undertaker's.

Q: Mr. Mootry, did you kill your wife?

A: No sir.

Q: Who killed your wife?

A: She killed herself.

The newspaper coverage in the times stated:

Notwithstanding his previous brazen behavior and his outlandish obstreperousness, he told his story well and made a very favorable impression. This was due in large part, doubtless, to his attorney's skillful handling of his examination.

The prosecution proceeded by putting on the rebuttal testimony of the slain woman's brother and father, both of whom testified that Mrs. Mootry "had never displayed any symptoms of melancholy or made any attempt to take her own life." It was now time for closing arguments to begin.

C.C. McComas, a senior prosecutor with the District Attorney's office, prosecuted the Mootry case. He had taken careful pains during jury selection to ensure a panel of God-fearing church-goers who would have little sympathy for the likes of Charles Mootry. It was of some interest that Rogers did little to prevent that particular makeup of the jury. Rogers' unwavering focus in each and every one of his cases was upon the impact that testimony would have upon a jury. Rogers realized that the jury would ultimately decide his client's fate.

Rogers knew that there was overwhelming evidence of Mootry's guilt. There was conflicting evidence of a possible suicide motive, and Mootry had testified emotionally in his own defense. But Earl knew that this case would be lost or won during the closing arguments. Rogers had done extensive research during jury selection into the backgrounds of the pious church-going jurors. When it came time for his closing argument, Rogers decided that his only chance of gaining an acquittal for his client was to give an emotional appeal to the jury which would cause them to disregard the evidence. Thus Rogers proceeded to give what even he regarded to be a corny, shameless appeal to the jurors' emotions in which he often referred directly to the jurors individually by name.

One could almost hear the heartstrings being plucked as Rogers said to the jury in part:

> Do you remember those days when you courted your girl who is now your wife and the thrill of that moonlit Sunday

night when you sat holding her hand? Charlie Mootry had
no such blissful background for his romance. No, when he met
that fate, when he realized how much he loved and cared for
Martha, she was a chorus girl in a seedy club. But he swept
her away from those horrible surroundings, he gave her his
name, married her and brought into her loveless life the only
happiness she had ever known. Which of us, had we suddenly
found ourselves loving a girl in such an environment would
have ignored her past, would have taken her to the altar, and
there entered with her into the holy bonds of matrimony? The
men with whom his lot had been cast sneered at him for his
weakness in marrying such a woman. He was really nobler in
his act than we would have been had we acted as he did in his
place. What greater proof could we ask of his love for Martha,
his wife? Mootry loved his wife. He did not kill her. No.

Martha was growing deaf. She was in ill health that made
her days a misery. She saw long years of pain and illness ahead
of her in a world where she could hear no sound. So she dared
to take her own life rather than be a burden to her husband.

My friends of the jury, has it come to pass in our day that
a man may be sent to the penitentiary, or even hanged, solely
upon the testimony of a pimp, a prostitute, and a policeman?

The lengthy closing argument was designed to emotionally manipulate each of the God-fearing and church-going
jurors. And the strategy proved to be successful. The jury,
regardless of the damning evidence, acquitted Mootry on the
very first ballot.

Outside the courtroom in the presence of several people
and some reporters, a relieved and appreciative Mootry
approached Rogers with outstretched hand to thank him.
With a palpable look of disgust, Rogers turned away from
Mootry and blurted, "Get away from me you slimy pimp, you're
as guilty as hell and you know it!"

Among those present who heard Earl's remarks was his
father, the Reverend Lowell Rogers, a man for whom Earl
had endless love and respect. To Earl, his father was nothing
short of a saint. In her book *"Final Verdict,"* Adela Rogers St.

Johns recalls what her grandfather told Earl shortly after the verdict in the Mootry case:

> There is a line as clear and broad to an honest man as the line between good and evil or right and wrong always is. You must draw that line, Earl. An attempt to save a man you know to be guilty from justice by dishonest or deceptive means crosses that line.

Apparently, this was a line that Rogers was willing to cross. During this time frame Rogers handled a barrage of cases. In a relatively unimportant murder case, but front-page news nonetheless, Earl achieved an acquittal for a client by the name of Chaudefosse, who was accused of murdering a man named Delbasty. Another of Earl's clients, George Blackman, was an official of a Los Angeles public utility corporation. He was charged with embezzlement in a case which no other lawyer would touch. Rogers defended his client, but Blackman was convicted. However, there was an issue regarding the admissibility of books and records which had been kept in the handwriting of a person who had committed suicide. These records had been admitted into evidence over Rogers' strenuous objections during the trial and proved to be the "smoking gun" which led to conviction. Rogers was able to have the conviction overturned on appeal; the appellate court agreeing that the proper foundation for the admission of the books and records had not been properly laid during the trial, and that the conviction had been obtained primarily on that evidence.

Reverend Lowell Rogers had a parishioner who used to come hear his services when he preached at a church in Colton named D.E. Mellus. Mellus was a freight conductor on the Sante Fe Railroad.

In the late 1800s and early 1900s, California was dominated by the railroad business. The path of railroad tracks and station locations controlled land and business values, giving the railroads enormous economic, social and political power. A transportation strike had taken place in San Bernardino in which it was ultimately decided that settlement would be achieved through an arbitration. A committee, comprised of citizens, railworkers, and management, was selected to attempt to resolve the dispute. Mellus was chosen to represent the railroad union. After some negotiations, Mellus voted to accept the offer, which he thought was fair, as proposed by management. Mellus was viewed as a traitor by other union members. A fight broke out between Mellus and a railworker by the name of Landon. According to Mellus, Landon fell during the fight and hit his head against a cast-iron stove in the train. Landon died of the resulting fracture to his skull.

Mellus was subsequently indicted for the murder of Landon. The coroner's surgeon testified that Landon was killed by a heavy blow against the side of Landon's head opposite the side of his head which struck against the iron stove. The coroner's conclusion was based upon a piece of bone which had broken loose from that opposite side of the dead man's skull. The prosecutor was successful in convincing the jury that Mellus had used a heavy metal object to smash Landon's skull, and he was convicted of murder. Unfortunately for Mellus, Rogers was not his defense lawyer during this trial.

Earl interviewed Mellus and was convinced of his innocence. He agreed to represent the convicted murderer. After an exhaustive effort, Rogers convinced the court to give him an order to have Landon's body exhumed for further examination. Rogers then convinced the court that sufficient new evidence existed and a new trial was ordered.

Sitting on a table during the new trial, in full view of the jury, was the skull of H.A. Landon. Rogers put on a defense with the aid of his experts, Dr. Day and Dr. Murphy, that contended that the piece of bone fracture that had been the evidence which convicted Mellus in the first trial was not the result of a heavy blow to Landon's head. Rather, the fracture was caused by the incompetent work of the autopsy surgeon when he had cut off the top of Landon's skull during the initial autopsy prior to the first trial. Rogers held Landon's skull in his hands as he explained for an awe-struck jury that the autopsy surgeon had drilled a hole into the skull. Then a saw was used to make a cut around the circumference of the top of the skull for its removal. As a result of an uneven cut by the saw, a triangular piece of bone had fallen out. Without knowing of this error, the autopsy surgeon had concluded in error that the bone fragment was the result of a blow to the opposite side of Landon's head from where he had been struck from the fall on the iron stove. Under cross-examination by Rogers, the autopsy surgeon admitted his error, and Mellus was found not guilty. This would not be the last time that Rogers' formidable medical knowledge would save a client from the hangman's noose.

Perhaps some of the words spoken to Earl by his father factored into his decision not to defend a seventy-three-year-old shoemaker named Methever accused of the grisly murder of ten-year-old Dorothy McKee. McKee was hacked to death with an ax at Long Beach. The details of the murder were gruesome, the little girl's body having been hacked to pieces.

Relatives of Methever approached Rogers and offered him a retainer of $1,400 (quite a substantial sum at that time) to represent the man accused of this heinous crime. Other members of Rogers' staff, knowing how badly the office could use the $1,400 fee, were confident that Rogers could get Methever acquitted and encouraged him to take on the case. Rogers refused. Perhaps it was his memory of the words imparted to him by his father which brought him to this decision. He may have been thinking of his own little daughter, Adela. In any event, another lawyer took on the case, and Methever was tried, convicted and duly executed.

J. D. Fredericks, District Attorney
"Courtesy of University of Southern California, on
behalf of the USC Library Department of Special
Collections."

CHAPTER FOUR

The Case of Murder at Acton

THE PARTICIPANTS

DEFENDANT:	Norman M. Melrose
PROSECUTORS:	C.C. McComas
	J.A. Donnell
	John Fredericks
DEFENSE ATTORNEYS:	Earl Rogers; Chief Trial Counsel
	Luther Brown; Co-Counsel
	Congressman James McLachlan,
	Co-Counsel
CHARGE:	Murder

The hate which two men can feel towards each other as the result of a longstanding feud culminated in the killing of W.H. Broome at Acton, California on January 20, 1903.

At that time, Acton was a small farming town divided into two basic social camps. On the one hand were the farmers, mostly of German decent, who had originally settled the town. On the other were newcomers who had recently arrived. One such newcomer was a southerner named Norman M. Melrose, who had become the assistant postmaster of the town. It was Melrose who killed Broome.

Some background on the feud between Melrose and Broome is illuminating in setting the backdrop against which the incident took place in which Broome was shot and killed.

Broome had previously had Melrose arrested on the charge that Melrose had shot and killed Broome's St. Bernard dog. This incident resulted in lawsuits between the two men. On another occasion the two men got into a fist fight at the post office after a verbal altercation had taken place.

In 1900, Broome started a company known as the Actonoma Oil and Development Company, of which he was president. Broome discovered that Melrose was advising people with whom Broome had corresponded that they should not do business with Broome. Broome then charged Melrose with opening the company mail. This charge led to an investigation of Melrose by the Post Office Inspector; however the charges made by Broome could not be substantiated.

Broome proceeded to file a lawsuit in the superior court against Melrose alleging three charges of libel. On the trial of the first of the three libel charges Broome lost and was extremely bitter.

Shortly after the libel case, Melrose had one of Broome's sons arrested on charges of malicious mischief, the claim being that Broome's son had vandalized Melrose's house. That case was ultimately abandoned.

The initial story of Broome's killing, according to Melrose, was self-defense. Melrose claimed that on January 20, 1903, he was pushing a wheelbarrow along the street in Acton, and that Broome got in his way and obstructed his passage. Melrose claimed that Broome had been shooting pigeons and was carrying a double barrel shotgun in his hand. As Melrose attempted to pass Broome, he claimed that Broome leveled the shotgun at him and they proceeded to fight.

Melrose claimed that as they grappled one shot from the shotgun was discharged, that Broome regained possession of the shotgun and pointed it at him for a second time. Melrose then supposedly pulled out a revolver and fired a warning shot that did not hit Broome. Upon seeing that Broome might shoot him, Melrose then shot Broome. According to Melrose, Broome did not die at once after being shot and yelled, "That son of a bitch shot me, I'll kill him." Melrose stated that he took the shotgun from Broome's hand and took it home for safekeeping. Melrose then contacted the justice of the peace in Lancaster and he and his wife drove there where he turned himself in.

One account from an eyewitness contradicted the story put forth by Melrose. In this account Melrose, without any fear of his own demise, shot Broome through the head; when Broome fell to the ground Melrose proceeded to shoot him point blank several times. It was said that Melrose then proceeded to kick Broome's body many times when it was on the ground after having been fatally wounded.

Broome was thirty-five years old with a wife and three children at the time of his death. His wife, a Western Union telegraph operator, was in poor health at the time of the shooting, and was initially only told that her husband had been badly hurt but not killed. Broome previously had been a high-ranking officer of the Order of Railway Telegraphers, and was from a fine family.

An autopsy was conducted on January 21, 1903. Coroner Trout and his deputy John Summerfield took charge of Broome's body and they had Dr. Anderson of Lancaster perform the autopsy. According to the autopsy report, four bullets were found in Broome's body, one of which had entered through the back of his head.

An inquest was conducted on January 21, 1903. The findings were that Broome had been murdered in cold blood by Melrose in a "deliberate, unwarranted and cowardly manner." The inquest jury found that "W.H. Broome came to his death January 20, 1903, at Acton by gunshot wounds inflicted upon him by Norman M. (*sic*) Melrose and that said wounds were inflicted with malice aforethought and with intent to kill and murder said W.H. Broome."

Six witnesses testified at the inquest that Melrose chased

Broome down and shot him in cold blood, beat him on the head with his revolver after he was on the ground, and then proceeded to fire three more shots into the body and to kick the body after the three shots were fired.

There were no powder marks on the body or the clothing indicated in the autopsy report and there were no witnesses who could corroborate any portion of Melrose's story. The lack of powder burns contradicted the notion that Melrose had shot Broome at close range as they scuffled. Rather, the lack of powder burns supported the theory that Melrose had shot Broom from a distance as he was running or laying on the ground.

The witnesses testified that it was Melrose who had run his wheelbarrow at Broome, who did have a shotgun in his hand at the time. However the witnesses stated that Broome put the shotgun against a fence, took his coat off, and challenged Melrose to "fight like a man." It was at this point that Melrose is claimed to have pulled out his gun and shot an unarmed Broome to death.

Melrose was taken into custody under the supervision of Deputy Sheriff Wilson and taken by freight train to the Los Angeles county jail pending trial.

Newspaper men at that time were regularly granted access to the jail to speak with prisoners. However, the newspapers were informed that they could not speak with Melrose on account of "instructions given the jailers by his lawyer." A local newspaper wrote:

> Never before has there been any trouble about seeing a prisoner in the jail, and never before have the newspaper men of this city been discriminated against while attorneys were allowed to talk to the prisoner by the hour if they chose to do so.

Many witnesses from Acton eagerly traveled to Los Angeles to meet with District Attorney Fredericks and provide him with first-hand accounts of the murder. The district attorney immediately made a public statement that ample evidence existed to support a charge against Melrose of murder in the first degree.

A preliminary hearing took place on February 5, 1903, in front of a standing room only crowd. The *Los Angeles Times* characterized the testimony given as follows:

> Seldom in any trial have the witnesses so entirely corroborated one another as in the case during the preliminary trial in Judge Austin's court today of N.M. Melrose for shooting W.H. Broome at Acton last month. In every material circumstance, and even in details such as the kicking of Broome's body by Melrose after the latter had shot Broome four times, the witnesses all tell the same story of deliberate murder. The cross-examination of these witnesses by defense attorneys for Melrose failed to shake the terrible testimony against the prisoner.

Deputy District Attorney J.A. Donnell called Mrs. Swanson to the witness stand. She testified that she heard loud talking in front of the hotel in Acton and went out to see what the trouble was. She went on to testify that she was standing near a gate, saw Melrose pull out his pistol and shoot Broome in the back of his head as Broome was running towards her. She then watched as Melrose walked up to Broome who was laying on the ground and shot him through the body with three more shots from his pistol. After firing the three shots, she testified that Melrose then proceeded to kick the victim's body "contemptuously." Mrs. Swanson saw her husband walk out of the gate. Melrose pointed his pistol at Mr. Swanson and told him "not to interfere." She then saw Melrose walk away carrying his wheelbarrow and Broome's shotgun.

On cross-examination, Earl Rogers simply asked Mrs. Swanson how rapidly Melrose fired the three shots at Broome. She responded that the shots were fired rapidly. Rogers took the gun and pulled the trigger rapidly three times in succession and Mrs. Swanson testified that the shots were fired that rapidly. Rogers' co-counsel, Luther Brown, timed how long it took Rogers to pull the trigger on the gun three times in rapid succession at "a little over one second."

Mrs. Ira Houser then took the witness stand and testified that:

> I saw it all from immediately after the firing of the first shot until it was all over with. I was before the window of my kitchen and was attracted by the scream of Mrs. Swanson. I looked up and saw Mr. Broome, followed by Mr. Melrose. Broome was in the act of falling and Mr. Melrose had a revolver pointed at him. When Mr. Broome fell Mr. Melrose pounded him on the head with his revolver and then he stepped back and shot him three times, and then he kicked him viciously.

At the conclusion of the preliminary hearing, Judge Austin ordered that Melrose be held for trial in the Superior Court on the charge of murder. His attorneys made a request that Melrose be allowed to post bail. The request was denied.

The trial was postponed due to the announcement in court on February 12, 1903, that Melrose had retained Congressman James McLachlan to represent him at the murder trial. McLachlan was in Washington D.C. awaiting the adjournment of congress and Melrose's trial date was delayed.

On February 25, 1903, Melrose was freed on $10,000 bail. The bail order was made by Superior Court Judge Smith. Although D.A. Donnell objected, Judge Smith acquiesced to the arguments of attorneys Earl Rogers and Luther Brown requesting that bail be set for Melrose.

According to the *Los Angeles Record* there was "standing room only" in Department I when the trial was set to begin on April 5, 1903. At this point in time Melrose had three attorneys representing his interests in the courtroom; Earl Rogers, Luther Brown, and Congressman McLachlan. As it turned out, the congressman was basically window dressing and did very little in the defense of the case. Jury selection was completed at the conclusion of the court session on April 6, 1903, and time had now come for the presentation of evidence and testimony.

On the eve of trial the conviction of Melrose for the murder of Broome appeared to be a certainty. With so many eyewitnesses to the brutal killing of Broome, how could Melrose escape conviction?

According to one news account, "over 100 people stood outside the railing watching with an intense morbid interest every move of the prisoner and of the prominent attorneys on each side."

The first witness called by the prosecution was county surveyor Leo Youngworth, who pointed out on a large map of Acton the exact location where the killing took place. He identified on the map the location and distances between the location of the killing and the various eye witnesses.

A small commotion was created during the middle of Mr. Youngworth's testimony when Mrs. W.H. Broome, the widow of the victim, and her daughter entered the courtroom, both dressed in black, and took seats near the jury box. At this point Earl Rogers stated loud enough for everyone including newspaper reporters to hear that " . . . I shall make a codicil to my will forbidding my wife to attend the trial of my murderer."

Dr. C. Ed Anderson testified regarding the location of the various bullet wounds and attributed the cause of death to the bullet wounds through the body.

By April 9th things were beginning to look hopeless for the defense. The various newspaper accounts indicated that both Melrose and his congressman attorney had displayed airs of confidence during the early stages of the trial. Witness after witness mounted the stand and swore to the details of the brutal cold-blooded killing of W.H. Broome by Melrose. According to one newspaper account:

> Congressman McLachlan stopped smiling yesterday in face of the terrible array of facts sworn to by the positive witnesses who are winding a rope around the neck of his client.

The Congressman actually participated in the cross-examination of Mrs. Selma Swanson who was one of the key percipient witnesses who testified at the preliminary hearing;

however; it was noted that it would have been "easier to shake the courthouse than Mrs. Swanson."

The prosecution proceeded to put on all of the witnesses who testified at the preliminary hearing and then some. All of the testimony supported the notion that Melrose had shot Broome, without provocation or justification, in cold blood.

During the trial one prosecution witness described in great detail how Melrose shot Broome in the head, without provocation. The witness described how Broome fell to the ground and that Melrose placed the muzzle of his gun against Broome's back while he was laying on the ground, and then fired a second bullet into Broome's body. Rogers then proceeded to have Luther Brown lie on the floor in the courtroom in front of the jury and had the witness describe exactly how Browne was positioned when Melrose shot him "point blank" on the ground. Rogers remembered that the autopsy report contained no mention of any powder burns on Melrose's body and had in fact concluded that the shots must have been fired from some distance to explain the lack of such burns. This point was brought out in the examination of the medical witnesses.

On April 11 th, the defense began to call witnesses. The first defense witness was J. Henry, who told of threats made by Broome against Melrose. On cross-examination it was simply brought out that the witness was a friend of Melrose.

Mrs. Flora Gorman was the next defense witness and she testified that Broome had once told her "not to be surprised if at any time she saw in the paper that he had killed Melrose." C.C. McComas cross-examined Mrs. Gorman and it was brought out that this statement had been made two years earlier.

W.F. Irwin, a rancher near Acton, also testified that he heard threats of violent intent made by Broome directed towards Melrose. A school teacher named Miss Bancher testified that Broome had told her that he would kill Melrose even if he "hanged for it."

Another witness, Paul Durkin, testified that Broome always carried firearms and that once Broome started a fight with him.

> I only escaped because I knocked the lighted butt of a cigar down his throat and he nearly strangled. Broome was a strong man; always looking for a fight.

The newspaper noted that the trial had never been so crowded as it was at this juncture, and that the courtroom was packed with a great number of women. On the morning of April 11th, the defense put fourteen witnesses on the stand, all of whom testified in one form or another about the comments and threats of violence towards Melrose that had been made by Broome.

A New England school teacher testified that she had witnessed the altercation from her home which was about one quarter of a mile from where the incident took place. Miss Plato testified that she had recently purchased a spyglass (small telescope) and that she was peering through it on the day Broome was killed. She testified that she saw Melrose and Broome in a physical altercation; and that at no time did Melrose shoot at Broome while he was laying on the ground.

Another witness, Detective A.W. March, testified that he had heard of a threat that Broome had made to kill Melrose.

When it came time for closing arguments, Luther Brown, Congressman McLachlan and Earl Rogers all gave argument in defense of Melrose. Rogers repeated the comments made by Broome to Melrose on the day of the killing; i.e., that Melrose's wife was no better than a "railroad whore." Said Rogers:

> "And Gentlemen! You may put it on record to refer in my own case if necessary, for if any man uses to me such language as Broome used to Melrose concerning his wife, I will kill him just as quickly as I can."

Rogers recapitulated all of the aggressions made by Broome according to the many witnesses put on by the defense; including the threats and the language used by Broome. He concluded that based upon the conflict of the evidence and the testimony of over twenty defense witnesses, that a reasonable doubt existed as to whether Melrose shot in cold blood, or in self defense. Rogers also drove home the fact that the autopsy report contained no findings of any powder burns on Broome's body and that in order to believe some of the eyewitness accounts you would have to believe that the coroner would have found gun powder burns. Yet the autopsy report was silent on that issue. This was just the case, according to Rogers' argument, of the old line faction of the town grouping together to make sure that "newcomer" Melrose would be punished. It was simply a continuation of the town feud, brought into the courtroom, with perjury having been committed by the witnesses to ensure the conviction of Melrose.

The jury deliberated for forty-five hours, and on April 20, 1903, they entered Judge Smith's courtroom in Department I of the Superior Court and informed him that they were hopelessly deadlocked and that they would never be able to agree on a unanimous verdict. The jury was deadlocked eight votes for acquittal and four votes for conviction. Judge Smith then excused the jury. The murder trial of Norman M. Melrose had ended in a hung jury. But this was not the end of the Acton murder saga, for Mr. Melrose was to be re-tried once again for Broome's murder.

Before the second trial had begun, the prosecution knew that it would have to bolster its case in order to obtain Melrose's conviction. In addition, there were news accounts that Melrose had been a supporter of the then D.A. John Fredericks, and Mr. Fredericks seemed bent on proving to the public that he was not providing any favors to Melrose. Thus he moved with vigor towards the retrial. He instructed his assistant, C.C. McComas, to exhume Broome's body and to conduct further examination. He wanted to see if Broome's body had any gun powder burns which would support the testimony previously given by witnesses that at least one of the shots was fired by Melrose from point blank range.

The exhumation was planned to be done in secrecy without the defense knowing anything about it. However, Rogers obtained a tip from an informant that the autopsy was going to be conducted. He contacted a newspaper man, and in middle of the night shocked everyone at the Evergreen cemetery when he showed up with not only his newspaper friend but a photographer from the newspaper who shot a picture of the bizarre scene.

Rogers demanded that he be allowed to be present when the further examination was conducted. The examination was delayed by several hours and Rogers was allowed to remain present with his own medical experts, Drs. Murphy and Day, along with co-counsel Luther Brown. Broome's head was cut off from his body during the examination. The prosecution wanted to establish that the bullet from Melrose's pistol had entered into the back of Broome's head, thus supporting the prosecution argument that Melrose shot him while he was running away.

Once the head was removed from the body, Broome's scalp was removed from the skull in order to examine the bullet hole in the skull. There seemed to be little question but that a bullet had entered Broome's skull, the only question was the exact location of entry. Dr. Anderson of Lancaster who conducted the autopsy had found the wounds on Broome's skull where Melrose had hit him with the butt of his gun. The question was whether the injury to Broome's skull was caused by a bullet or some other means. Dr. Anderson had included in his prior report that a bullet had entered the skull but provided no further detail since it seemed, based on the overwhelming eyewitness accounts, that the bullet wound to the head would not be much of an issue.

On the reexamination of Broome's skull there were some

holes found, but it could not be determined for certain if the holes were caused by the entry of a bullet. McComas then instructed the physicians to saw the skull into pieces to look for further evidence that the holes were connected to a bullet wound. This was done and the contents of the brain were poured out as well. Despite this effort, there was no further evidence found. In addition, the skin on Broome's body near the area of the entry of the other bullets was too badly decomposed to determine the existence of any gun powder burns. The body of Broome was then pieced back together and re-buried in his grave in the cemetery.

On July 5, 1903 the retrial of Melrose began, Earl Rogers and Luther Brown were present on the opening day of trial to defend Melrose. In his statement of the case to the jury, C.C. McComas stated that:

> The people will prove that Melrose shot, maliciously and designedly, one W.H. Broome to his death. He would not have been picked by a stranger as the villain of the tragedy from real life.

Appearing for the prosecution at the second trial were McComas and Donnell again, together with H.W. Allender and the District Attorney himself, John Fredericks. The jury selection began and was a tedious affair due to the previous notoriety of the case.

Once the trial began, the prosecution put on the same array of witnesses as in the first trial. Witness after witness again repeated their testimony from the first trial; that Melrose had shot and killed Broome for no reason, shot him while he was laying on the ground and savagely kicking the lifeless body.

On July 7, 1903, D.A. Fredericks added some flair that was not present at the first trial by calling Broome's widow to the witness stand. This was a surprise move on the part of the prosecution. The scene was choreographed such that Broome's bloodstained garments were sitting close to the widow as she took the stand. She was dressed in heavy black clothing and appeared the grieving widow.

Mrs. Broome was not a percipient witness to the actual shooting. She was put on the stand to testify as to collateral events which would establish circumstantial evidence as to Melrose's intent and state of mind when the killing of her husband took place. The widow testified as to the prior problems her husband and Melrose had encountered. Mr. Fredericks then pulled out a stack of letters that had been written by Melrose to third parties and then given to Mrs. Broome. Letters in which Melrose characterized Broome as a "clever swindler", and a letter in which Melrose stated that Broome "has too long infested this earth." The Court then shut down the prosecution's effort to have any of these letters read any further to the jury and ruled that all of the letters were inadmissible. Fredericks proceeded to attempt to have each letter, one by one, admitted into evidence, and proceeded to argue with the court as each letter was denied admission into evidence. There was some speculation that the D.A.'s efforts in this regard were to rebut any future allegations that Melrose was treated in a preferential manner due to his prior political support of Fredericks. Wrote the *Los Angeles Record* on July 8, 1903:

> Chagrined that the court would not permit him to introduce his letters, attorney Fredericks offered them one by one, had them labeled and put Judge Smith upon record as turning them down. The only reason for the act was a future vindication of the District Attorney's office against any charge of laxity in a prosecution in which the cry of politics had been raised.

Mrs. Broome went on to testify about a prior incident in which Melrose had shot their family dog to death. According to her testimony, Melrose shot and killed the dog while her little son was astride the back of the dog. That concluded the testimony of Broome's widow.

The defense put on many of the same witnesses as they did in the first trial; once again to establish that Broome had threatened Melrose on many occasions and stated that he hated Melrose and would kill him. Then, to the surprise of everyone, the defense called Earl Rogers as a witness.

Rogers left the counsel table for the witness stand over the objections of District Attorney Fredericks to testify as an expert regarding the autopsy of Broome. Rogers had previously been extensively educated in medical sciences and testified that he had actually assisted in performing over thirty autopsies and had been present for 70 others that had been conducted. He testified about his education and knowledge regarding science and autopsies in general. Judge Smith ruled that Rogers could testify on behalf of the defense and offer his opinions.

Rogers' testimony covered with minute detail the first autopsy. Filled with technical terms of the different parts of the body, with a flow of physiological language at his command, Rogers went into detail as to what he believed happened. The important part of the testimony was that no probe had been passed through the two holes, that the scalp had been cut before Undertaker Weh and Coroner Trout had arrived. Rogers testified that he had carefully examined the space between the two holes in the head and that there was not the slightest evidence of any abrasion which would have been present from a bullet wound. Rogers also testified that when he made his surprise visit to the second secret autopsy after the body had been exhumed that the D.A. had brought with them "a hammer, a chisel and a saw."

The prosecution was attempting to prove that if the first bullet hit Broome in the head, rendering him unconscious but not dead, that there could have been no possible basis for self defense based upon fear to justify the subsequent shots being fired by Melrose into Broome's body which actually caused his death.

Melrose took the witness stand in his own defense. He testified that on the day of the killing, Broome had followed him, shotgun in hand, swearing and calling him and his wife vile names. He told Melrose that his wife was no better than a railroad whore. He stated that Broome proceeded to place his shotgun against a fence, and that he then put up his fists and dared Melrose to fight him. He said that Broome then started back towards his shotgun and that Melrose then pulled his pistol and shot a warning shot into the air intending to scare Broome. As Melrose would have it, Broome then grabbed his shotgun and a struggle ensued between the two men for its possession. During the tussle, Melrose then emptied his revolver into Broome's body.

The defense also recalled Miss Lillian Plato to the stand. She was the New England school teacher who testified at the first trial of having seen through her small telescope the altercation which took place between the two men in corroboration of Melrose's version of events. Miss Plato took the witness stand in the second trial on July 12, 1903, and testified consistent with her prior testimony. She said then when she heard the shooting, she picked up her telescope and saw Broome and Melrose in an altercation on the ground. She testified that at no time did Melrose stand over Broome and fire any shots. This directly contradicted the accounts of the many prosecution witnesses.

With substantially the same evidence and testimony that had been produced during the first trial both sides wrapped up their cases in the second trial.

> It was an appeal to passion and sympathy and at its close one juror was wiping tears from his eyes drawn by the attorney's picture of Melrose as a defender of his own life and the reputation of his wife.

A courtroom packed like a sardine can was on hand to listen to Rogers' closing argument in defense of Melrose. Unlike the first trial in which the jury deliberated for forty-five hours, with a hung jury voting eight for acquittal and four for conviction, the jury in the second trial deliberated for only thirty minutes before returning a verdict of not guilty at 6:00 p.m. on July 17, 1903.

As it turned out, Melrose went on to work for Earl Rogers in a number of capacities, including investigator and personal bodyguard. He would surface in public several years later during Rogers' defense of Patrick Calhoun and Tierry Ford in the famous San Francisco graft cases.

CHAPTER FIVE

The Case of Three Bad Cops?

THE PARTICIPANTS

DEFENDANTS:	Bert Cowen James J. Hawley J.W. Murphy
PROSECUTOR:	William P. James, Assistant District Attorney
DEFENSE ATTORNEYS:	Earl Rogers, Chief Trial Counsel Judd Rush, Co-Counsel Le Compte Davis, Co-Counsel
CHARGE:	Manslaughter

In the latter part of 1903, William Randolph Hearst started a new daily newspaper in Los Angeles, *The Examiner*. The *Los Angeles Times* was owned by General Harrison Gray Otis, who was very anti-labor. Hearst, on the other hand, was pro labor union. The entry of *The Examiner* into the Los Angeles market was difficult. The *Los Angeles Times* and other business leaders made concerted efforts to boycott *The Examiner*, refusing to buy advertisement space and encouraging others to refrain from doing so as well.

The Examiner practiced a brand of newspaper hyperbole known as yellow journalism, with larger-than-life headlines. It created stories with more interest to increase circulation, and thus induce advertisers to buy ad space.

In December of 1903, sixty-year-old Joseph Choisser and his twenty year old son, Louis Choisser, were in Los Angeles, staying at the Broxburn Hotel. They had arrived from Illinois, where Joseph was supposedly a successful businessman. The police received a telegram from the sheriff of Hardin County, Illinois, asking for assistance in the arrest of Joseph Choisser for his participation in defrauding money from investors in Illinois. Three Los Angeles police detectives were sent to the Hotel Broxburn to apprehend the elder Chossier. According to the account given by the detectives, they met resistance when they announced their presence at the hotel. They said that the elder Choisser was sitting on his bed in the hotel room and that he had reached for a gun when they announced themselves. Reacting quickly, the police officers shot and killed Choisser as he sat on his bed in the hotel room. At that point, his son Louis pulled a gun and began firing at the detectives, who retreated into the hallway. As they positioned themselves in the hotel hallway, Louis rushed out to pursue them, gun in hand, and was then shot to death as well.

On December 18, 1903, Dr. George W. Campbell performed an autopsy on the Choissers at the Bresee Brothers undertaking establishment. He found that Louis was five-feet, six inches tall, weighed about 135 pounds, and had five bullet wounds in his cadaver. The bullet wounds indicated three points of entry into the body and two points of exit.

Coroner J.H. Trout and Deputy Coroner JW. Surnmerfield presided over the inquest on the body of Louis Chossier on the evening of December 18, 1903, the autopsy having been conducted earlier that afternoon. The inquest resulted in the exoneration of the three policemen who were involved in the shooting. The three officers were patrolman J.W. Murphy, Detective James J. Hawley and Detective Bert Cowen.

The Examiner sent several reporters to the hotel to sniff around for information regarding the events and circumstances of the deaths of the two Choissers. What followed were a series of sensational front page articles in which the three officers were accused of having murdered the two men in cold blood. Feature stories were published that key eyewitnesses had been offered bribes to leave the state and avoid being called as witnesses in any proceedings against the three officers. The articles demanded justice and warned the public that Los Angeles had a police force with thugs and murderers on the loose. Article after article was printed with major headlines declaring that an array of witnesses had been located who had seen the cold-blooded murders of two innocent men.

Public interest and awareness of the incident was aroused and the District Attorney's office charged Murphy, Cowen and Hawley with manslaughter. Earl Rogers, along with prominent local attorneys Judd Rush and Le Compte Davis, were retained to represent the policemen. Assistant D.A. William P. James was assigned to prosecute the case.

On January 1, 1904, a front page article appeared in *The Examiner* alleging that two of the key prosecution witnesses

W. P. James, District Attorney
"Courtesy of University of
Southern California, on behalf
of the USC Library Department
of Special Collections."

had been offered bribes in connection with their prospective testimony. Albert Lowell and Leroy Smith both asserted that they were offered money to "leave town" and be unavailable to testify against the police officers. The two men provided detailed accounts of the bribery offer to Ona Morton, an attorney who had charge of interests of the Choisser relatives, and to the former State's Attorney of Hardin County, Illinois who was in Los Angeles to help investigate the killings. The bribery offer was made by a man whose name was unknown to Lowell and Smith; but he told them he would get back in touch with them concerning the offer.

Ona Morton made a statement to *The Examiner* that:

> I think the employment of detectives by us has frightened this would be briber into temporary inactivity.

The Examiner insinuated in its article that the would-be-briber was possibly connected to another detective by the name of S.H. Verrill, who had been retained by defense attorneys Rush and Le Compte. Both Lowell and Smith claimed to have been contacted by the would be briber on January 6, 1904. He was described as approximately forty-five years old, tall, broad shouldered, with dark hair, dark complexion, and a mustache mixed with gray. He wore a black derby hat and a big heavy gold watch chain. The incident was initially described by the two men to a detective Appel, who had been hired by attorney Morton. Appel in turn took the men to meet with attorney Morton. As the front page *Examiner* stories would have it, the defendants and their attorneys were resorting to illegal tactics in an attempt to avoid prosecution.

On January 9, 1904, the preliminary examination of detectives Hawley, Murphy and Cowen, charged with manslaughter in the case of Louis Choisser, began in Justice Chambers' courtroom which was packed to capacity with spectators.

The key prosecution witnesses were actually individuals uncovered by reporters from *The Examiner* during their investigation of the incident. Joseph Atkinson was in his room two doors away from the Choissers when he heard a shot. He ran to Choisser's room to see what had happened. The elder Choisser, Joseph, was on the closet floor being attended to by his son Louis. Atkinson helped Louis move his father to the bed. Louis then indicated to Atkinson that he was going to go summon a doctor to help his father and proceeded to run out of the hotel room into the hall. A moment later, according to Atkinson, several more gunshots rang out from the hallway area. Rogers cross-examined Atkinson:

Question (By Rogers): Mr. Atkinson, what were you doing when you heard the last shots, the shots out in the hall?

Answer (By Atkinson): I was stamping the fire out of Mr. Choisser's vest—the elder Choisser.

Q: Aren't you using the word stamping in that particular because your original idea was that the vest was on the floor and you were stamping it with your feet?

A: No sir.

Q: How many shots did you hear from out in the hall?

A: Three.

Q: You say that you and young Choisser picked the old man up from the closet area and then threw him on the bed?

A: Yes sir.

Q: But not sufficiently violently so that even a man that was vitally shot would be hurt by it?

A: I don't think it hurt him.

Q: Did you see anything on the clothing when you picked him up or afterwards?

At what time afterwards?

Q: Or at any time you were in the room?

A: I think there was blood on his shirt.

Q: You think there was?

A: Yes sir.

Q: Did you see it?

A: Yes, something red like blood.

Q: You signed a statement previously about what you saw?

A: Yes, that's correct.

Q: Where were you when you signed your statement about what you saw?

A: In a room at the Broxburn.

Q: Was it your room at the hotel?

A: No sir.

Q: Whose room were you in when you signed that statement?

A: Mr. Appel's room.

Q: Mr. Appel's room?

A: Yes sir, in his room.

Q: That's the same Mr. Appel who is working for Choisser's family members?

A: I'm not really sure who he works for.

Q: Do you know whether or not the young Choisser had a revolver in his possession on the night of the shooting?

A: Well, I didn't see him with a revolver in his possession.

Q: Do you remember you testified earlier that the young man was wearing a dark coat and then you changed your testimony?

A: Yes, but I was thinking of one thing and saying another; I meant to say dark vest and pants.

Q: How did you confuse a vest with a dark coat?

A: I don't know but what I meant was vest and pants.

Q: Do you recall that prior to living at the Broxburn Hotel that you lived on the corner of south Main and Second streets?

A: Yes sir.

Q: Do you recall that your landlady's name was Mrs. Medlar?

A: Yes sir.

Q: Do you remember an occasion where you and some of your friends were making something of a rough house over there and Officer Murphy, one of my client's in this case, was called over there and put you out of the house?

A: No, I don't remember that.

Q: Never happened?

A: No.

Q: Sure about that?

A: It didn't happen, at least not that I can recall at this time.

Q: Is it possible that you have just forgotten about what happened between you and Murphy?

A: I don't think so.

Q: Will you swear that young Choisser didn't have a revolver in his possession when he left the hotel room for the hallway just outside the room?

A: If he did, I didn't see it.

Q: What time was it when you heard the first shots that evening?

A: Somewhere between nine thirty and ten o'clock.

On January 12, 1904, the prosecution put Arthur Clough on the witness stand. Clough testified that when he heard the initial shot he was in his room in the hotel and proceeded to stand on his bed and look out into the hallway through the transom of his hotel room door. He stated that he observed young Louis Choisser leave his hotel room and enter into the hallway area. He saw Choisser running down the hallway unarmed. He then saw Detectives Murphy and Cowen both shoot the young man; each a distance away from the victim of about four feet.

Question (By James): Did you, Mr. Clough, pay any special attention or direct—have any reason to direct your observation to Louis Choisser's hands as he came down the hall?

Answer (By Clough): Yes.

Q: And what was that reason?

A: I had heard shooting, seeing the officers hiding behind the corner of this hall, seeing the boy come out of room 63, run rapidly down the hall, and I was very curious to know if there would be more shooting. I seen guns in the officers hands and was wondering whether he was running down the hall to shoot at those officers or what he was doing, or whether he was trying to escape.

Q: Now, when you looked out of the hall and as you say, saw the young man fall, or about to fall, what was the position of his hands and how did he fall?

A: When I looked out in the hall he was in that position where he had his hands above his head and legs together and he fell forward on his face.

Q: At that point in time was there anything in Mr. Choisser's hands?

A: No sir.

Q: When you got to the body did you see anything—I mean firearms or any instrument of any kind lying about the body of the young man?

A: The only firearms I seen were in the hands of Mr. Cowen and Mr. Murphy.

Despite cross-examination which delved into Clough's drinking problems, past suicide attempts, and acts of dishonesty, Clough stuck to his story and maintained that he was stone sober when he witnessed the shooting. An example of the cross-examination of Clough follows.

Question (By Rogers): Do you ever go by any name save that of Arthur B. Clough?

Answer (By Clough): No sir.

Q: Never did at any time?

A: No sir.

Q: Haven't you ever made use of the name J.A. Smith?

A: No sir.

Q: Do you remember one occasion when the police here accused you of having stolen some jewelry from your wife?

A: I had forgotten that. I didn't steal any jewelry from my wife, but I had some jewelry of mine.

Q: She reported it stolen, didn't she?

A: No sir.

Q: You took the jewelry and you did sell under the name of J.A. Smith, didn't you?

A: No, I pawned it in the name of A. Bennett, Arthur Bennett, my first and middle names.

Q: Do you know whether you sold or pawned the jewelry?

A: Pawned.

Q: You know that Mr. Murphy and Mr. Hawley, two of the men who stand accused here today, are the two men who recovered that jewelry when it was reported stolen?

A:I found that afterwards.

Q: You found that out prior to the time that you agreed to come forward on behalf of the prosecution and testify in these proceedings, though, correct?

A: Yes sir.

Howard Mix was called to the witness stand and testified that he was in Mr. Atkinson's room at the time of the shooting and that he saw young Choisser running down the hallway in the hotel just before he was shot. Mix testified that he could observe Choisser's hands and that he was not in possession of a revolver.

D.F. Abel was then called upon by the prosecution to testify. On the night of the shooting he was staying at the Broxburn Hotel. He was in town from Nevada having brought with him a car load of horses to sell in Los Angeles. Mr. Abel was in the process of getting undressed for bed when he heard a gunshot.

Question (By Assistant D.A.): What were you doing when you heard the first gunshot?

Answer (By Abel): I was sleeping at that time; the sound of the gunshot woke me up.

Q: Do you recall the time?

A: It had to somewhere near ten o'clock.

Q: Then, what next after the gunshot, what did you hear next?

A: Then I heard some running in the hall.

Q: Did you open your hotel room door?

A: Yes.

Q: What did you see?

A: I saw a man standing around the corner with a gun in his hand, head poked around the corner, and he was saying "Hi there, come out of there; what are you doing in there, you son of a bitch?"

Q: I will direct your attention, if I may, to Mr. Murphy, who sits here, one of the defendants in this case, and ask you whether or not the man that you saw resembles him, and if so-

A: The man sitting there in the center?

Q: Mr. Murphy, will you stand up please?

A: That is the man I saw.

Q: Did Mr. Murphy say anything to you?

A: No sir.

Q: Did you say anything to him?

A: No sir.

Q: Now what was Mr. Murphy's language?

A: He says: "Hi there, what we you doing in there? Come out of there YOU son of a bitch."

Q: What did you do then?

A: I closed the door and went back into my room.

The prosecution then called Deputy District Attorney Flemming to the witness stand. He testified that after the three detectives had been exonerated at the coroner's inquest that he went with them to the hotel and that they described where all of the shooting had taken place in the altercation with the Choisser's. Flemming described in detail and with the aid of charts as to the exact locations described by the detectives as to where the shootings had taken place.

Mrs. Adelle Milk was called to the witness stand by the prosecution. She gave her age as forty-two, her status as married, her occupation as a chamber maid at the Broxburn Hotel. She had worked at the hotel since November of 1903.

Question (By Asst. D.A.): Now what were your duties at the hotel in connection with the room occupied by the Choissers?

Answer (By Milk): Doing the chamber work; taking care of their room.

Q: Now, did you ever see any revolvers in that room during the time you that they were in occupancy there?

Yes sir.

Q: How many guns did you see?

A: Two.

Q: Where did you first see them?

A: Under the pillow.

Q: When?

A: The first morning I did their room up.

Q: How were they arranged?

A: They were just lying under the pillow.

Q: Both under one pillow?

A: No, sir; one under each pillow.

Q: What did you do with them when you handled them?

A: I put them in a small grip.

Q: What made you put them in a small grip?

A: Because I saw them there; found them there afterwards; that is where they kept them.

Q: On the 17th of December, 1903, did you see the revolvers?

A: Yes sir, I did.

Q: What time of day did you see them and where?

A: Between four and five o'clock.

Q: Where did you see them?

A: In the grip.

Q: Did you ever see more than two revolvers; revolvers other than these two revolvers in their room?

A: No sir.

Q: After the shooting what was the condition of the bed clothing and the bed?

A: There was one blood stain on it.

Q: Where and upon what?

A: It was through the quilt and was about three inches round.

Q: Did you clean the closet in that room?

A: Yes sir.

Q: Were there any stains there, and if so what were the number and size of the stains?

A: There were two small stains on the floor and one on the wall.

Q: What type of floor covering was in the closet?

A: Linoleum.

Q: What did you do with respect to the blood stains that were on the floor, if anything?

A: I washed them up.

Q: What were the sizes of the two stains?

A: One was the size of a quarter and the other the size of a nickel,

Q: How high up on the wall of the closet was the other blood stain?

A: About eight to ten inches from the floor.

Q: Can you describe that blood stain?

A: Yes, it was smeared on the wall.

Another witness was put on the stand by the name of G.A. Schneider to corroborate some of the prior witnesses testimony. However, the prosecution was somewhat startled when on direct examination he revealed something else that he observed on the day of the killing; a gun in the possession of young Louis Choisser.

> Question (By James): Now, Mr. Schneider, just tell in your own way all that you saw and heard and did immediately after the shooting commenced.
>
> Answer (By Schneider): I heard a scuffle which sounded like it was coming from, the adjoining room which adjoins the corner of my room. I heard what you might call a scuffle or struggle fiorn the other room. I then heard two or three shots and when I heard those shots I immediately went out of my room into the hall from my room and I turned and went towards room 63. When I passed out into the hall from my room towards room 63, 1 saw Mr. Atkinson. He was standing at the door of his room. From there I passed to room 63 and I saw the young Choisser-that is the boy; and he was-a-he asked for help.
>
> Q: Tell us what he said.
>
> A: Yes sir. He said "the son of bitch he shot my father. Come help me boys." And as he was speaking, I saw him there, and he had a gun in his hand, and I didn't understand the situation exactly, but I could clearly see the gun. It was a nickel-plated gun. It was a nickel-plated revolver that was in his hand.

The prosecution rested their case on September 16, 1904. They had presented numerous eyewitnesses, including Joseph Atkinson, Howard Mix, Arthur Clough, Harry Rosco, Mrs. Clough, Robert Rice, and David Abel, all of whom testified that Louis Choisser was unarmed when he was shot in the hallway of the hotel; once in the chest and one bullet in the back. However, there was the one witness, Mr. Schneider, who had testified contrary to all of the other witnesses when he testified that the young Choisser had a nickel-plated revolver in his hand when he saw him running down the hall.

On April 16, 1904, the defense called J.B. Hawley, an assayer and expert on firearms and ammunition to the stand. He testified as to his analysis of two bullets that had been found at the scene of the shooting, one bullet having been removed from the doorjamb of Arthur Clough's room which was said to have been fired by Louis Choisser at Detective Murphy. Hawley testified that the chemical analysis of the composition of those two bullets were different and did not match the composition of the bullets used in the guns possessed by any of the three detectives. He testified further, that the two bullets did match the composition of the bullets which remained in the gun used by the young Choisser. His conclusion was that at least two bullets had been fired in the hallway of the Broxburn Hotel from the gun which had been in the possession of Choisser.

Hawley's testimony was novel if not revolutionary, for the science of ballistic testing had never been used before in a West Coast courtroom.

The defense put two witnesses on the stand: one Detective Paul Flammer and the other, Los Angeles Chief of Police Elton, to corroborate the testimony of Flammer. Flammer testified that he examined the sill of the transom over the door leading to the room occupied by Clough soon after the shooting had taken place. He found that the dust in the area around the transom had an accumulation of dust which was virtually undisturbed. This obviously could not have been the case if Clough had, as he had testified earlier, rested his arms on the sill, while witnessing what transpired outside in the hall. Elton's testimony simply corroborated that of Flammer; that he too had inspected the area on the sill and that there was an undisturbed accumulation of dust thereon.

Earl Rogers was convinced that the only reason his clients were going through this entire ordeal was based upon the creation and hyperbole created at the inception of the incident by the tactics of reporters from *The Examiner* to create a sensational story. Part of creating the sensational story were the public claims of two men who claimed that they had been offered a bribe by a mystery man to leave town in order to avoid being available to testify against the defendants. Earl Rogers called Leroy Smith to the stand in an effort to expose this concoction.

Question (By Rogers) Now you were not even at the hotel when the shootings took place were you?

Answer (By Smith): That's correct.

Q: You were at the theater and didn't return to the Broxburn hotel until after the shootings took place and the two men were already dead, correct?

A: That's correct.

Q: Did you see your picture in the Los Angeles *Examiner* on January 9th?

A: Why, surely I did.

Q: Did you make, on or about January 8th of this year, in the city of Los Angeles, to a reporter of *The Examiner*, or any person employed by *The Examiner*, a statement to the effect that someone had attempted to bribe you by offering money for you to leave the state to avoid testifying in this case?

A: Yes I did.

Q: Was it true?

A: Yes.

Q: Did you sign a statement and swear to it?

A: I signed a statement; but I didn't swear to it.

Q: Who was this person who you say offered you this bribe?

A: I don't know who he was, sir.

Q: Had you ever seen this man before or since?

A: No I have not.

Q: Don't you know this was a fake, pure and simple just to make a little stir, a little muss? Don't you know that?

A: Was it?

Q: You knew it was a fake didn't you?

A: No.

Q: Describe the man who offered a bribe to you?

A: Well, he is a man about six feet, broad shoulders, dark hair, had a brown suit of clothes on, mustache, derby hat.

Q: Did he tell you who he was?

A: No he did not.

Q: At the time that you say this offer was made to you, did you report it to anyone with the district attorney's office?

A: No sir, I did not.

Q: Who did you report it to?

A: The first man I said anything to was Appel.

Q: Mr. Appel didn't take you to the district attorney's office did he?

A: No he didn't.

Q: So you had been offered an illegal bribe and you didn't go directly to the district attorney?

A: That's correct.

Q: How did you wind up telling the story to *The Examiner*?

A: Appel relayed what I said to him to Mr. Morton.

Q: And that's the same Mr. Morton who is attorney for the interests of the relatives of Mr. Choisser?

A: I think that's correct.

Q: How long after you first told your story to Mr. Appel did you have an interview with *The Examiner*?

A: Within a couple of hours.

Q: So instead of going to an officer of the law with your story so that the briber could possibly be apprehended, you decided to have your picture taken and story told to the public which would ensure that the mystery briber would never again surface?

A: (No answer).

Q: Did you tell the reporter at *The Examiner* that you wanted them to wait on the story, let this man come back and try to bribe you again and have him watched?

A: I told him just like this; I says; I don't want to tell you the story, I says, I don't know whether it is right to tell you —

Q: What did he do? Did he chloroform you to get the story?

A: Do I look like I need to be chloroformed?

Q: Yes.

A: Do I?

Q: Did you give up this story by the long, sad, serious process of extraction, or did you spring it along with the photograph?

A: If you will let me tell you, I will tell you.

Question (Cont'd): the mystery briber would never again surface?

A: (No answer).

Q: And you were a very valuable prosecution witness in this case were you not? You arrived at the hotel after all the shooting took place, when the event was all over and you knew nothing about what happened that had not been told to you by other people. Yet you are the target of the briber who is willing to pay you to leave town to avoid being called as a witness; such an important witness that you are interviewed by *The Examiner* and make the front page picture and all. You were part of this fraud weren't you?

A: No sir.

Detective Murphy took the stand. He testified again how at the Broxburn hotel he and the two other detectives had gone to at the direction of Captain Bradish to arrest Joseph Choisser, and that they had with them a telegram from law enforcement in Illinois requesting that the arrest be made. He went on to recount the story he told at the inquest. When the officers entered into the hotel room and announced themselves, Joseph Choisser was sitting on the bed and reached for his gun and was then shot. They then ran out of the room when the younger Choisser brandished a weapon at them. Murphy testified:

Answer (By Murphy): About a niinute or a minute and a half after I reached this corner of the hall young Choisser left his room and ran down the hall toward me. First I was going to shoot him in his door. Then I waited, thinking that I would overpower him. When he came up to within two feet of me he shot at me. Then I shot at him. I hit him in the breast. Cowen also shot. Young

Choisser fell about twelve feet from me down the hall. I ran up and took the gun out of his right hand. I had been shot at twice before I shot. Once in the room and once in the hallway. The only words that were spoken in the hall were the words I spoke to Cowen. I says, "I think Hawley's shot." Cowen then says "I think he is."

Q: For what purpose did you draw your revolver in the hall?

A: To defend myself.

In summation before Justice Chambers the prosecution claimed that the evidence to support the three detectives being held to answer on charges of manslaughter was conclusive. They summed up their case by arguing that Joseph Choisser, a well-to-do cattle buyer from Harrisburg, Illinois and his son Louis, were sought for arrest by Hawley, Murphy and Cowen without any valid warrant. Joseph was killed without warning, and that Louis was killed as he was on his way for a doctor to attend to his father and that at the time he was killed he was not armed with any weapon.

The defense summed up their argument by stating that the officers went to the hotel with a telegram from out-of-state law enforcement officials to arrest Joseph Choisser, who they shot in self-defense when he reached for his gun. Louis Choisser fired at the officers while they were inside the hotel room causing them to retreat into the hallway, where Louis was subsequently shot in self-defense when he fired upon the officers. The defense argued that scientific testing had proved that at least two bullets were found at the scene which had not come from the officers' guns but from the gun of Choisser; thus bolstering their claim of self-defense.

Judge Chambers found that probable cause did not exist to hold any of the men over to Superior Court on the charge of manslaughter and the case was dismissed on January 23, 1904. That ended any effort to prosecute Murphy, Cowen or Hawley for the deaths of Joseph and Louis Choisser.

The Captain of Detectives, A.J. Bradish, summed it up this

way in his statement after the court ruling was issued:

> The officers were wholly justified in shooting. If they had
> not been they would justly have been branded as inefficient
> and cowardly. I deplore the circumstances that make it nec-
> essary for human life ever to be taken, but there are times when
> it has to be done, and the affair of the Broxburn was one of
> them.

This, of course, would not be the last time that the Los
Angeles media would be accused of trying a high-profile criminal prosecution in the press, nor of allegations being made
against the Los Angeles Police Department of a thuggish,
"shoot first, ask questions later," mentality. And, as usual, Earl
Rogers was there, center stage, as the modern era of Los Angeles was being invented.

CHAPTER SIX

The Case of the Crazy Colonel

THE PARTICIPANTS

DEFENDANT:	Colonel Griffith J. Griffith
PROSECUTORS:	District Attorney, John Fredericks
	Ex-Governor Henry T. Gage,
	Special Prosecutor
	Isadore B. Dockweiler,
	Special Prosecutor
DEFENSE ATTORNEYS:	Earl Rogers, Chief Trial Counsel
	Luther Brown, Co-Counsel
	Major John F. Jones, Co-Counsel
CHARGE:	Attempted Murder

Griffith J. Griffith was born in a small town near Cardiff in south Wales on January 4, 1850. His parents were of very modest means and he lived his childhood in relative poverty. Through the larges of some relatives, Griffith moved to the United States in 1866; to Scylkill City, in Pennsylvania. He was taken in by the Mowry family and went to public school.

Later, Griffith moved to New York where he got a job and went to school to study journalism. In the 1870s he moved to San Francisco and obtained a job as a manger for the Herald Publishing Company, which owned and operated a number of newspapers, After holding down this job for some time, Griffith became a newspaper reporter. He developed a specialization in writing stories on matters concerning the mining industry and ultimately became a mining industry correspondent for the newspaper. In this capacity, Griffith traveled around the country writing detailed reports on the various mining ventures of interest. His reports became highly respected for their detail and accuracy and he developed many important contacts in the mining industry.

In 1876, Griffith was actually retained by an investment consortium and paid a small fortune to perform an extensive report on some of their holdings. Afterwards, Griffith continued to work as a mining correspondent; however he was also retained to perform special projects for mining investors for which he was handsomely compensated.

In 1879 and 1880, Griffith invested in some silver mining ventures in Utah and Mexico, making a substantial sum of money as a result. In 1882, Griffith, who had previously made visits to Los Angeles, purchased the Rancho Las Feliz which was a tract of land comprised of about 4071 acres for an amount which is not known precisely but which was speculated to be between $8,000 and $50,000. He purchased the land from Thomas Bell on December 8, 1882. Subsequently Griffith received all or more of his investment back when he sold water rights connected to the land to the city for $50,000.

While living in Los Angeles Griffith met Louis Mesmer, a very wealthy and influential man and the patriarch of one of Los Angeles' most respected and prominent families. Mesmer had a daughter, Mary Agnes Christina Mesmer, whose nickname was Tina. A courtship was begun between Tina Mesmer and Griffith which led to their eventual marriage on January 27, 1887. Through inheritance, Tina was estimated to be worth in excess of one million dollars at the time she married Griffith in 1887; an astronomical sum of money at that time. The newspaper coverage in the *Los Angeles Times* on January 28, 1887, said of the union:

Col. Griffith J. Griffith
"Courtesy of University of Southern California, on behalf
of the USC Library Department of Special Collections."

A wedding which may be said to possess more than usual
local and social importance took place in this city yesterday
morning. By this marriage two immense estates were united,
the large possessions of G.J. Griffith and a vast amount of Los
Angeles property, owned by the charming bride, Miss Mary
Agnes Christina Mesmer, daughter of Mr. and Mrs. Louis
Mesmer, familiarly known among her most intimate society
friends as "Tina." Besides the Los Feliz rancho, Mr. Griffith
is the fortunate possessor of a number of rich gold, silver and
lead mines. The bride's Los Angeles property which she owns
in her own right, will certainly not be worth less than
$1,000,000.

The two had a son, Vandell Mowry Griffith, who was born
on August 29, 1888. Griffith's fortunes had certainly been

enhanced by his marriage to Tina. Griffith continued to wheel and deal in Los Angeles, greatly enhancing his fortune. He took control of his wife's fortune and arranged a sale for a portion of her real estate holdings for close to a million dollars.

Although Griffith was known as being a shrewd business man and was regarded as being socially significant, he was also viewed as an egomaniac who was exceedingly full of himself, and he went to extremes to gain advantage in business dealings with others. One such situation almost cost the Colonel his life on October 28, 1891.

A man by the name of Frank Burkett leased a portion of land on the Los Feliz ranch with an option to purchase. When Griffith heard that Burkett had entered into an agreement with a third party to sell his parcel, he sent out notification that Burkett's rights had been forfeited. Burkett brought suit to protect his rights but the case ended in a non-suit. He wanted to appeal but was advised by his then partner, Henry T. Gage, not to take an appeal. Burkett lost several thousand dollars as a result of Griffith's actions and had become very angry regarding his financial loss and derogatory statements made by Griffith to others about him.

Griffith was at a graveyard when he was approached by Burkett who shot at him with a shotgun causing superficial injuries to his head and shoulders. Burkett then took a pistol and shot himself fatally in the head. Coroner Weldon conducted an inquest, and the cause of death was officially determined to be a suicide. Griffith, having survived his brush with death, continued as a major Los Angeles business player and subsequently began discussions with the city about a proposed donation of a tract of his land. On March 5, 1898, Griffith donated, and the city of Los Angeles accepted, 3,015 acres of land which is now Griffith Park and Observatory. It was one of the largest private gifts of land ever made in the world.

It was against this backdrop that a most shocking and spec-

Mary Agnes Christina
"Tina" Mesmer
Courtesy of Van Griffith

tacular event took place while Griffith, his wife and his son were on vacation at the Arcadia Hotel in Santa Monica on September 3, 1903. Colonel Griffith J. Griffith held a revolver in his hand and shot his pleading wife Tina in the head!

On the evening of September 4, 1903, Mrs. Griffith, gave an account of what happened to one of her relatives, who related the information to a reporter with the *Los Angeles Times*. Mrs. Griffith reported that she was in her hotel room at the Arcadia in Santa Monica, packing her trunk in preparation for the trip back to Los Angeles when her husband entered the room. He pulled out his revolver, pointed it at Mrs. Griffith and said: "Get your prayer book and kneel down and cover your eyes. I'm going to shoot you and I'm going to kill you."

According to Mrs. Griffith's account, she then begged him to lay down his revolver, saying: "Oh, Griffith, don't, please don't!"

Arcadia Hotel in Santa Monica, where the Griffith shooting occurred.
The Griffith's room was at the center of the hotel, with the wooden roof
of the suite directly below where Tina fell.
Courtesy, *Santa Monica Public Library Image Archives*

At that point, having just made her plea for mercy, Griffith
J. Griffith shot his wife in the face. After being shot she sprang
towards her husband and scuffled with him, noticed that the
window in the room was open, let go of her husband, then ran
to the open window and jumped out. She fell on the porch roof
after a fall of about ten to twelve feet and fractured her shoulder. She got up, walked on the roof to an open window on the
second floor of the hotel, climbed through the window to someone's room and then collapsed. She was initially treated for her
injuries at the hotel by Dr. Crawford of Santa Monica.

According to the account of the story which appeared in
the September 5, 1903, issue of the *Los Angeles Times,* Mrs.
Griffith revealed that her husband had threatened to kill her
previously and she believed him to be insane.

Mrs. Griffith was taken in a special car to the California

hospital, where she was treated for the gunshot wound and a compound fracture to her shoulder resulting from the fall from the third to the second story. By the time she arrived at the hospital she had lost consciousness. After making a careful examination, Dr. M. L. Moore decided that an immediate operation was necessary.

An operation was performed to remove the bullet. In the process it was deemed necessary to remove Mrs. Griffith's entire left eye. According to her surgeon, Dr. Moore, the bullet struck Mrs. Griffith at the outer edge of her left eye, and hit the bone at the edge of the eye socket, fracturing it and splitting it into fragments. One piece of lead passed directly through the eyeball and others glanced along her skull and under her scalp. Had the bullet struck a sixteenth of an inch farther to the right, it would have caused instant death for it would have penetrated the brain.

Colonel Griffith dismissed the incident as an accidental discharge of the revolver by his wife. He claimed that while she was packing her trunk in the hotel room, the gun was accidentally discharged, the bullet hit her in the head, and that she fell to the floor and broke her shoulder bone.

Members of Mrs. Griffith's family, including her brothers; immediately told the press that the Colonel's version of events was false; that their sister had not shot herself by any accident and that her broken shoulder was sustained by falling out the window, not by falling to the floor of her hotel room.

Griffith maintained that any story that his wife's injuries were the result of anything other than an accident were "wholly false." Griffith's version was as follows:

> Mrs. Griffith spent a part of the afternoon on the beach while I called on friends in Santa Monica. I returned to the hotel about five o'clock. Mrs. Griffith had arrived there before me, and was engaged in packing a trunk, preparatory to our intended departure for Los Angeles. I entered our rooms and began to help her, folding up clothing of my own and doing

other little things of that sort. Suddenly, a revolver—a hammerless weapon of mine, I believe—was discharged, the bullet striking my wife in the face and inflicting a glancing wound across the right side of the forehead as I afterward ascertained. Mrs. Griffith cried out "I am hurt," or some words like that, and ran to the window. Almost immediately afterwards she fell out of the window. Looking out and down, I saw her rising to her knees from the roof of the veranda. There was blood on her face. I at once called the bellboy and gave the alarm, following him presently to the hotel office, where I stated that there had been an accident in which Mrs. Griffith had unfortunately shot herself, and that she also had fallen from the window."

That is all there is to the story, and I cannot see why any attempt should be made to create a sensation about it. It is a most unfortunate affair, most unfortunate, indeed, but purely an accident, and one in which the public is not concerned.

A reporter asked Griffith, "Where in the room was Mrs. Griffith standing, or sitting, at the moment the revolver was discharged?"

Griffith responded:, "Now I am not sure—I was so stunned and bewildered. But I think she was bending over the trunk and placing clothing in it. The hammer of the pistol must have struck against the edge of the trunk."

The reporter inquired further: "Then it was a hammerless revolver?"

"Why—ah—yes, I think it was. Yes, I think so. But I cannot be perfectly sure. Yes sir, the weapon belongs to me, and I have had it for some time. No, I cannot say why Mrs. Griffith had the pistol—but she must have had it in her hand at the time. I am quite sure she had it in her hand."

"What was Mrs. Griffith doing with the weapon?"

"Indeed I cannot tell. She certainly had not made any demonstration with it. I tell you the whole thing was an accident."

"The story is in circulation Colonel, that immediately prior to the shooting an altercation was in progress between yourself and your wife. Is that correct?"

"It is not correct. My wife and I have never quarreled. The poor thing is a—is a Catholic—don't believe in that sort of thing—doesn't know any better; and—well you understand. But on this occasion there was no quarrel between us."

"Where were you standing with reference to Mrs. Griffith's position at the time the shot was fired?"

"Now, I couldn't tell you that. I was startled, stunned, utterly bewildered by the shot. I cannot remember where I stood."

"How close to the window was Mrs. Griffith when the shot was fired?"

"She was very close to it—right beside it in fact."

"Not bending over the trunk then?"

"Yes, I think she was."

"How near the window was the trunk?"

"Oh a couple of feet away. Very close. Right at the window."

"The window is at the far end of a narrow gableway at the side of the room is it not? And this gableway is at least ten feet long? And the trunk was standing in the room proper not in the gableway?"

"Those statements are correct," responded Griffith.

"The story that has gone out," the reporter continued, "is to the effect that you were drinking heavily on Thursday and that when you entered your room an altercation arose between yourself and Mrs. Griffith and that the revolver was discharged while you and your wife struggled for its possession. Is this story wholly incorrect?"

"Wholly so," responded Griffith, who had always prided himself as someone who was not a drinker. "I was sober and I can prove it by friends on whom I called that afternoon. I have told you there was no quarrel with Mrs. Griffith. I have no idea why she had the gun in her hand. There was no struggle of any kind between us. The whole thing bewildered me."

"Do you know why, after having been shot, your wife ran to the window, instead of throwing herself on the bed or waiting while you summoned help?"

"No, I don't know why she went to the window, but maybe it was to get fresh air. The whole thing was a most unfortunate accident, and I regret it more than anyone else. I have scarcely eaten a thing since it happened, and I could hardly sleep last night."

The newspapers commented on what they observed to be odd behavior on the part of Griffith on the day of his wife's operation. He visited the hospital briefly in the morning and then went to lunch at the Jonathan Club. He then attended a meeting at the City Hall of the Board of Park Commissioners.

The *Los Angeles Times* wrote on September 6, 1903:

> Few men in Los Angeles are more generally known than Col. Griffith. He has been a prominent figure in this city for many years. He is the owner of the famous Los Feliz rancho, a portion of which was deeded to the city as Griffith Park. As to public spiritedness, he has given frequent evidences of the possession of that quality and he has often taken a leading part in pubic affairs. However, he has long been regarded as peculiar in some respects. When in his normal condition he has been the personification of geniality, but when in his cups and he has not frequently been in that condition he has been known to give way to a display of violent temper when crossed even about little things.

The newspaper went on to describe Mrs. Griffith's late father, Louis Messmer, as "one of the most widely known of the pioneers of Los Angeles County who had amassed a fortune and owned the United States Hotel."

A group of Mrs. Griffith's family members saw to it that certain information was leaked to the press concerning their opinions regarding the Colonel.

It became publicly circulated in the newspapers shortly after the shooting that Griffith had used extortive means to obtain property worth many hundreds of thousands of dollars from his wife shortly before their marriage.

It was reported in the press that after the Griffith's were publicly engaged to be married and the wedding invitations had been sent out, when the soon-to-be Mrs. Griffith was placed in an intolerably embarrassing situation were the wedding to be canceled, that the Colonel demanded that she deed over to him an extremely valuable piece of real estate known as the Briswalter tract. The property was deeded over to the Colonel who then controlled a substantial portion of his wife's fortune in addition to his own.

The press also reported that Griffith hated Catholics "worse than poison." Mrs. Griffith was Catholic and apparently the two had arguments regarding the religious upbringing of their son, Van.

At first, Colonel Griffith didn't believe that he was in harm's way in terms of criminal prosecution. He truly believed that due to his wealth and social standing that the District Attorney would never charge him with any crime. Griffith was dead wrong.

His wife's outraged family members arranged for the retention of prominent Special Prosecutors to assist District Attorney John Fredericks in the prosecution on the charge of attempted murder. Retained were Isidore B. Dockweiler, a very well-known and successful attorney, and Henry T. Gage who had previously served as the Governor of California. Ex-Governor Gage was considered one of the state's foremost trial lawyers, close in reputation to the late Senator Stephen White.

Griffith finally began to realize the severity of his circumstances. A conviction of attempted murder could result in a prison term in excess of twelve years. On February 12, 1904, just four days before his scheduled criminal trial, Colonel Griffith J. Griffith retained Earl Rogers to defend him against the charge that he had attempted to murder his wife on September 3, 1903.

Especially in light of the press interviews that Griffith had given after the incident, the defense of Colonel Griffith was quite a challenge. Rogers developed a novel defense theory of "alcoholic insanity" in which he would argue that Griffith had been a closet alcoholic for many years. The effect of alcohol on Griffith led him to have delusions that his wife was in a conspiracy with the Pope to poison him; and that his wife was not faithful to him.

It would be argued that the effect of the long years of drinking up to a pint of whiskey every day had resulted in these delusions on the part of Griffith, and that on the day of the shooting he believed that his wife was trying to poison him.

The irony and agony for Griffith of his lawyers' strategy was the impact it had on his self-esteem and ego. As he sat in court he had to listen to witness after witness describe him as having delusions of his own self-importance and place in society; whose drinking problem was so severe that he spent a great deal of his life in a drunken haze suffering from the most severe of delusions.

He was described as a man "sitting at the end of the attorneys' table, humbly out of the way, his face contorted with shame, and his lips twitching—a picture of utter woe and dejection—a man crushed."

During his opening statement, District Attorney Fredericks told the jury that "it must be understood that fifteen years ago Griffith would not have married Mrs. Griffith if she had not given him her fortune."

Fredericks went on to tell the jury that on three separate occasions Griffith had been violent with his wife during arguments concerning financial affairs, and that the final shooting took place shortly after an argument he had with Mrs. Griffith in which she demanded an accounting and settlement in connection with funds from her late father's estate.

Fredericks told the jury that the prosecution would provide evidence to establish the motive for Griffith to kill his wife and that the state would prove that Griffith was sane when the shooting took place.

The prosecution put Dr. Joseph Kurtz on the witness stand who testified that there was a difference between insanity and being a common drunk, which was the description he attributed to Griffith. Dr. Kurtz testified that anger and jealousy regarding infidelity of a spouse did not constitute insanity. He said, "If jealousy were an insane delusion the insane asylums could not hold all of the insane."

During his cross-examination of Dr. Kurtz, Rogers was distracted by a strange sound coming from someone in the overcrowded courtroom audience. The newspaper account stated:

> "While attorney Rogers was delivering one of his most impressive questions to the witness, a woman in the audience was loudly snickering."

Rogers stopped his examination to complain about the woman's behavior to the judge and realized that the offender was the sister of W.H. Broome, the man killed in Acton by Norman M. Melrose, who was acquitted after being represented by Rogers at trial. Fortunately, the woman quickly exited the courtroom and the trial proceeded without further interruption. In any event, Dr. Kurtz maintained that Griffith was not insane at the time he shot his wife.

The prosecution paraded one medical expert after another, each testifying that Griffith was not insane and that he was not suffering from "alcoholic insanity."

L.M. Grider, a real estate broker/dealer, took the witness stand and gave testimony as to large sums of money obtained by Griffith prior to the shooting in connection with various sales transactions of property which belonged to Mrs. Griffith. The prosecution wanted to establish the financial motive for the shooting.

Mrs. Griffith was called to testify. In a moment of high drama, she took the stand wearing a black veil over her disfigured face. She was dainty and responded in a very soft voice to the questions put to her.

She was asked questions about her family background and her responses clearly established that she was from a wealthy and prominent family. The questions led up to the fact that, just prior to the shooting, she had told her husband that she wanted to personally assume management control of some of the assets left to her by her father, and that she wanted an accounting from the Colonel with regards to some of her holdings.

> Question (By Ex-Gov. Gage): At the time of the shooting had you made a will?
>
> Answer (By Griffith): No.
>
> Q: Then if you had been killed by the shot inflicted upon you that day, you would have left no will?

At one point during her direct examination, the prosecutor asked Mrs. Griffith to face the jury and lift up her black veil. She began to tremble somewhat, and she was assisted in slowly raising her veil exposing the gruesome disfigurement to the jury and everyone in the courtroom. In 1904 the benefits of plastic surgery were obviously not available.

Much to everyone's surprise, Rogers informed the court that he intended on cross-examining Mrs. Griffith. His cross-examination was a gentle attempt to simply bring out certain points. Mrs. Griffith confirmed that her husband had for several years, and without the slightest provocation, accused her of infidelity.

She spoke of the Colonel's drinking problems, that her husband hated the Catholic church and had made comments to her to the effect that he thought the Catholics were trying to poison him. She told how he sometimes would change plates or cups with her at meals to be certain that he would avoid being poisoned.

When she left the witness stand on February 16, 1904, Mrs. Griffith fainted and had to be attended to by physicians as Judge Smith ordered the courtroom cleared.

The prosecution called Irving Sayforth to the stand. Mr. Sayforth was the newspaper correspondent who had interviewed the talkative Colonel the day after the shooting had taken place. He repeated and confirmed the story given to him by the Colonel previously; that he was not drinking on the day of the shooting, that he had no quarrel with his wife, that she accidentally shot herself, and that she somehow fell out of the window from the hotel after having shot herself. The prosecution rested and it was time for the defense to put on its case.

One witness was put on to establish that Griffith had purchased hundreds of cases of whiskey over a period of time. Jacob Liser, Griffith's barber, was called to the stand to give his opinion as to the oddities of the Colonel.

Question (By Brown): What is your occupation, sir?
Answer (By Liser): I am a tonsorial artist.

There was laughter in the courtroom.

Q: Do you mean that you are a barber?
A: Well, that's a short name for my professional occupation.
Q: Where is your place of business?
A: At the Palace Barber shop.
Q: Have you had occasion to perform any services for Colonel Griffith?
A: I have shaved the Colonel almost every single day for many years.
Q: Well, being a barber, did you sometimes allow Colonel Griffith to take a small part in conversation?
A: Yes, he often participated in the conversations.

Liser went on to testify that Griffith was constantly complaining that the Catholics were trying to poison him, especially his wife, who was influenced to do so by the Catholics.

"People used to always ask me who my nutty friend was," Liser concluded.

Frederick George Purssord, a masseuse and bathrubber, was called to testify. He told how Griffith used to come to his establishment to sleep off fogs and that he never saw Griffith when he was sober. He saw Griffith three days before the shooting, who had seemed "terribly nervous and excited, fairly beside himself".

Griffith's manicurist came to court and testified that the Colonel had bitten his fingernails clear down to the cuticles prior to the shooting incident.

Mrs. M.T. Moll, who was a neighbor of Griffith's in Hollywood, related having an encounter with the Colonel in a trolley car a few days before the shooting . She said that Griffith complained of pains in his head and thought he must have been suffering from sunstroke.

Dr. J.H. Crawford, the Santa Monica physician who treated Mrs. Griffith at the hotel immediately after the shooting, was called to the stand. He quoted Mrs. Griffith as stating to him just after the shooting:

"Oh, the Colonel is crazy; he is surely crazy."

The doctor proceeded to testify that Mrs. Griffith told him that she thought she was going to die as a result of the gunshot wound and that she wanted to make a death statement. That's when she had stated that her husband was crazy. The significance of this was that on direct examination, Mrs. Griffith had previously testified that when she made that comment it was merely an offhanded remark; one not to be taken seriously. Dr. Crawford's testimony put the comment into the context of that of a dying declaration.

In his opening statement Rogers had previously told the jury that it would be shown by a preponderance of medical testimony that Griffith's delusions as to being poisoned and of his wife's unfaithfulness to her marriage vows were characteristic of a certain brand of insanity when combined with his drinking problems.

Dr. N.H. Hamilton of Santa Monica testified that Griffith was insane, and had come to him two years before the shooting absolutely convinced that he was slowly being poisoned by the Catholic Church.

Dr. H.G. Brainerd took the stand and testified that Colonel Griffith's delusions were common to "alcoholic insanity." He stated:

> When a man comes to see me with the statement that someone is trying to poison him and that his wife is unfaithful to him, giving trivial reasons for his belief, I often find that the person has alcoholic problems. I met with Griffith for an hour or more and in all my experiences with the insane I never heard more insane conversation crowded into such a short period of time. He told me that a Sister of Charity had come to him several years ago and attempted to poison him in order to obtain the Briswalter real estate for the Catholic Church. He told me that the Catholics had conspired to and had in fact poisoned the late Senator Stephen White causing his death.

Dr. Granville MacGowan, an expert on nervous conditions, took the witness stand next. He was a member of the insane commission in Philadelphia and was on the staff at the insane ward of the Charity Hospital there.

He testified that Griffith drank a pint of whiskey each day and that Griffith told him that his wife was having improper relations with a "Negro" porter at a hotel, that poison had been placed in a wine bottle of his, and that his wife was in concert with Catholic interests in an effort to see to his demise. Dr. MacGowan's opinion was the same as Dr. Brainert's.

Numerous medical witnesses were called by the defense in addition to those already mentioned; each of which provided a diagnosis that Colonel Griffith suffered from alcoholic insanity which manifested itself in delusions concerning his wife's infidelity and conspiratorial plans to have him poisoned.

When Earl Rogers gave his closing argument to the jury, the courtroom was "crowded almost to suffocation." The gallery was opened and was reserved for women, who crowded its limited dimensions. Every foot of space was taken and there was hardly a sound as the large audience listened with "almost breathless interest to the magnetic address of the young Earl Rogers."

Rogers spoke of the statement that Mrs. Griffith had made while she was in "fear of her impending death"; that statement being that her husband was crazy. He said:

> Realizing that her last moment was about to come, she made this statement, and it tells the story of this entire case. I do not care that after she had been brought back to the city and influences which were perpetrated in this prosecution, brought to bear that little by little she has worked away from that statement. It was made at the time under the sense of impending death, and as such was the ultimate truth, no matter how much subsequent events and subsequent influences have changed her mind.

Rogers continued in his argument to the jury:

> Fifteen minutes after these most unfortunate circumstances, Mrs. Griffith, in the presence of Dr. Crawford and Mr. Wright said: "I am about to die. I feel that my death is at hand. I want to make a statement. Send for the materials." And over and over again she repeated what she had know for all those years, "Colonel Griffith is crazy" she said. Not once, but six or seven times did she repeat it. You will remember how hard it was tried to keep you from learning this, but the evidence went in and therein is the ultimate truth from Mrs. Griffith.

Rogers went on to argue that the angle of the gunshot wound to Mrs. Griffith's face was not consistent with a shot having been fired by someone standing over a victim. Rogers argued that Griffith did have the gun in his hand but that it was not his intent to kill his wife. Rather, when Mrs. Griffith feared she was going to be shot she struggled with her husband and the gun accidentally discharged causing her injury.

Rogers proceeded to recount for the jury the opinions of the many defense experts who had testified that Griffith suffered from alcoholic insanity at the time of the shooting. And ironically Rogers, an alcoholic who would eventually succumb to the disease, argued to the jury that:

> While society leaves liquor on every street corner, and while it leaves the doors open so that the man going down the street who would rather have a glass of whisky than all the money in the mint, it must suffer the consequences. That stuff has an attraction, has a hold that no man who has not felt it tighten on him can realize and I say, as long as society passes it right under a man's nose where the lights shine on it night and day, society cannot rise in righteous indignation and howl for vengeance when it does its deadly work.

Rogers concluded by stating that Griffith should not be convicted of the attempted murder of his wife because he was suffering from alcoholic insanity at the time of the shooting. He argued that Griffith should go to a sanitarium and secure treatment to restore him to a healthy condition of mind once more.

The following day the courtroom was jampacked to hear former Governor Gage make his closing argument to the jury. Gage argued that the pistol, being a hammerless weapon, with a safety device, would be almost impossible to discharge by accident.

He argued that the Colonel had set about to murder his wife for financial gain and that as such he was guilty of her attempted murder. With his hands clasped, trembling above his head, the former California governor exclaimed:

> And he led her there in that hotel, to the brink of eternity, and while she prayed with clasped hands to God to save her from his murderous fury, he shot her. Did he have mercy?

A moment later there was a clicking of a revolver and the jurors were shown how it was almost impossible to discharge the gun in a struggle, unless the holder meant to shoot and pushed the safety device. Mr. Gage, in a demonstration, struggled with several of the jurors for the revolver, the latter trying to discharge it, but they could not. Gage continued:

> The defense claims we have shown no motive for the shoot-

ing and therefore you should acquit. But I will show you motive. It was to retain control of her fortune. What does the evidence show? It shows that he had been unusually kind to his wife that day of the shooting. Why did he go among his friends and show affection for the woman he did not love? And while he was going around all this time, he was planning on shooting her. This was not a mental explosion. He intended to shoot her and he shot her!

The arguments having ended and jury instructions read, deliberations began. After two hours of deliberations the court was informed that the jury wanted to ask the judge a question. Judge Smith and everyone in the courtroom listened as Jury Foreman, C.P. Patterson of Long Beach, asked: "We want to know what the penalty is for assault with a deadly weapon."

Judge Smith informed the jurors that the penalty for the crime of assault with a deadly weapon was imprisonment not to exceed two years and a fine. This was a lesser crime than the one for which Griffith had been tried of attempted murder. The jury then resumed it's deliberations. After what amounted to a total of six hours of deliberations the jury requested that they wanted to report.

"Have you agreed upon your verdict?" asked Judge Smith.

"We have," replied Foreman Patterson.

"Declare it," stated Judge Smith.

"We the jury in the above-entitled action, find the defendant guilty of assault with a deadly weapon."

After the jury verdict was pronounced, Sheriff White took charge of Griffith and escorted him to the county jail.

It turned out that for the first several hours, the jury was evenly deadlocked with six jurors voting guilty on the charge of attempted murder and six jurors voting to acquit on the basis of alcoholic insanity. A compromise verdict was agreed by finding Griffith guilty of the lesser crime of assault with a deadly weapon.

The jurors who had originally voted to acquit could live with a guilty verdict for the lesser offense, with a maximum sentence of two years, infinitely less than the penalty for a conviction of attempted murder. The jurors who had voted to convict were willing to compromise, knowing that Griffith would serve time and that a hung jury was avoided.

Griffith was sentenced to two years in prison. After serving twenty months he was released from San Quentin prison on December 3, 1906. Upon his return home to Los Angeles he told a reporter with the Los Angeles *Record*:

> I am glad to be in good health, with my own people and in Los Angeles again. I shall simply drop into the ordinary ways of business, looking after the many interests which I have here. I really have nothing further of special interest to say for publication.

The result in the Griffith trial was regarded by most as a major victory. By dodging a conviction for attempted murder, Griffith avoided a prison sentence which would have been well in excess of ten years. However Earl Rogers, ever holding himself up to a higher standard, confided to those closest to him that he considered the outcome to be a humiliating defeat.

Mrs. Charles Canfield
"Courtesy of University of Southern California,
on behalf of of the USC Library Department of
Special Collections."

CHAPTER SEVEN

The Case of the Reluctant Prosecutor

THE PARTICIPANTS

DEFENDANT:	Morris Buck
PROSECUTORS:	John Fredericks, D.A.
	Henry T. Gage, Special Prosecutor
	Earl Rogers, Co-Special Prosecutor
DEFENSE ATTORNEY:	A.D. Warner
CHARGE:	Murder

Although Rogers had failed to secure an acquittal for Griffith on the alcoholic insanity defense, the jury verdict of guilty on the lesser offense of assault with a deadly weapon showed the willingness of a jury to compromise a verdict when persuasive evidence of insanity was established. Griffith could have easily been convicted of attempted murder absent the insanity evidence. With the parade of witnesses put on by the defense, Griffith got off with a guilty verdict on a lessor crime and a far lighter sentence.

On January 27, 1906, Mrs. Charles Canfield was murdered on the front porch of her home on the corner of Ninth and Alvarado Streets in Los Angeles. Mrs. Canfield was the wife of oil magnate Charles Canfield, partner of Edward L. Doheny. Mrs. Canfield dedicated her wealth to an extensive assortment of charities, which brought her into leadership in the highest circles of the city. Her generosity and kind heart endeared her to many others.

Mrs. Canfield's slayer was Morris Buck, her former servant. She had granted Buck a meeting upon his request. He was hopeful that Mrs. Canfield would provide him with a business loan. Paul Johnson, a waiter in El Paso Texas, gave a newspaper interview several days after the shooting, stating:

> I worked with Buck in El Paso four months ago. He continually referred to his wealthy friends in Los Angeles and said that he was coming here and that they would set him up in business.

Apparently when Mrs. Canfield turned down Buck's request for a loan, he pulled out his revolver in anger and pointed it at his former employer. As Mrs. Canfield rose from her chair to object to his behavior, Buck shot her in the chest. As she staggered forward and grasped at the gun, he fired a second shot and she fell to the floor, mortally wounded. She died approximately thirty minutes later.

A number of neighbors and passersby stood at the scene of the crime where Buck proceeded to place his revolver to his temple and stated with a crazy sounding laugh: "Shall I shoot?" Although some in the crowd did, indeed, encourage him to take his own life, he lowered the gun, seated himself on a chair and simply stared at Mrs. Canfield's quivering body.

Buck after attempting to flee the crime scene, was taken into custody where for several days he simply slept, stared stupidly, and spoke to people in monosyllables. He was interviewed by Dr. A.M. Smith, to whom he told many things concerning his past life and family. His mother had been a matron of an insane asylum. Buck had never been treated for mental illness, he did not drink, smoke or use drugs of any sort.

At the time of his wife's death, Mr. Canfield was traveling in Mexico; but upon learning of the news of his wife's demise he made immediate plans to take the Southern Pacific back to Los Angeles, and made record time in his return trip.

Arrangements were made for Buck to be interviewed by several other insanity experts prior to his arraignment for the murder of Mrs. Canfield. Buck's two sisters in Arizona, Mrs. Walter Dorsey and Mrs. G. L. Davison made immediate arrangements to travel to Los Angeles, along with his brother, William Buck. It was learned shortly after the murder that it was their intent to retain legal counsel for their brother, whom they felt was insane, and to put on a proper legal defense for him on that ground.

After an exhausting train journey, Mr. Canfield returned to Los Angeles to bury his wife; the funeral services being conducted by Francis Murphy. Wanting to make sure that Buck would receive the death penalty for the brutal murder of his wife, Canfield arranged for the retention of former Governor Henry T. Gage to act as special prosecutor and to assist District Attorney Fredericks. Buck's preliminary hearing took place on February 1, 1906. Buck appeared without an attorney and when the Judge asked if he was ready to proceed, Buck sat silent for an entire minute, and then catatonically looked towards the judge and stated: "yes sir."

"Have you an attorney?" asked the judge.

Buck sat like a stone wall with no response or protest as the hearing went forward. He showed absolutely no interest as Coroner Trout and Dr. Ralph Hagan testified as to their identification of the victim and the precise manner of her death.

Canfield and the prosecution knew that Buck would retain an attorney prior to his trial and that his only viable defense would be insanity. To Canfield, anything short of a trip to the gallows for Buck would be a catastrophic result; he wanted to avoid a compromise jury verdict at all costs. Governor Gage was instructed to approach Earl Rogers and request that he act as co-special prosecutor in the case against Buck. Canfield did not want to take any chance that Rogers would be retained by Buck's relatives to put on an insanity defense. The result in the Griffith case was a good reminder as to how a jury could arrive at a compromise verdict if a persuasive insanity argument could be presented. Canfield didn't want Buck to be saved from hanging with the possibility of a manslaughter conviction. Rogers was approached and for the first time in his career, acted as a prosecutor in a criminal case. At first he was reluctant to take on the case because he had never before acted as a prosecutor. In addition, he was opposed to the death penalty, which in this case would be the result he would be retained to secure. However, he was an admirer and friend of the late Mrs. Canfield, and so took on the role played, thus far in his career, by his adversaries. He quickly assembled an array of expert witnesses who would attest during trial that Buck had been sane at the time that of the killing.

Nineteen prosecution witnesses were lined up to testify regarding the sanity of Morris Buck. Attorney A.D. Warner was retained to represent Buck and, to no one's surprise, his strategy was to contend that Buck was insane at the time of the killing.

One newspaper account reported that when the trial began on March 1, 1906, the courtroom was packed to utmost capacity. People crowded the aisles until every inch of standing space was occupied. The buzz of whispered conversation was so great that it was necessary to partially clear the room before the trial could go on.

Public interest in the trial grew ever greater as the days wore on, with one newspaper account describing the scene on March 13, 1906:

> As strenuous as a rush of the football warriors on the grid-iron was the rush Tuesday morning on the entrance to Judge Smith's court, where Morris Buck the slayer of Mrs. Charles Canfield is on trial. Deputy Sheriff Frank Cochran did his best to stem the tide, and finally succeeded in checking the

onrush so that, when court opened, the aisles were fairly clear, but all the standing room at the rear as well as all the seats in the courtroom was occupied"

The newspapers described Buck as having a demeanor that seemed to care little about the proceeding; who simply sat without expression looking towards the courtroom floor.

Lizzie Billingsly, who was the cook at the Canfield residence, was an eyewitness to the shooting. She took the stand and identified Buck as the slayer of Mrs. Canfield.

Eugene Cronk who was the coachman at the Canfield residence testified that he was called from the barn by Mrs. Canfield's youngest daughter who said there was a man there. As he approached Mrs. Canfield warned him that Buck was in possession of a gun. Cronk then ran back to the barn to get his gun, and while he was running he heard two gunshots.

Dr. J.H. Davidson testified as to the condition of Mrs. Canfield when he arrived and described the gunshot wounds which caused her death.

Dr. R.E. Cohn who was the superintendent of the Napa insane asylum testified that he believed Buck to be sane and that his physical appearance in court was a ruse to deceive the jury into believing that he was insane.

Additional doctors were called by the prosecution to testify that Buck was sane. A variety of different former employers of Buck were called to the stand; each testifying that Buck was a solid employee and had never manifested any signs of insanity.

Buck's former brother-in-law, Jacob France, took the witness stand. He had previously been married to Buck's sister, Minnie, but the marriage was later dissolved. Buck had previously worked for France on a ranch. France testified that Buck was a good worker and that he always appeared to be a rational and sane person.

Special Officer Charles Foster testified that he was responsible for taking Buck into custody on the day of the shooting and that Buck did not exhibit any abnormal behavior at the time he was first apprehended.

On March 15, 1906, at approximately 11:50 a.m., Dr. Barber was in the middle of his testimony; another in the parade of witnesses for the prosecution to attest to the sanity of the defendant, when Buck suddenly collapsed in his chair. His head fell backwards, and the chair in which he was sitting tipped over. Buck was laid out on the floor, court was adjourned, and the room was cleared. He appeared back in court the next morning fully recovered from the incident. Perhaps he was beginning to realize the predicament he was in.

The defense put on various medical experts to attempt to prove Buck was insane. On cross-examination, Rogers came across to the jury as more of an expert in the field than the doctors as he methodically picked their testimony apart. The value of Rogers not being the defendant's attorney was readily apparent.

The defendant's brother, William Buck, was placed on the stand and testified that his brother Morris had been severely cut at the base of his skull by a cleaver at the hands of a drunk while the two had lived in Arizona. On cross-examination Rogers brought **out the** fact that William Buck had killed a man in Arizona with a cleaver, had been sentenced to life in prison, but had avoided his sentence based upon technical considerations.

Another relative of Buck's testified that the defendant had been kicked in the head by a horse when he was a child. Additional witnesses testified as to various head injuries of Buck and at one point his defense counsel showed the jury members all of the scars which appeared in the back of Buck's head. It would in later years be scientifically shown that aggressive, violent behavior can result from brain damage caused by blows to the head; however, at this early date no such connection had been established.

On March 20, 1906, Morris Buck was found guilty of first degree murder, with no recommendation of mercy being given by the jury.

On March 23, 1906, Morris Buck appeared before Judge Smith for sentencing. "Morris Buck stand up," stated the judge as the condemned murderer came slowly to his feet.

"The judgment of this court is that you shall be taken to the state penitentiary at San Quentin within the next ten days and there detained awaiting further order of the court, and that upon a date hereafter to be fixed, and not less than sixty nor more than ninety days from this time, you shall be, by the warden of said penitentiary, hanged by the neck until you are dead."

And so Earl Rogers, who ironically was opposed to the death penalty, appeared as a special prosecutor in the case of the slayer of Mrs. Charles Canfield and ultimately assisted in delivering Morris Buck to his execution.

Rogers became somewhat obsessed that he had participated in the prosecution of a man who was to be executed. He attended the hanging of Morris Buck and then apparently made arrangements to be present in the room when the prison surgeon performed an autopsy. Rogers assisted while the surgeon cut Buck's head open to determine if there was any evidence of brain damage or enlargement resulting from the prior injuries to Buck's skull that had been testified to during the trial. Rogers found at least some consolation that no evidence of brain damage was found in the post mortem examination and that he had not participated in sending an insane man to the gallows.

Patrick Calhoun
"Courtesy of University of Southern California, on
behalf of the USC Library Department of Special
Collections."

CHAPTER EIGHT:

The Case of the Bay Area Pay Offs

THE PARTICIPANTS

DEFENDANTS:	Tirey Ford
	Patrick Calhoun
PROSECUTORS:	William Langdon, D.A.
	John O'Gara, Asst. D.A.
	Francis Heney, Special Prosecutor
DEFENSE ATTORNEYS:	Earl Rogers
	Garrett McEnerny
	A.A. Moore
	Lewis F. Bylington
	Porter Ashe
	Alexander King
	William Abbott
	Luther Brown
	Jerry Geisler
	George Francis
	Stanley Moore
	John J. Barrett

On April 15, 1850, the first legislature of California incorporated the mining town into the city of San Francisco. The city's government was beset with corruption from its very inception, and the legislature was soon petitioned to change the charter. The petition recited:

> Without a change in the city government which shall
> diminish the weight of taxation, the city will neither be able
> to discharge the interest on debts already contracted, nor to
> meet the demands for current disbursements. The present con-
> dition of the streets and public improvements of the city abun-
> dantly attest the total inefficiency of the present system.

The legislature passed the "Consolidation Act," and from 1856 to 1900, city and county were governed as one political unit. The tax-paying populace saw their money squandered as public improvements proceeded at a snail's pace. It took twenty-five years to complete the city hall at a then stagger-ing cost of $5,500,000!

Repeated attempts were made by the citizens of San Fran-cisco to get a new charter, those efforts finally succeeding in 1900. Executive responsibility was centered in the powerful mayor's office. The foundations were established for munic-ipal ownership of public utilities, and legislative power was vested in a board of eighteen supervisors elected at large.

A grand jury was convened, which prepared a report indi-cating that the present administration was trafficking in favors sold to gamblers, prize fighters, and criminals; illicit profits were being reaped from illegal contracts. Every department of the executive branch was "honeycombed" with corruption.

Notwithstanding this report, Mayor Eugene E. Schmitz, a former violin player and member of the musicians union, was re-elected mayor of San Francisco in 1905 as the candi-date of the Labor Union party. His former vocation was indeed appropriate; for Schmitz, like Nero, was metaphorically fid-dling away as corruption spread like a wildfire throughout every district of his city.

The investigation into political corruption continued after Schmitz was re-elected, revealing that graft permeated the local government in almost every conceivable way. Govern-ment officials went into partnership with dishonest contrac-tors; sold privileges and permits; shared profits from brothels;

black-mailed gamblers and promoters of prize fights; sold franchises to wealthy corporations, leased offices for municipal operations at inflated rentals generating "kick-backs," and took bribes from just about anyone who wanted an illegal favor and was willing to pay for it.

Abe Ruef, an intelligent, well-connected San Francisco attorney, had engineered the political fortunes of Mayor Schmitz. Various individuals and companies retained Ruef and paid him exorbitant retainers to provide them with "legal" advise (more likely "illegal" advice) and counsel in connection with their business activities.

The investigation into San Francisco's corrupt political machine was interrupted on April 18, 1906, by the San Francisco Earthquake which caused massive destruction and chaos. The city rebounded with a sense of civic pride and enthusiasm and the rebuilding of San Francisco took place with great fervor. Of course, the massive rebuilding effort presented myriad opportunities for corrupt profiteering.

Through the persistence of private citizens, including the former mayor of San Francisco, James D. Phelan, and prominent businessman, Rudolph Spreckels, a grand jury was summoned to continue the investigation of political graft. B.P. Oliver was selected grand jury foreman, and two important individuals were brought in to assist in the investigation and potential prosecutions of grafters. William J. Burns was brought in as a detective, and Francis J. Heney was employed as a special prosecutor.

Burns was renowned in his field from coast to coast, and would ultimately go on to head the United States Secret Service. Francis Heney a favorite of President Teddy Roosevelt, was a tough and accomplished prosecutor who had just recently completed a successful prosecution for the federal government of timberland graft in Oregon. Heney had previously been the Attorney General for the Arizona territory, where he was known for having shot and killed an Arizona political boss in a gunfight.

The grand jury issued indictments and Mayor Schmitz and Abe Ruef were both convicted at trial on charges of bribery. Those convictions were overturned on appeal for technical reasons, and Ruef was again charged on other bribery counts and a trial date was set.

The United Railroad chief, Patrick Calhoun, and his attorney, Tirey L. Ford, were both indicted on bribery charges. It was alleged that Calhoun had provided for Ford to take control of $200,000 in bribe money. Ford then funneled the money to Ruef and several influential members of the city's board of supervisors, who in turn divied up the bribe money amongst the other supervisors. The United Railroad Company was to then receive the supervisors' votes to grant Calhoun's company the lucrative overhead trolley franchise in San Francisco.

The wealthy and powerful Calhoun was the prosecution's prize target. His plight became more serious when Louis P. Glass, the chief of the Pacific States Telephone and Telegraph Company, was convicted on bribery charges. On top of this, the prosecution was in the process of negotiating immunity deals with Ruef and two key supervisors to appear as prosecution witnesses against Ford and Calhoun.

Calhoun's camp had previously retained the full-time services of Luther Brown, Earl Rogers' law partner, to help in the jury selection process. Brown was known to conduct exhaustive investigations of potential jurors' backgrounds and prejudices. After the conviction of Glass, desperation being the mother of retention, it was decided that Earl Rogers should be added to the United Railroad's defense team, and he was retained shortly thereafter to act as the chief defense counsel for what was reported to be the largest legal fee ever paid to a lawyer.

The retention of Rogers required him to move his family and his legal staff, lock, stock and barrel, to San Francisco. In addition to his wife and two children, Adela and Bogart, and other members of his staff, he brought with him a young law student from his office by the name of Jerry Giesler. Rogers was put up at the St. Francis Hotel, was given the exclusive use of a home in a well-to-do suburb, and was provided with chauffeurs, servants, and whatever other creature comforts he desired. He also had the exclusive use of a chartered ferry where he prepared for court in the middle of San Francisco Bay. This was necessitated after someone fired shots at Rogers while he and his daughter Adela were walking near the Presidio one evening.

Due to extensive earthquake and fire damage to the court-house in San Francisco, the graft trials all took place at the Sherith Temple where a make-shift courtroom had been created.

On September 6, 1906, the arraignments for a number of alleged grafters took place, among them Patrick Calhoun and Tirey Ford. In court that day the prosecution announced that they would proceed with the trial of Mr. Ford first, to be fol-lowed by that of Calhoun. Ford's trial was set for September 12, 1906. The prosecution wanted to try Ford before Calhoun for tactical reasons. They hoped that a conviction of Ford would lead him to testify against Calhoun in some sort of a deal that the prosecution could then work out with him.

On May 15, 1906, the trial began before Judge William P. Lawlor with the reading of the charges against Tirey L. Ford. His felony was allegedly having offered a bribe to then super-visor Thomas F. Lonergan in the amount of $4,000 to cor-ruptly influence his vote on an ordinance authorizing the United Railroad Company to change its cable railroads to an overhead trolley system.

Rogers immediately made a motion to the court that Patrick Calhoun's case be tried first, and to abate the trial of Ford until the conclusion of Mr. Calhoun's trial. Judge Lawlor denied the motion, ruling that the prosecution had the right to try their cases in any order that they chose. The motion having been denied, jury selection began.

The fireworks in the first trial of Ford began early during jury selection on September 13, 1906, when Earl Rogers examined a juror, asking:

> If it should appear that Rudolph Spreckels, District Attorney Langdon and Mr. Heney, through the prosecution, had secured the control of the city government in order that the Spring Valley Water Company might sell its plant to the city, would that effect your impartiality as a juror?

As will be seen later, Rogers would attempt to show that the graft prosecutions were financed and motivated in large part by Mr. Spreckels, who was a business competitor of Mr. Calhoun. The following is an example of a portion of Rogers' *vore dire* of one prospective juror:

> Question (By Rogers): Now Captain, I don't want to pry, but have you any stock in a rival street railway company, formed by any member of the Spiracles family?
>
> Answer (By prospective juror): I have not.
>
> Q: Are you a stockholder in the Spring Valley Water Company?
>
> A: I am.
>
> Q: Own much or little of that stock?
>
> A: Medium amount.
>
> Q: You have testified that you have never had any business dealings with the special prosecutor, Francis J. Heney, yet do you not know that Heney was at one time an attorney for the Spring Valley Water Company?
>
> Comment (By Heney): I was attorney only on certain occasions and was not employed by the company.
>
> Comment (By Rogers): You were an attorney for the company, however, and were employed by an agent of the company.
>
> Q: (By Rogers): If it should appear that former mayor Phelan, Mr. Spreckels and Mr. Heney were planning to order the board of supervisors to buy the plant of the Spring Valley Water Company, would that affect your verdict?
>
> A: (By prospective juror): No.
>
> Q: As a stockholder you would be rather glad?

At this point, the District Attorney, his assistant and Mr. Heney all rose to their feet voicing objections to the line of questions being pursued by Rogers, who immediately retorted: "If you will withdraw the objection I will prove that the first official act of the Board of Supervisors appointed by Mayor Taylor was to prepare for the purchase of the Spring Valley Water Company. I will prove that James D. Phelan, Rudolph Spreckels and their board of supervisors—"

Protestation(By Heney): Will you try to prove it?

Reply (By Rogers): Yes.

Further comment (By Heney): You can't prove a thousandth part of it!

Further Reply (By Rogers): We will prove nine-tenths of it!

At this point Judge Lawlor jumped in and temporarily stopped the attorneys from arguing in front of the prospective jurors. These types of arguments between counsel for prosecution and defense persisted throughout jury selection which made the process tedious and exhausting.

To add to the already chaotic atmosphere of the jury selection was the epilepsy attack suffered by a courtroom spectator who was in a pew adjacent to where the defendant was located. M.B. Young was taken to the General Emergency Hospital after the attack and courtroom proceedings were temporarily halted while the situation was attended to.

On September 16, 1906, Rogers, in open court, accused the prosecution of improperly listening in on conversation between defense lawyers and the defendant and requested Judge Lawlor to prevent William Burns and his operatives from sitting in close proximity to the defendant and his lawyers.

Mr. Heney responded by stating to the court that the defense financed by United Railroad was employing: "the most desperate characters in the state of California as an adjunct to its defense."

Judge Lawlor granted the request made by Rogers and ordered the agents of Burns who were seated next to Tirey

Ford to move their seats and he also cleared the first two rows of the area directly behind the defendant and his attorneys.

The jury selection was completed and the first prosecution witness was called to the stand on September 24, 1906. Hundreds of spectators were attracted to the makeshift courtroom at the Temple and when the doors were opened, throngs of eager spectators filled the passageways on the lower floor of the edifice. Men and women struggled for good seats and/or locations and a stampede followed. Several persons fell to the floor and were trampled upon. Two policemen on hand were knocked to the floor by the rush of spectators. Sheriffs deputies were finally able to restore order to the courtroom and proceeded to provide for orderly seating.

Heney gave an opening statement for the prosecution in which he outlined the case and the evidence that would be proven against Mr. Ford. He stated in part:

> Defendant Ford is being charged with having paid Thomas F. Lonergan, the sum of $4,000 to influence his vote and action in a matter to come before the board for action upon; to wit; an application for the construction maintenance and operation of an overhead trolley system. We do not expect to prove that Mr. Ford personally made this offer to Lonergan, but do expect to prove that the offer was made to Lonergan by Mr. Wilson who was authorized by Mr. Gallagher, and through Gallagher to each supervisor by Abraham Ruef and that Ruef was authorized to make the offer by Tirey L. Ford.
>
> We expect to prove to you that Ruef took the matter up with Ford in February and March, 1906, prior to the great fire. At the time the question was discussed between Ruef and Gallagher as to whether it was possible to put the matter through the supervisors. Gallagher made inquiries and reported back that each supervisor wanted ten thousand apiece.
>
> We intend to prove that the matter was taken up again after the fire. It was agreed that the time was right to pass the ordinance and it was further agreed that each supervisor would receive $4,000, that Gallagher would receive $15,000, that Mr. Wilson would receive $10,000, making the total bribe to the board $85,000.

We will prove that after the bribe was agreed upon, that on May 14, 1906, Mr. Wilson introduced the bill on a petition signed by Patrick Calhoun, who had come to San Francisco on April 29th, and is still here. On May 21st, the overhead trolley ordinance was passed by a unanimous vote of the supervisors.

Two hundred thousand dollars was transferred by Patrick Calhoun to the United Railway account which was transferred to the San Francisco mint on May 22nd, the day after the trolley ordinance was passed. We expect to show that money was the price paid to Ruef to secure the ordinance—$85,000 to the supervisors, $50,000 to Mayor Schmitz, and the balance retained by Ruef.

Patrick Calhoun went to the superintendent of the mint a few days after receipt of the money and said that he wanted to arrange for the money to be withdrawn by Tirey Ford. The evidence will show that the money was all withdrawn by Mr. Ford. Every dollar of the $200,000 was drawn by Tirey Ford, expressly in currency, not a dollar showing on the books of the corporation.

The first witness to testify for the prosecution was John E. Behan, who was an assistant clerk for the Board of Supervisors in May of 1906. He had taken the minutes for the board meeting which had taken place on May 14th, showing entries of the passage of the overhead trolley ordinance and of the entries on May 21st, showing entries for the final passage of that ordinance.

The originals of these documents, which established the award of the trolley car franchise to United Railroad by a unanimous vote of the board of supervisors, were admitted into evidence.

Ex-supervisor Thomas F. Lonergan was the prosecution's first witness on September 25, 1907, which turned out to be an interesting day in court. Lonergan testified as to the amounts of money he had received during his tenure of office in return for his votes on various items brought before the board.

He then testified as to his arrangement on the vote in connection with United Railroad's application for the overhead trolley system. He told of his finding an envelope in his vest jacket pocket containing a substantial sum of money of various denominations and that he presumed the money had been placed there by supervisor Jim Gallagher.

On cross-examination, Rogers got Lonergan to admit that he had never actually discussed with Gallagher the reason the money was put in his pocket and that he did not actually see Gallagher put the money there.

Rogers then asked Lonergan if he had signed a statement recently in which he denied taking any bribes in connection with the overhead trolley ordinance. Lonergan replied that he was not aware of any such document. Rogers then proceeded to show Lonergan a document which had a signature thereon and asked him if it was his signature. Lonergan looked at the document and confirmed that it was his signature. Lonergan explained that he was interviewed by a man named A.E. Dorlan who represented himself as an East Coast magazine writer. Dorlan told Lonergan that he wanted to do an interview with him to get his side of the story and that the article would not be published until after the trial had concluded. In the statement signed by Lonergan it stated that he had not received nor been offered any bribes in connection with the overhead trolley system, and that his vote was based upon what he believed to be best for the city. Lonergan admitted he signed the document but pointed out that it was not attested to under oath.

Rogers then showed Lonergan a court document which he had executed under oath in which it was stated that he had neither received money nor conspired against any person or corporation in connection with any of his votes as a supervisor. Lonergan stated that he had signed the sworn statement falsely and that he knew that as a result, he had committed a felony. He testified that he had been promised immunity from prosecution for any crimes he had committed, and that he had been shown an immunity contract by supervisor James L. Gallagher.

> Question (By Rogers): Did you believe the overhead trolley was the need of the time?
>
> Answer (By Lonergan): I did.
>
> Q: Would you have voted for it had you not been paid for your vote?
>
> A: I believe I would have, yes.

On re-direct examination, Lonergan was asked by Francis Heney if he had been followed and contacted by anyone recently. Lonergan responded that he had been followed for several days by a particular individual. Heney then asked if the man who had been following him was Mr. N.M. Melrose, to which Lonergan answered that he did not know who Mr. Melrose was.

> Question (By Heney): Do you see the man who has been following you here in the courtroom today?
>
> Answer (By Lonergan): Yes.
>
> Q: Please point him out sir. Is he the man that is seated right behind the defendant, Mr. Ford?
>
> A: (pointing): Yes, he is that man seated right over there behind Mr. Ford.
>
> Statement (By Heney): May the court please take notice that the witness had identified a man, who we know to be on the payroll of the railroad company and we know that his name is Norman Melrose and that this same man was previously defended on murder charges by Earl Rogers!

On further re-direct, Lonergan testified that Mr. Dorlan, the supposed East Coast writer, had wined and dined his entire family, took them on automobile rides, and to fine restaurants, and that he had not carefully read the statement which Dorlan had him sign. It turned out that Mr. Dorlan was really none other then Rogers' operative, Norman Melrose, who posed as a writer!

Ex-superintendent James Gallagher was the next witness to take the stand. He testified that he had first met the defendant when he was Attorney General. Abe Ruef had asked him to ascertain how the supervisors stood on the overhead trolley ordinance, and what amount of money it would take to secure its passage. This conversation with Ruef was before the fire.

Gallagher further testified that after the fire, Ruef approached him again and stated that the United Railroads desired passage of the overhead railroad measure and that he should find out how much it would cost to assure passage. Ruef could obtain $4,000 for each supervisor.

Gallagher went on to state that he was authorized to offer supervisor Wilson $10,000 to use his influence on the other supervisors and that he was to retain $15,000 for himself.

Gallagher then testified that he received possession of $45,000 in currency in Ruef's office and had placed the money into envelopes and distributed them to the supervisors in the latter part of July, 1906.

On cross-examination Rogers asked Gallagher to tell the jury how much money he had received in bribes as a supervisor. He then asked Gallagher how much his living expenses had been for the prior year and a half. Rogers calculated that the witness had $10,000 in safe deposit boxes which exceeded the amount of the bribes minus the witness's living expenses.

> Question (By Rogers) How do you account for that extra $ 10,000. 00; from where did you receive that money?
>
> Answer (By Gallagher): Out of my earnings as a lawyer.
>
> Q: Are you sure of that?
>
> A: Yes, quite sure of it.
>
> Q: Are you sure you didn't get that unaccounted for $10,000 in connection with your testimony here in these proceedings?
>
> A: I am certain of it.
>
> Q: Where did you get that kind of money if you didn't get it from Mr. Spreckels?
>
> A: I already answered the question Mr. Rogers; I told you I earned that money for legal services rendered in my capacity as a lawyer,
>
> Q: Did you have any meetings with Mr. Spreckels concerning the subject matter of your immunity from prosecution in return for your testimony in these proceedings?

A: Yes.

Q: Where did the meeting take place?

A: The Presidio gate was selected as the meeting place.

Q: Why there?

A: Because it was the most secluded spot we could think of in the city to hold a private conversation without being observed or overheard.

Q: What did Spreckels tell you in this conversation?

A: He told me that the prosecution's goal was not to prosecute the political bosses because they come and go; that their real goal was to prosecute public service corporations, because the corporations stayed on forever.

Q: What about Mayor Schmitz, was he included in the immunity discussions?

A: No, I don't know anything about Schmitz and any immunity discussions; Abe Ruef was the only person outside the supervisors about whom immunity was discussed.

Q: Did Abe Ruef ever tell you that he had given any money to Mayor Schmitz in connection with the overhead trolley system?

A: No he did not.

On re-direct examination, Gallagher testified that he had never received any money from Rudolph Spreckels. He also testified that during his meeting, Spreckels had told him that several of the other supervisors had already confessed to having received bribes, and that immunity could be obtained for all of the supervisors if they came clean and provided confessions to their having received bribes.

Gallagher also testified that he had been approached by a man who identified himself as a "Mr. Dorland," an east coast magazine writer who requested an interview, and that he had denied Mr. Dorland's request.

The next witness to take the stand was former supervisor, Samuel Davis. He stated that he had a conversation with former supervisor Wilson who had approached him to discuss the subject of the overhead trolley system after the fire; that

Wilson told him that there was $4,000 in it for each member of the board. He said that he voted for the overhead trolley franchise because he was already in favor of the ordinance, but that he expected to be paid the $4,000 notwithstanding. Davis testified that he knew Tirey Ford "slightly," but was not acquainted with Patrick Calhoun.

On cross-examination, which was brief, Davis stated that his testimony in the proceeding was given subject to a contract of immunity from prosecution which he had entered into prior to the commencement of the trial.

The prosecution called twelve supervisors to the witness stand, all basically telling the same story, that they would have voted in favor of the overhead trolley ordinance even if no bribe money was involved. Each of the supervisor witnesses testified that they believed the trolley ordinance was in the city of San Francisco's best interest. Each testified that they had been told of the money in connection with the trolley car vote from Jim Gallagher.

None of the witnesses could establish knowledge on the part of Tirey Ford that any money had been given to any supervisor by Gallagher, Ruef, or anyone else for that matter, in connection with the vote by the supervisors on the overhead trolley ordinance. All of the supervisors testified that they had received immunity agreements in connection with their testimony.

After the former supervisors had all completed their testimony, the prosecution spent several days putting on detailed and tedious testimony from the Director, the Assistant Director, the Cashier, the Assistant Cashier, and the Bookkeeper of the United States Mint. This testimony covered every minute detail of the monies transferred by Calhoun to the mint, including his instructions to the mint as to the authority of Mr. Ford to receive the money, the exact manner in which Mr. Ford collected the money, how the money was packaged, what denomination of bills were used, and so forth.

In his opening statement to the jury, Heney had promised

that the prosecution was going to prove that Ford had entered into an illicit agreement with Ruef to cause the supervisors and mayor of the city to be bribed to obtain passage of the overhead railroad ordinance. Over three thousand spectators showed up at the makeshift courtroom at the Temple Israel to see Ruef testify near the end of the Ford trial. However, the crowd was disappointed when they learned that the prosecution rested its case without having called Ruef to the witness stand.

Speculation was made that the prosecution was holding Ruef back to be called as a rebuttal witness after the defense put on its case. Others theorized that Ruef had refused to change his grand jury testimony which was to the effect that he had received legal fees from Ford for services rendered on behalf of United Railroad, but that he had never discussed any bribes with Ford and further Ford had no knowledge of any bribes.

Without calling one witness, without the utterance of one word of testimony, and without the introduction of any evidence, Earl Rogers stood up in court and stated that "We decline to put in any testimony and rest." It was argued during closing argument by the prosecution that:

> The material questions in this case are: Was Lonergan offered a bribe by Abe Ruef or his lieutenants, Gallagher or Wilson, with the intention of influencing his vote on the trolley ordinance; secondly, was Ruef when that offer was made, acting under an agreement with the defendant Ford, contemplating the giving or the taking of such an offer? If gentlemen, you decide that question in favor of the people there is nothing left to the case but a verdict of conviction.
>
> Are you going to say by your verdict, "Well done, Tirey Ford, do it again. If you want a franchise, arrange with the supervisors and get what you want and stop not there. If you have a case in court, go there too; go to prosecutors, go to the jurors in the box, go to the Judge on the bench, make your arrangements and pay your money and you shall be immune.
>
> Are you going to render a verdict like that, or are you going

to say this thing must stop? Gentlemen, I ask you in the name of the People of the State of California, to find Tirey L. Ford guilty as charged.

Over three thousand people were present as Earl Rogers gave his dramatic and emotional closing argument to the jury. He said in part:

> The first man to bring a biscuit to this city after the fire was a United Railroad employee, Thomwell Mullaily. The man who walked the streets until he died was George Chapman, general manager of he United Railroads. Who were the men who stood by this city when it lay in its ashes? Tirey Ford and Patrick Calhoun and others like them. For days they worked until they dropped in their tracks. They took their money and their life's blood and they worked and they strived as no man ever did before. And now, Tirey Ford is to go to the penitentiary?
>
> Why? Because Rudolph Spreckels wants the street car system. What did he do, what did this man do? Who came here on the first train after the fire? Patrick Calhoun. Who brought every dollar he could rake up and asked for more, and said, "My fortune goes to San Francisco?" Pat Calhoun was that man. Now the penitentiary waits for him and Tirey Ford. Why? Because Thomas Lonergan lied and lied like a trooper. You think I strain myself when I do this. No! When I was a boy, I am not much more yet; when, I went into the Supreme Court as a boy to get my license, who was the Attorney General who sat there? Tirey L. Ford. And I never thought the day would come when I would stand up before a jury and ask for his life."
>
> Did they need to buy this franchise? Not a bit of it. Every one of these supervisors would have voted for it. Every newspaper in the city was crying that something should be done. And the first spadeful of dirt was turned over by the United Railroads, and after Rudolph Spreckels made them stop taking people for free, they turned over the receipts to the Relief Corporation.
>
> We are living in a condition of things brought about for a purpose. It is fictitious. This prosecution is like the inquisition of the old ages. In those days, when they wanted a man

to talk they put the screws on him and said "When you tell us thus and so we will take the screws off," and some of your ancestors and mine told lies to get those awful screws off. And the men who put those screws on believed they were doing themselves and God a service. And so Lonergan, before the screws were put on, went and met with Spreckels who told him that all he had to do was go in there and testify against Ford and Calhoun, and his toenails can stay on.

And have you asked yourself why the prosecution did not call Ruef to testify? The reason was that although they believed that they could make him say that Tirey Ford did this thing, they found out at the last moment that when he came into this court and looked General Ford in the eye, he could not do it. That's why! It was a lie! He looked at General Ford in the eye and he knew it was a lie!

I do not care whether this crowd goes out of here and says Rogers made a bad speech or a good speech. I want to help you to arrive at what I believe to be the only possible verdict. If you sign a ballot of guilty you have got to say that when Mr. Heney told you that he was going to prove that Tirey L. Ford authorized Ruef to offer a bribe to Gallagher he has proved it beyond a reasonable doubt.

Rogers suddenly swung around and, pointing his finger at Rudolph Spreckels, continued his argument:

I will not say that this man who sits here is corrupt; I will not say that he is doing what he ought not to do. I will say that whatever his motives have been he has done some good, but, like many men who have done good, he is intoxicated by a sense of his own power and carried on by a purpose which is debased.

He told Gallagher out at the Presidio that he was after the public service corporations. It appears in evidence in this case, that he has a rival street car company. It appears in this case that it is his money that he is using to go after Mr. Calhoun and Mr Ford, and it appears in this case that he is a private citizen, without the sanction of the law, promised Gallagher that if he would induce the supervisors to come over on the proposition that they might go free, and that's their reward.

Who prepares the evidence in this case for the prosecution? A man who does not live here and takes private money for his services. He is a man, a private prosecutor of national reputation, hired for the purpose not of enforcing the law, not of demonstrating facts to you; he is here to convict and does not care about the facts or the truth he only cares about obtaining a conviction regardless of the facts.

And gentlemen of this jury, when I sell my profession to coin the blood of General Ford, the blood of his weeping wife and his poor children, into dollars, you come out and kill me and bury me.

Rogers paused for a moment, turned and looked Francis Heney square in the eye and said: "Mr. Heney, that's what you have done!"

At that point Rogers turned and rushed down the aisle into the corridor, while over three thousand spectators watched in amazement.

Heney gave the prosecution's rebuttal, the jury was given instructions, deliberated, took over thirty ballots, and were hopelessly deadlocked. Every vote was eight for acquittal and four for conviction, with the exception of one ballot which was nine for acquittal and three for conviction. Seeing that the jury was dead-locked and that the chance for a unanimous verdict was not possible, Judge Lawlor dismissed the jury. The prosecution announced they would re-try Ford and a new trial date was set.

On October 22, 1907, jury selection was completed in the second Ford trial. John Behan, the clerk of the Board of Supervisors was again placed on the witness stand and he testified as to the various dates that petitions were signed and ordinances passed in connection with the overhead trolley system.

Ex-supervisor Jennings P. Phillips took the stand and testified that "Big" Jim Gallagher had told him that there would be $8,000 in it for him to vote on the trolley car ordinance, but that Gallagher only gave him $4,000. He could not remember exactly when he received the money, nor could he recall the denomination of the bills he received. He could not link up his receipt of the money from Gallagher in any direct way to the defendant.

The prosecution put on the same array of witnesses as had been put on during the first trial to establish that Calhoun had transferred $200,000 to the mint, that he had given authorization for Tirey Ford to withdraw the funds, that Ford had in fact received the money in the form of currency, that most of the supervisors received $4,000 each from "Big" Jim Gallagher, and that the supervisors had all voted in favor of the trolley system ordinance. Still there was no direct linkage to Ford. That is, until the prosecution called some surprise witnesses.

Robert H. Perry was put on the stand. He testified that he was employed by Detective William Burns and had been assigned the task of shadowing Abe Ruef during the months of June, July and August of 1906. He told the jury that during his surveillance of Ruef, he had actually kept pace and been able to follow Ruef's famous car known as the "Green Lizard." He had seen Ruef leave his car and enter the offices of Tirey Ford during the same general time period that Ford had made cash withdrawals from the mint. Although circumstantial, this testimony put Ruef and General Ford together at a time when Ford had possession of large sums of currency he had taken from the mint.

While on the stand Perry consulted his notes in a book which he said he had made while he had been tailing Ruef. Perry testified that on July 31st, he saw Ruef leave his home at about 10: 10 a.m. and enter his notorious Green Lizard automobile. Perry operated on a hunch that Ruef's destination was the United Railroad office, so he hurried over to their headquarters only to see Ruef's car parked outside in front. Ruef didn't leave the building until 12: 10 p.m.

During this three month time period, Perry followed Ruef from dawn until sunset.

On cross-examination, Rogers accused Perry of faking the

notes and creating them "after the fact" to help the prosecution make its case. Rogers pointed the witness's attention to entries in his book which seemed to appear in crowded spaces and differ in writing style.

> Question (By Rogers): I see that the entries are written up the sides and not in the same pencil; how do you explain that?
>
> Answer (By Perry): I put Ford's name into the report later in order to make it more complete and accurate.

Rogers asked that the notebook of Perry be admitted into evidence but Heney vehemently objected on the basis that the book contained entries which were of importance to other investigations being conducted. Those portions relevant to the Ford case were admitted.

> Question (By Rogers): You are a detective are you not?
>
> Answer (By Perry): No I am not a detective, I am an assistant to William Burns who is a detective, I am simply his assistant.
>
> Q: You shadowed Ruef didn't you? You shadowed him like a man's shadow follows him when the sun is shining. Don't you call that detective work?
>
> A: It all depends which way the sun is shining.
>
> Q: If you were working on Ruef, how come you put Ford's name on the margins?
>
> A: I put it there to identify him with.
>
> Q: There is nothing here in your notes which indicates that Ruef actually visited Ford's offices, isn't that correct?
>
> A: Correct.
>
> Q: You put the name in the margins of the book specifically for this case, isn't that what you did!?!

Two waiters, William Adamy and John Baker, were called to testify by the prosecution. They had both been employed at the Cosmos club after the fire and testified that they both saw Ruef and Ford there in the month of May.

On cross-examination Rogers was able to establish that after the fire, the Cosmos club was very popular and many prominent people frequented the place. Neither man saw any money change hands nor did either overhear any conversation between Ruef and Ford.

The trial was interrupted for one month during the Thanksgiving holidays and resumed on December 2, 1907. Once again, the prosecution rested its case without putting Abe Ruef on the witness stand.

On the evening of December 3, 1907, after deliberating for five hours, the jury in the second Ford case had reached a verdict. The judge took the bench, then the door to the anteroom opened and the twelve jurors filed in and took their places.

> Question (By the judge): "Gentlemen of the jury, have you reached a verdict?
>
> Answer (By Jury Foreman Russell H. Judson): We have, your honor.

The juror handed a slip of paper on which the verdict was written to the clerk. It was given to the judge who opened it up, transcribed it in the record without a word, and then handed the piece of paper back to the clerk. Then the following words were read out loud in the courtroom:

> We, the jury, find the defendant, Tirey L. Ford, NOT GUILTY.

An outburst of cheers broke out amongst the spectators and tears of joy filled Ford's eyes as he approached the jury members and shook each of their hands in gratitude. Francis Heney and Rudolph Spreckels looked at each other with shock and disappointment.

However, the saga was not yet over for Tirey L. Ford. On December 4, 1907, the district attorney's office announced that they intended on trying him a third time for another act of alleged bribery, and that this time they intended on putting Abe Ruef on the witness stand as a state's witness. The D.A.'s offices released this confident statement:

> We will put Abe Ruef on the witness stand in the next trial
> to testify against him, and Ford will be convicted beyond a
> doubt.

In the third Ford trial the prosecution did call Abe Ruef and Patrick Calhoun as witnesses for the State. The only problem was that both elected to exercise their constitutional right not to testify since both men were awaiting their own criminal trials. The third attempt at Ford had lost the enthusiasm and steam of the two earlier efforts; in addition to which, the public support of the graft prosecutions seemed to be waning.

A record of sorts was established when, on May 2, 1908, the jury in the third prosecution attempt to convict Tirey L. Ford, brought back an acquittal to a cheering crowd after deliberating for exactly five minutes and forty-five seconds. The twelve jurors left the courtroom to begin their deliberations at 11:37 a.m. and a few seconds before 11:43 a.m. they knocked on the door of the jury room and sent word to Judge Lawlor that they had arrived at a verdict. With slight exaggeration, it almost would have appeared like a scene out of a slapstick comedy, where the first jurors to leave the courtroom return with the verdict before the last of the twelve jurors had filed out.

In theory, the prosecution could have tried Ford in separate trials in connection with the bribery of each of the fourteen supervisors who were alleged to have taken bribes. However, Ford's prosecutorial nightmare had now come to an end. The prosecution knew that they could never obtain his conviction and it was decided not to attempt to try him again.

Ford stated:

> The jury of twelve men has placed the stamp of disapproval
> upon the efforts that have been made through the District
> Attorney's office to injure my good name. It would seem that
> the verdict of two American juries ought to be a full vindica-
> tion before the American people.

Although Ford's ordeal was ended, Heney was moving forward with the prosecution of Abe Ruef and then Ford's boss, Patrick Calhoun. The game plan for the prosecution at this point was to prosecute Ruef first, and then concentrate their efforts on obtaining Calhoun's conviction.

During Ruef's trial in November of 1908, the home of "Big" Jim Gallagher was blown up just prior to the date he was to testify against Ruef. Fortunately for Gallagher, he and his wife were out on a stroll when the dynamite blew up their house. Ruef's lawyers contended that the incident was a set-up to make Ruef look bad and that it was more than coincidence that Gallagher was not at home when the explosion took place.

But the most dramatic event in the San Francisco graft trials took place on November 13, 1908, at approximately 4:25 p.m. during a brief courtroom recess.

During the break Heney was conversing with Jim Gallagher, who had been on the witness stand, and Chief Clerk Al McCabe of the district attorney's office. A man walked right up to Mr. Heney in the crowded courtroom, pulled out a .38 caliber revolver, and shot Heney in the head as he was speaking.

The assailant, Morris Haas, was immediately apprehended and taken into custody. Heney, who was rushed to the hospital, was fortunate that the shot was not fatal and he survived. In fact, Heney's life may have been saved by a joke, for he was laughing at the moment of the shooting, his jaw moving just so as to deflect the bullet from a potentially fatal trajectory.

Haas was a former prospective juror in one of the earlier graft cases, whose previous felony record was exposed by Heney during his examination of Haas during jury selection.

Haas was taken into custody and placed into the county jail, where thirty men, armed with rifles and under the command of Lieutenant Mullender of the Mission Police Station, were placed on guard to protect him from a possible mob attack. The shooting of Heney brought about much sympathy and outrage. A personal letter of sympathy, outrage and shock written by President Theodore Roosevelt was printed in the newspapers. Everyone wanted to know why Haas had shot Heney and if he was in conspiracy with others in the assassination attempt.

However, whatever questions anyone may have to put to Haas were to go forever unanswered. More than one half-century before another assassination attempt, this one successful, would give fodder to conspiracy theorists, Haas was found dead in his jail cell, a gunshot to the head, a revolver laying on the jail cell floor. It was stated that the cause of death was suicide, but the prisoner was allegedly searched before he was placed into his cell.

The trial of Ruef went forward with attorney Hiram Johnson, who later was to become California's governor, filling in for Heney as the prosecutor. Ruef was convicted and sent to prison.

Heney recovered from his injury in time to return to the courtroom and try the case against Patrick Calhoun. The injury didn't seem to slow Heney down and he aggressively pursued the case against Calhoun.

On April 28, 1909, Rogers was in the middle of a telling cross-examination of one of the ex-supervisors. During the middle of the cross-examination Heney and assistant D.A. John O'Gara stood up and interrupted the examination and accused Rogers' young aide, Jerry Geisler of "making smiles and sneers" at the jury. Geisler had been sitting and conferring next to Calhoun at the time of the accusation. The six-foot-four Calhoun stood up and addressed the court:

> I am on trial for my liberty. I desire to enter a protest to the conduct of the district attorney as unbecoming and contrary to every rule of law as practiced anywhere among the English-speaking people. I desire further to say that the

object was manifestly to bring a controlling influence over the members of the jury, for the purpose of holding a threat over them that some cabalistic figure was being made on this desk. It is my liberty that is at stake and I look to your honor to protect it.

The prosecution's attempt to break the momentum of Rogers' cross-examination seemed to backfire. Young Mr. Geisler, who at that point was a virtual errand boy for Rogers, became a valuable member of his staff in the years to come. In later years after the death of Earl Rogers, Geisler became one of the most influential and successful lawyers in Los Angeles, representing such celebrity figures as Charles Chaplin, Errol Flynn, Bugsy Siegel and many others.

Geisler commented later in his life that the accusations made against him by the district attorney in the Calhoun case was the first time that his name ever appeared in print. In fact, his name appeared in the headlines of several San Francisco newspapers on April 29, 1909, in connection with the incident.

After months of jury selection and five months of testimony, the jury in the Calhoun case was deemed to be hopelessly deadlocked on June 20, 1909, after twenty-four hours of deliberation, with the final jury vote at ten for acquittal and two for conviction. Rogers let the press know that he was upset that the judge had dismissed the jury after only twenty-four hours of deliberation with a 10 to 2 vote and stated that with further deliberations the jury could have reached a verdict.

It took three months and two days to select the Calhoun jury. 2,310 jurors were summoned, 998 jurors were examined, 441 jurors were challenged for cause, 844 were excused by the Court, and 13 were accepted for jury duty.

In the four combined prosecutions against Ford and Calhoun, the defense did not put one witness on the stand and never offered any evidence. The political climate was going through a change. Francis Heney ran for district attorney of

San Francisco and lost. The graft prosecutions had lost their momentum. During the time that he was in San Francisco, Rogers has his own brushes with the law. He would often get drunk. One night, he and his good friend, famed writer Jack London, got arrested twice for brawling on the Embarcadero. This was just one of several incidents during this time period that Rogers was arrested for participating in drunken brawls. Earl Rogers, nontheless returned to Los Angeles, without doubt the most prolific, famous and successful lawyer on the West Coast.

CHAPTER NINE

The Case of Sulphuric Acid

PARTICIPANTS

DEFENDANT:	William McComas
PROSECUTOR:	Deputy D.A. Flemming
DEFENSE ATTORNEYS:	Earl Rogers, Chief Trial Counsel
	Paul Schenk, Co-Counsel
	W.W. Dodge, Co-Counsel
CHARGE	Murder

After the last of the Ford cases had concluded in San Francisco, Earl Rogers returned to Los Angeles and tried the McComas murder case prior to going back to San Francisco to defend Patrick Calhoun.

William McComas had a tragic childhood. His mother, father and brother were slaughtered by Indians in a massacre in New Mexico.

McComas had been in the mining business, mostly in Arizona, when he was charged with the murder of his lover, Charlotte Noyes. The prosecution had a simple theory of the case. McComas was in a dire financial condition and killed his lover in a fit of rage because she refused to give him money. The prosecution was in possession of several letters written by Ms. Noyes in which she had stated: "It may happen today for his threats are becoming murderous."

When the police investigated the scene of the killing they

found the dead woman along with quantities of carbolic acid. Both McComas and the decedent had acid burns on their bodies. The prosecution contended that McComas threw acid on the woman and shot her. McComas claimed that the acid was thrown in his face and that he had then pulled a gun and started shooting which resulted in his girlfriend's death.

The trial began on May 18, 1908, in Los Angeles Superior Court. A jury was quickly selected. A number of mysteries had developed surrounding the circumstances of the killing. Why were the acid and the murdered woman found in different rooms? The police were claiming that the murder occurred in a part of the house where no acid had been found. There were two cartridges in McComas' revolver that were discharged; but they were not adjacent in the gun's cylinder. One cartridge was directly under the hammer and the other directly opposite. Did a struggle occur in which fingers caught the hammer and caused the cylinder to whirl, or was the revolver reloaded after the killing? What was in the mysterious cup found on the kitchen stove? Was it sulfuric acid or olive oil?

The prosecution called Policeman Wyatt to the stand. He testified that the defendant had told him on the day of the killing that he had shot his girlfriend, and he identified the room where the shooting had supposedly taken place. Curiously, however, no acid was found by the police in that room.

Dora Willy testified that she was in a neighboring house attending a patient who was dying, when she heard three shots and a scream. She could not determine if the scream was a man or a woman.

A night watchman, C.J. Sawyer, testified that he was sitting on a dry goods box in front of a grocery store when he heard the fatal shots. Since the location of the shots was not on his beat he did not investigate, and only went to the scene of the killing at a later time when law enforcement was already on the scene.

Lila Vance testified that she lived just across the way from Mrs. Noyes' flat, and that one day, just before Christmas, she heard Mrs. Noyes screaming, saw her come to an upper window, and saw McComas grab her and pull her back. "I won't do it! I won't do it! I won't do it!" she had heard Mrs. Noyes exclaim.

Mrs. Horace Burr testified that she had overheard part of the incidents of the night of the murder. She lived in the flat below the Noyes flat. Her bed was directly under the telephone. She said she was asleep early that night. She was awakened by the voice of McComas crying out through the telephone, requesting an ambulance.

Mrs. Burr's husband, Horace, testified that one night in January he heard a disturbance in the Noyes flat upstairs and that it sounded like a body falling down the stairs. He stepped to the door of his flat and saw Mrs. Noyes and Mr. McComas come out. Mrs. Noyes was clinging to his neck and was sobbing. They went down towards Ingraham street; she was clinging on to him the entire way. Then they came back and he could hear Mrs. Noyes pleading that McComas not leave her.

Several other witnesses testified as to hearing shots at the time that the killing was believed to have taken place and then detective Valentine Carey was called to testify.

Valentine Carey, a detective for the district attorney's office, testified that he was the first one to arrive at the scene. He had been at a dance at the Pepper Hotel. McComas had entered the hotel, covered with acid, and announced that he had shot and killed a woman. Carey found Mrs. Noyes at her apartment lying dead, stretched out with her toes extended and her arms doubled under her as though she had been dragged. Her head was on a pillow. At the time he said that McComas was walking around, swabbing his face with a towel, and that he admitted that he had shot and killed her. McComas told him that Noyes had thrown acid in his face, that he shot once just to scare her and that she "ran" into the second shot, which killed her. Carey went to the telephone and found it dripping with acid. McComas told him that he had already used the phone to call the police. Carey assisted McComas in applying oil to his face, and continued to examine the rest of the residence.

Carey went on to testify that he found a cup half-filled with sulfuric acid sitting on the gas stove in the kitchen. He found acid splattered on the kitchen door. More acid was found in the bedroom on quilts and the floor. Spots of acid were also found on the floor leading to the room where the body was found.

On cross-examination Rogers asked Carey if he had found a gun in the woman's bedroom. Carey responded that he had not found a gun during his initial examination of the room, which was not very exhaustive or complete.

> Question (By Rogers): Aren't you just saying this because you know the police claim to have subsequently found a gun in the bed in that room?
>
> Answer (By Carey): Well, I know there was a lot of talk at the preliminary about it. I didn't pull the clothes down very far, otherwise I would have found the gun.

Part of the defense theory was that Mrs. Noyes not only threw acid on McComas, but shot at him with a gun that she owned. Rogers asserted flatly that the police found the gun, reloaded it so that no used chambers existed, and then planted it in the slain woman's bed in order to give the impression that the woman had not fired it during the murder. Rogers was able to establish the possibility of this scheme through his cross-examination of witnesses associated with the police investigation of the murder.

Detective Joe Ritch took the witness stand for the prosecution. He testified that Captain of Detectives Flammer had found the gun in the bedroom, but then put the gun back into the bed. Later, he took the revolver to the police station after everyone at the scene had left. Rogers cross-examined Ritch.

Question (By Rogers): We were all out there together at the scene, police and defense lawyers?

Answer (By Ritch): Yes, the detectives, yourself and some reporters were all there after the shooting took place, that's correct.

Q: It was understood that our discoveries were to be mutually shared, isn't that correct?

A: So understood.

Q: Do you know why our attention was not called to the finding of that gun?

A: I'm not really certain.

Q: That gun was found when both myself and my associate Mr. Schenk were present at the residence, when we were in another room looking through some papers, isn't that correct?

A: Well, yes.

Q: While the pistol was being located in the bed in that room adjacent to where Mr. Schenk and I were located, you closed the room to that door, correct?

A: Yes.

Q: Were you told not to inform me that the gun had been discovered?

A: Yes.

Q: You knew we had been insisting that a gun had been found and calling upon you to dig it up, correct?

A: Well no, that's not true.

Q: Well the ultimate fact was that the finding of that pistol was to be keep a secret from us, isn't that true?

A: Yes sir, that's true.

Captain Flammer took the stand and under cross-examination by Rogers admitted that he had been told to keep the finding of the gun a secret. He testified further that he had met personally with McComas before the shooting took place at a time when Flammer was acting Chief of Police. McComas had come with a letter of introduction from Mayor Harper. According to Flammer, McComas told him that he was living with a woman named Mrs. Noyes and that he wanted to leave her, but that he was afraid of her and wanted an officer sent out to keep the peace while he took his clothes away from the apartment. Flammer testified further that McComas had informed him that Mrs. Noyes owned a revolver.

> Question (By Rogers on cross-examination): Where did you find the gun?
>
> Answer (By Flammer): I found it between the sheets and the coverlet.
>
> Q: Where was I and Mr. Schenk at the time you found the gun?
>
> A: In the adjacent room.
>
> Q: Why didn't you tell me anything about finding the gun?
>
> A: I would have called you in myself, but Mr. Flemming told me not to say anything about it, so I took his advice.
>
> Q: If you had it your way you would have called Mr. Schenck and myself in, instead of putting back the revolver under the covers?
>
> A: I thought it proper to call you in. Mr. Flemming well, you know how those things are... We don't all use the same judgment.

Detective Grant Robert was the next witness cross-examined by Rogers.

> Q: Now I understand that you found the bullet hole in the wall; what was the condition of the bullet hole before it was tampered with?
>
> A: That bullet hole was never tampered with in any way.
>
> Q: Is it your testimony that the bullet hole had not been enlarged to make it appear that the hole was created from my client's gun?
>
> A: That's my testimony.
>
> Q: Do you remember the Sunday after our investigation when you and I had a conversation at the police station?
>
> A: Yes.
>
> Q: And you told me that no revolver had been found at the flat?
>
> A: Well, if I did I don't have to tell you my business.
>
> Q: You thought you could lie to me with impunity?
>
> A: I didn't know that you were serious.
>
> Q: What did you think I was doing?
>
> A: Thought you were trying to get information I had no business

to tell you.

Q: On the witness stand do you believe in concealing everything you are not actually asked for if it would be helpful to the defendant?

A: No sir, no sir, absolutely not.

Q: Would you volunteer anything to help the defendant from the witness stand?

A: If I thought of anything I would tell it

Q: Do you know why Mr. Schenck and I were not told about the gun?

A: No, I don't know.

Q: Do you know who dropped the revolver into the bed?

A: No.

When the prosecution rested its case, Rogers gave a short but dramatic statement of the defense case. Said Rogers in part:

> Mrs. Noyes and McComas had mutually agreed that their relations should cease. The defendant was preparing to break with her on the advice of his friends and upon his own better judgment. Sometimes Mrs. Noyes seems to have been unwilling to let him go. Sometimes she wanted him to leave her. She was a highly emotional woman. Sometimes she was very loving; sometimes she was desperately angry with him, and for no cause. McComas experienced all the vagaries of a jealous woman. She quarreled with him; not him with her.
>
> On the day of the killing she had been at the races. She had been playing the races for some time with all the abandonment of a woman gambler. She had been playing a system. Without going into details it is enough to say that it is the old cumulative system that would take the combined capital of John D. Rockefeller and Andrew Carnegie to win. She lost. She kept demanding money of McComas all of the time with which to continue to play at the races. The night of the killing she became angry because he went to dinner at the home of some friends instead of with her. At his friend's house he had dinner and played some cards.
>
> As he came out of the house and took the car he noticed

a woman in a rain coat and an old hat—at least a hat not in fashion—well an old hat—pulled down well over her eyes. She got on the same car and sat down on the outside; McComas then recognized her. He changed his seat in the car and sat down next to her. He asked what she was doing out so late. She told him something about taking a transfer from another car. To make her story hold good she took an old transfer from her purse and handed it to the conductor who laughed and threw it on the floor. McComas then paid both of their fares.

She insisted that he go home with her. She said she was afraid to go home alone. He finally consented and they got off at Figueroa and Sixteenth street. She was looking at McComas in a strange and unaccountable way. Arriving at her flat, McComas took off his overcoat and hat and they sat down in her living room. They were talking there about her racing system. Being a mining engineer and something of a mathematician, McComas tried to show her that her system led only to bankruptcy.

At that time, Mrs. Noyes got up and walked back into the dining room where there was a man's office desk. Supposing she was getting something in this desk, McComas walked though into the bedroom. The woman must have gone through the silent swinging door into the kitchen.

It was absolutely dark in the kitchen and the bedroom. Suddenly, out of the utter darkness from no one knows where—Just out of the dark—flashed this burning liquid fire—without threat of previous word.

Startled beyond my power of description, deaf partly from other causes and partly because of the acid that was burning his left ear—a burn from which the flesh was afterward taken off in strips-both blind and deaf—McComas tried to get away. As he groped his way out, another or blinding douse of acid struck him. As he was fighting to get away—to keep this awful stuff from his face—came a third dose. McComas is a western man and he reached for his gun. In his blindness and momentary stupidity, he began squeezing the thing; he commenced shooting, although he could not see and did not know at what, or whom, he was shooting.

In his blindness he elbowed his way around not knowing where he went and finally got to the bathroom where he found a towel. He wiped off his face as best he could, but he knew there must be something he could put on his face. He had made little salads in the kitchen and groped his way out there and found a bottle of olive oil. Then tortured with excruciating pain—his mouth, ears, eyes and face burned so the flesh came off in strips—he made his way to the telephone, where he rang up the police and cried, 'my God, I'm dying.' He didn't know if he shot twice or if the woman had shot at all.

Two days before this Mrs. Noyes told a woman friend that she intended to burn out McComas' eyes with vitriol. We will introduce testimony to show she first threw acid upon McComas and then added a cup of water. We will show that she had discovered that water added to sulfuric acid will intensify the burns. We will show that the pain suddenly became agonizing as she lashed water in his face. We will show that McComas had no thought of ever killing Mrs. Noyes. We will show that—aside from this affair—he was a man of exemplary character.

We intend to trace his life from the time he was a little boy—when he came to Arizona with his father and brother—will trace him through fights with Indians and through the turbulent life of the frontier. McComas always carried a revolver. He had a permit from Mayor Harper to carry one at the time of this killing.

We will show that Mrs. Noyes knew that the penalty for throwing acid was fourteen years in prison. She knew she was doing something more terrible than killing a man. It was only God's mercy that she did not carry out her threat to blind him.

We will conceal nothing. The defendant is going to take the witness stand before you. We will ask you to acquit him on the ground that he had no intention of killing this woman; that, through fright and stupefaction, he did not know whom he was shooting at; we ask that you acquit even if you believe that he did know and did intend to kill her. The average man is not going to stand still and have any person burn his eyes out. We will show that under the law, no man has to stand still and have acid thrown on him."

W.H. Lyford, general counsel of the Chicago and East Illinois and various other railroads in the Rock Island system testified that his wife was a cousin of McComas and that he knew him through that relation. He stated that in 1892 McComas came to his house in Chicago from somewhere in New Mexico to be treated for a terrible injury to his right eye. He testified that the eye at the time was clear out of the socket and looked like "fresh liver." He testified that McComas stayed at his home for four months during his recuperation; two of which were spent in a room that was perfectly dark.

Mrs. Lyford testified as to the severity of the injury to McComas' right eye and told that he was practically blind in that eye. Since the acid was thrown in his left eye on the night of the shooting, the defense wanted to establish that McComas was virtually blind on the night of the shooting.

Dr. Burt Ellis, a well-known specialist, testified that McComas had been his patient for months before the shooting on account of this same eye. He said that McComas had about twenty-five percent of the normal sight in the eye that had been injured; was very defective in one ear, and somewhat shy of hearing in the other.

D.L. Hough, assistant police surgeon, testified that when water was combined with sulfuric acid the combination would have greatly exacerbated any injury to McComas. In this way Rogers accounted for the fact that there was no acid, but only an empty cup in the room in which the woman was found dead. Dr. Hough testified that water added to sulfuric acid intensifies the burning and the heat, and thus the pain.

McComas was put on the witness stand. Rogers took him through a detailed direct examination which tracked the story told by Rogers in his opening statement. McComas described in detail how he was writhing in pain, acid burning his face, disoriented; that he pulled his gun shooting instinctively, insane from his pain. He did not intend on killing Mrs. Noyes. After the detailed and exhaustive direct examination, the prosecution was not able to shake the story on cross-examination.

There was a mob scene at the courthouse when Earl Rogers gave his closing argument, with people literally fighting for seats in the courtroom. Rogers gave a dramatic and colorful closing argument. The jury deliberated for over ten hours, and when the jury foreman, on May 29, 1908, declared that the jury was hopelessly deadlocked on a ten-two vote, Judge James excused them and told them to go home; a hung jury. McComas was retried with the prosecution and defense evidence virtually identical to that put on in the first trial. Once again Earl Rogers defended McComas. At the conclusion of the second trial the jury brought in a verdict of not guilty and McComas was a free man.

Clarence Darrow on the witness stand.
Courtesy, *Herald Examiner Collections/Los Angeles Public Library.*

CHAPTER TEN

The Case of the Great Defender Defended by the Great Defender

THE PARTICIPANTS

DEFENDANT:	Clarence S. Darrow
PROSECUTORS:	John Fredericks, D.A.
	Joseph Ford, A.D.A.
	Arthur Keetch, A.D.A.
	C.C. McComas, A.D.A.
DEFENSE ATTORNEYS:	Earl Rogers, Chief Trial Counsel
	Horrace Appel, Co-Counsel
	Clarence S. Darrow, Co-Counsel
CHARGE:	Bribery

The period between 1890 and 1900 saw a tremendous growth in the population of Los Angeles. New business opportunity, cheap real estate, and temperate climate attracted people to Los Angeles from places all across the country.

In 1882 partial ownership of the *Los Angeles Times* was acquired by Civil War veteran General Harrison Gray Otis. Los Angeles saw an economic slump in 1890, at which time Otis asked his staff to take a temporary cut in pay. The International Typographical Union stepped in on behalf of the

Times' employees, refused to take the requested pay cut, and went on strike. Otis decided to fight, brought in scabs and strikebreakers and defeated the union's efforts.

Otis then became a celebrity as union foe and advocate of Industrial Freedom. At the time his newspaper had a daily circulation of approximately 55,000 and an 85,000 Sunday circulation. Los Angeles became known as an open shop city with powerful interests galvanized against organized labor and unions. The Merchants Manufacturers Association was formed in Los Angeles, whose primary goal was to ensure that businesses in Los Angeles only employ non-union labor.

Boycotts and other reprisals of various forms were threatened to local businesses which employed or did business with union members. A vigorous effort was made to assure that no union organization would take place in Los Angeles.

In sharp contrast to Los Angeles, San Francisco was a city infiltrated and strongly influenced in many respects by a variety of unions. Slates of candidates on labor tickets had been elected to public office and local government in San Francisco was dominated by labor interests. In order for labor unions to gain a foothold in Los Angeles, a decision was made by labor organizers in San Francisco to organize metal workers in Los Angeles to come under the control of the International Association of Bridge and Structural Iron Workers. Members of that union were employed in extremely hazardous work in connection with, among other things, the construction of multistory high-rise buildings. It was reported at that time that over 100 metal workers died on the job each year in various accidents; most notably they would simply fall from scaffolds to their death on the street below; and all this on the meager wages of $2.50 per day.

Between 1908 and 1910, labor organizers participated in a form of terrorism by planting and exploding dynamite at various locations around the country in an attempt to intimidate those resisting the promotion of union organization and recognition. In the many dynamite explosions which had taken place, minor property damage had occurred with no loss of human life. Yet the explosions had proven to be an effective means to frighten people and businesses into recognition of the unions.

Olaf Tvietmoe was the secretary treasurer of the California Building Trades Union. He became head of the General Strike Committee in the effort to break the open shop of Los Angeles and to organize union efforts there.

A general strike was called by the metals workers on June 1, 1910. Picket lines were set up and tension was omnipresent between pro-union and anti-labor sentiments in the city.

The Merchants and Manufactures Association retained Earl Rogers to act as its general counsel and instructed him to draft a prospective ordinance designed to restrain union activity in Los Angeles. Rogers proceeded to draft an ordinance which was intended by its author to curb union activity in Los Angeles which created safety risks to the city's citizens. On July 16, 1910, the city council unanimously passed the ordinance which Rogers drafted. The newly passed ordinance outlawed picketing in the city of Los Angeles.

Labor organizers defied the ordinance and continued to set up and participate in pickets. Numerous arrests followed at picket line locations. One arrest of twenty-five picketers was followed by the arrest of over 80 others. The *Los Angeles Times* wrote articles condemning the activities of the union lawbreakers. Union organizers charged the *Times* and its publisher with criminal liable and litigation was initiated.

Union organizers decided to set off a dynamite explosion near the offices at the *Los Angeles Times* building. John Joseph "J.J." McNamara was the youthful and successful Secretary of the International Association of Bridge and Structural Iron Workers Union located in Indianapolis. Arrangements were made for his brother, Jim McNamara, along with several others, to travel to Los Angeles to accomplish this task.

Prior to his arrival in Los Angeles on September 30, 1910, he traveled to San Francisco and other west coast locations to prepare for the bombing under the alias of James Brice. He checked into a local hotel under his alias, then proceeded to plant sixteen sticks of eighty-percent dynamite in an alleyway behind the *Los Angeles Times* building. The dynamite was set to explode by means of a timing device at 1:00 a.m. in the morning. Unfortunately, McNamara was ignorant of the nickname given to the location where he planted the dynamite. Not far from where the dynamite was set to explode were numerous barrels of printers ink stored in the alley; thus it was called "ink alley."

When the dynamite detonated a massive explosion occurred which in turn caused the ink barrels to explode and cause an enormous fire; larger than ever experienced in Los Angeles up to that time. The *Times* building had extensive damage from the explosion itself, but far worse, it was soon engulfed in flames. Many staff members of the newspaper were in the building when the explosion took place and were trapped inside by the fire. Fire trucks soon arrived at the scene. Employees of the *Times*, trapped in the building, jumped from their office windows into safety nets waiting for them below. Some of the people who jumped missed the nets and were killed. Still others jumped from the building to their deaths, despite no safety nets below, to avoid the horrors of the inferno. In all, twenty people died as a result of the October 1, 1910 dynamiting of the *Los Angeles Times* building, including the young city editor, Harvey Elder, a close, personal friend of Earl Rogers.

The *Times* published a one-page edition the following morning, brimming with emotion, pinning the blame for the bombing on the unions, and calling those responsible cowardly murderers. Los Angeles Mayor Alexander sought out the help of famed investigator William J. Burns, met him in

Los Angeles, and retained him for the singular purpose of finding and apprehending those responsible for the deaths of those killed by the bombing. Burns was the investigator who would had assisted the prosecutors in the cases against Earl's clients Tiery Ford and Patrick Calhoun in the San Francisco Graft trials. Prior to those cases, Burns had been assigned by President Theodore Roosevelt to assist Francis Heney in the successful prosecution of graft and corruption in a variety of cases in the Oregon timberlands.

The *Los Angeles Times* disaster attracted national attention in the media. Labor leaders claimed that the explosion was either a set up by anti-union factions to create public anti-labor sentiment, or was the result of faulty gas mains and negligence on the part of General Otis in not properly maintaining his building.

After an extensive investigation, J.J. McNamara was arrested at his union's headquarters in Indianapolis. The arrest was an unusual affair. Burns had obtained a written extradition request signed by the governors of California and Indiana. A police officer showed up at the union offices on April 22, 1911, and told McNamara that his presence was requested at police headquarters. Upon arrival at the police station, he was served with the extradition papers and taken before a police court where the judicial officer granted Burns permission to take the prisoner to Los Angeles. Despite McNamara's plea that he be afforded a hearing and an attorney, the judge was satisfied, once McNamara's identity was established, that the next step was for him to be transported to Los Angeles.

Arrested in Detroit was J.J.'s brother, James McNamara, and an accomplice of his in various bombings by the name of Ortie McManigal. Burns was able to secure a confession from McManigal who gave detailed accounts of the times and places of various bombings, including the bombing of the *Los Angeles Times* building. His confession established that it was James

McNamara who actually purchased and planted the dynamite, and that he was acting at the direction of his brother, J.J. McNamara.

The trip from Indianapolis to Los Angeles took strange and circuitous routes, by automobile and train under heavily armed guard. Burns was concerned that union organizers would attempt to hijack him in his attempt to bring the McNamara brothers to justice in Los Angeles, so he devised these circuitous means to get to his destination. Under intense public interest and outcry, the McNamara brothers were successfully brought to Los Angeles by William Burns to face charges in connection with the explosion of the Los Angeles Times building, and for the twenty deaths resulting therefrom.

During the several days time period that it took for the prisoners to be transported across the country to Los Angeles, union leaders arranged for the retention of legal counsel to defend them at trial. Chicago-based Clarence Darrow, the most famous trial lawyer in the United States, was summoned to Los Angeles to defend the McNamara brothers.

Clarence Seward Darrow was born on April 18, 1857, near Kinsman, Ohio. He attended law school for only one year before being admitted to the Ohio bar in 1878. He moved his residence to Chicago in 1887, and immediately participated in attempts to free the anarchists charged with murder in the Haymarket Riot of 1886. His friendship with Judge John Peter Altgeld, later to be governor of Illinois, led to Darrow's appointment as Chicago city corporation counsel.

Darrow then became general counsel for the Chicago and North Western Railway. He left this post in 1894, in order to defend labor leader Eugene V. Debs, who was head of the American Railway Union, and had been charged with violating federal court orders during the Pullman Strike. Although Debs and his associates were convicted, Darrow established a national reputation as a labor and criminal attorney.

Switching his allegiance to the side of the unions, Darrow defended Thomas I. Kidd, of the Amalgamated Woodworkers Union, at Oshkosh, Wisconsin, on the charge of conspiracy and secured an acquittal in 1897. In arbitration hearings during the Pennsylvania anthracite coal strike in 1902, Darrow represented the striking coal miners. During cross-examination he was able to shed light on the oppressive working conditions in the mines, as well as the degree to which child labor was used. Subsequently, in 1907, he represented labor leader William D. "Big Bill" Haywood, charged with the assassination of former governor of Idaho, Frank R. Steunenberg, and secured his acquittal.

A substantial war chest was provided to Darrow with which to defend the McNamara's; money to be used to pay Darrow and his entire staff, and money to be used in connection with any and all anticipated costs associated with the defense efforts.

Much was at stake with the prosecution of the McNamara brothers. If they were acquitted, the perception was that they could and would continue to have impunity to inflict further damage upon anti-labor forces with acts of terror. If they were to be convicted, a serious blow would be dealt to the public sentiment towards organized labor.

On November 28, 1911, Charles Lockwood was to appear in downtown Los Angeles Superior Court to be examined as a prospective juror. However Lockwood was unable to appear as scheduled due to his arrest along with a former deputy U.S. Marshall and a former Los Angeles County chief jailer. The former federal officer was Bert Franklin, who was known to be a private detective who had been acting as the chief detective for the McNamara defense team since October 11, 1911. Franklin was charged with having taken part in a scheme to hang the jury in the McNamara dynamiting case by bribing Lockwood. The former chief jailer was Charles E. White, who was a longtime friend of both Franklin and Lockwood, and was acting as a middleman in the transaction by holding on to a portion of the bribe money until after a jury verdict was reached.

As it turned out, the arrest was part of a sting operation. Franklin had allegedly approached Lockwood with an offer to bribe him. The terms were that Lockwood would get $500 up front; if he was actually selected to be on the jury he would receive the balance of $3,500 when the jury came back hung.

It was agreed that White, a mutual friend of both men, would hold the $3,500 to be paid to Lockwood if and when the judge in the case declared a hung jury. Lockwood had allegedly gone to John Fredericks, the D.A. at the helm of the prosecution team, and told him of the bribe offer. The D.A.'s office then worked with Lockwood to have him arrange for the meeting to take place with between himself and his prospective briber at 9:00 a.m. at the corner of Third and Los Angeles streets.

Detective Samuel Browne, and a number of his assistants in the D.A.'s office, were placed on the street corner such that they were able to hear and observe the bribe as it would take place. They overheard the conversation between Lockwood, White and Franklin that the initial $500 was Lockwood's to keep upfront, and that he would get the $3,500 balance at such time as the jury came back hung in the McNamara trial. The sting went as planned and the arrests took place shortly after 9:00 a.m.

Franklin was immediately arraigned before Justice Young on two charges of bribery and released upon the deposit of $10,000 cash bail. The bail was posted by attorney LeCompte Davis, who was assisting Clarence Darrow in the defense of the McNamara brothers. As a matter of fact, Davis dropped what he was doing at the courthouse and made haste in getting to the county jail to post the bail.

Samuel Browne, who was the chief investigator in the District Attorney's office, initially reported to the public that the D.A. had evidence that Mr. Franklin gave $500 to Lockwood, with a promise for an additional $3,500 if the McNamara trial resulted in a hung jury. He reported that the D.A.'s office was in possession of the actual bribe money and had enough evidence to secure Franklin's conviction for bribery.

Darrow was in an awkward position. Here he was in the middle of jury selection as the chief defense counsel in defense of the McNamara's, and his chief investigator had been arrested and arraigned on charges of having bribed a prospective juror.

Darrow made immediate arrangements to secure former California Governor Henry T. Gage to act as Franklin's defense counsel; including the payment of a $10,000 cash retainer taken from the McNamara defense fund. On November 29, 1911, Gage requested a postponement for the date of the preliminary hearing. Deputy District Attorney Joseph Ford immediately told the court that the D.A.'s office was opposed to any type of delay, and that the state needed the matter to go forward immediately due to witness problems and other considerations.

Ford requested that the Court set the hearing for Friday, December 1, 1911. Gage appeared surprised by the position taken by Ford and told the judge that it was not fair to force him to have only one day to prepare for the court hearing. After intense argument by both sides the Court essentially granted Ford's request for a speedy hearing date and set the matter for Monday, December 4, 1911.

On Friday, December 1, 1911, shock waves reverberated around the country, and national labor leaders stood in disbelief when word got out that, pursuant to a plea bargain negotiated by Clarence Darrow, both McNamara brothers had entered guilty pleas, and their trials would not go forward. The plea bargain called for James McNamara to serve a life sentence and for J.J. McNamara to serve between 10 to 15 years in prison. The event was a major blow to the forces of organized labor because it brought to an end any controversy as to the responsibility for the deaths of the twenty *Los Angeles Times* employees. And so on December 1, 1911, Clarence Darrow was sitting with two convicted clients; powerful forces in organized labor were irate at him for allowing the guilty pleas; and his chief investigator was about to go on trial for the alleged bribery of a juror and of a prospective juror in the case he had just concluded by virtue of his clients' guilty pleas.

The grand jury immediately began to investigate possible knowledge and involvement that Darrow may have had in connection with the alleged bribery of jurors and/or prospective jurors by Bert Franklin. On January 26, 1912, Darrow announced that he had retained Earl Rogers to act as his attorney in connection with any action the grand jury might take. Rogers released the following statement:

> It is true that I have been employed by Mr. Darrow to care for his interests in anything arising from the present county grand jury investigation of the McNamara trial. We do not know that any situation requiring my services will arise, but we are prepared for any eventualities.

On January 28, 1912, it was leaked to members of the media that investigations had uncovered that money given to juror Robert Bain and prospective juror George N. Lockwood was part of a fund maintained in San Francisco, and that a man alleged to be intimate with the workings of the McNamara defense acted as agent between the alleged bribe takers and givers. On the morning of January 28th, Clarence Darrow returned to Los Angeles from a trip to San Francisco and went into a lengthy meeting with his attorney Earl Rogers.

On January 29, 1912, Clarence Darrow was indicted on the charge that on November 28, 1911, he "willfully, unlawfully, corruptly and feloniously," gave the sum of $500 to George N. Lockwood and promised to give Lockwood the further sum of $3,500 to vote for an acquittal in the case of the People of the State of California vs. J.B. McNamara. A second identical indictment was filed against Darrow charging him with the bribery of Robert Bain.

The indictments were drawn under sections 92 and 95 of the California Penal Code where it was deemed criminal conduct where any person "gives or offers to give a bribe to a juror with intent to influence his vote as a juror." The penalty for conviction of this crime was up to ten years in the state penitentiary.

Darrow appeared in court with Earl Rogers by his side at 4:00 p.m., before Judge Conrey who was sitting on the bench in the absence of Judge Hutton. Foreman Hubbard of the grand jury informed the court that they were ready to present indictments. A poll was taken of the grand jury, the court ordered the indictments received, warrants were technically issued, and Darrow was placed under arrest. The issue of Darrow's bail was next addressed. Assistant D.A. Ford addressed the court: "We feel that this is a serious offense your honor, and we would like the bail fixed at $10,000 on each indictment."

Rogers had come prepared, the bail was posted, and Darrow was free to go as he pleased. There was some commentary over the fact that Darrow had retained Rogers to defend him. Rogers had acted as the legal counsel for the Merchants and Manufacturers Association, an avidly anti-union organization, and he had helped in the drafting and passage of legislation which outlawed union picket lines in Los Angeles. Rogers had also acted as a special prosecutor in the investigation of the McNamara brothers in connection with their role in the dynamiting of the *Times* building. Now here he was defending the Great Defender of organized labor. To the apparent inconsistency of this scenario, Rogers made this statement to reporters as he was walking with Darrow outside the courtroom, just after the indictment:

> When I believe a man innocent I have a right to defend him. My previous connection with the McNamara case has no bearing on this matter.

When Darrow was questioned in connection with his indictment, he stated to reporters:

> Just what I have said from the first, and that is that I know nothing of this bribery charge; know nothing of any attempt to approach one of the prospective jurors, and knew absolutely nothing of this thing at all until Franklin was arrested.

A reporter questioned Darrow further, "Do you believe that Bert Franklin gave certain evidence to the grand jury which caused your indictment?"

"I am not going to discuss this case now in that way, not at all in that way," said Darrow.

"But in view of the fact that you state your entire lack of knowledge of any alleged bribery do you not believe that no indictment could have been returned against you unless some person gave evidence against you—that is direct evidence implicating you in the charges alleged by the State?"

Darrow responded, "I haven't seen the evidence that was given before the grand jury. I have no transcript of it and won't have for several days. But then, what is the use of discussing the case in this way?"

It was widely reported on January 30, 1912, that Bert Franklin had confessed to the bribery of both Robert Bain and George Lockwood and that he had received immunity from prosecution for his testimony implicating Clarence Darrow in the crime. The D.A.'s office refused to discuss the matter on the record. The following day, Bert Franklin confirmed that he had confessed and would testify against Darrow at the time of trial. Darrow was at Earl Rogers' office when he heard word of Franklin's intention to testify against him and stated that he hoped the public would forego an opinion on his guilt until the evidence amassed by the D.A.'s office was introduced. He further stated: "I am not guilty, and time and a fair jury will prove."

Jury selection in Darrow's case began on May 15, 1912, in Judge Hutton's courtroom in Department 2 of the Superior Court.

On May 24, 1912, District Attorney John Fredericks delivered his opening statement in the bribery trial of Clarence Darrow. Fredericks told the jury that Darrow was the director-general in a wholesale bribery plot, and that the state would prove that the $4,000 of bribe money which was to be given to the prospective juror, George Lockwood, by Bert Franklin, was handed to Franklin by Darrow on the morning that $500 of the money was alleged to have been placed in Lockwood's hands. Fredericks also stated that Darrow placed large sums of money in the hands of hired agents from the East and that it was used for the purpose of bribing jurors and witnesses and inducing State witnesses to leave the state or testify falsely. Fredericks stated that the evidence would show that Bert Franklin offered Lockwood $500 up front and $3,500 more to be delivered after he had voted not guilty in the McNamara case. Fredericks stated:

> We will show that Franklin met Lockwood by appointment at his ranch home one night and conferred with him about the bribe money in the presence of several detectives who were stationed nearby. No money was passed that night. Lockwood agreed to meet Franklin to receive the money on the following Monday morning at Third and Los Angeles Streets. C.E. White, a mutual friend, was selected to hold the money. Franklin was to give Lockwood $500 down and the balance on the day a "not guilty" verdict was returned. We will show you that it was Clarence Darrow's money that Franklin had in his possession. We will show you that the money used in this instance was part of a large fund raised by Darrow's

agents in the East and sent direct to him. We will show that Darrow was the directing spirit in all of the attempted briberies. We will show that the Lockwood deal was one of a series of many acts engineered by Darrow to prevent justice in the McNamara case. Now, gentlemen of the jury, all of the charges I have made to you this afternoon I hope to prove to you beyond a doubt before the close of trial. The judge will instruct you that the charges in my address are not to be considered as evidenced in this case. In closing I want to congratulate you of the jury that the case is really under way and the time for the introduction of evidence is at hand.

Several times during Fredericks' opening statement to the jury, Earl Rogers jumped to his feet, loudly sounding objections of prosecutorial misconduct for making these types of inflammatory conclusions in an opening statement. Judge Hutton overruled the objections, but proceeded to inform the jury that the inflammatory charges being made by the District Attorney were not to be considered as evidence by them.

The first witness called to the stand by the prosecution was George Munroe, the clerk in Department 9 who testified and established the fact that George Lockwood was drawn and subsequently sworn in as a venireman in the McNamara case.

During the middle of the examination of George Lockwood, Rogers brought to the court's attention that he had obtained information that Robert J. Foster, a detective for the National Erectors Association, had attempted to smuggle inflammatory and prejudicial newspaper articles concerning Clarence Darrow into the jury room. The judge ordered the appointment of a special prosecutor to investigate the matter.

George Lockwood testified in detail regarding his conversations with Bert Franklin, how Franklin had offered him a bribe of $500 up front with an additional payment of $3,500 once he was on the jury and had voted to acquit. Lockwood was questioned during a detailed direct examination explaining how an acquaintance, Mr. White, was to act as the middleman in holding the $3,500 deferred payment. Lockwood also testified in great detail how the exchange of the money went down on Third and Los Angeles streets. He also explained how he had informed the D.A.'s office about Franklin's offer to bribe him and of how he had assisted the district attorney's office in helping to set the stage for the actual arrest of Franklin. Lockwood's testimony supported the assertions made by the district attorney in his opening statement of the case.

Bert Franklin was called to testify for the prosecution. On direct examination Franklin's testimony corroborated that of George Lockwood. He also testified that Darrow gave him money for the purpose of payment to prospective jurors to vote for the acquittal of the McNamara's if they were selected to be on the jury. In fact, Franklin testified that all of the money which had been given to him by Darrow was for the express purpose of bribing jurors.

On cross-examination of Franklin, Rogers was able to bring out that substantial monies had been paid to Franklin by Darrow which was to be used and was actually used for legitimate and honorable purposes. It had become publicly known during the time period that Franklin was on the witness stand, that the prosecution was going to call LeCompte Davis as a witness for the prosecution. Davis had acted as co-counsel along with Darrow for the McNamara brothers during their trial. During his testimony on May 31, 1912, Franklin stated that Davis had initially been utilized to defend him in connection with the bribery charges and that a meeting had taken place shortly after his arrest which was attended by Franklin, Davis and Darrow.

Franklin testified that during the meeting Davis had proposed that Franklin should plead guilty to one of the indictment counts and that his fine would be paid out of the McNamara defense fund.

On June 3, 1912, Franklin dropped a bombshell on those present in the courtroom when he testified that Darrow had told him that the $4,000 used in the alleged bribery of Lockwood had come directly from Samuel Gompers, the president of the American Federation of Labor. Franklin was not able to confirm whether Gompers had actual knowledge that the money was to be used for bribery.

Question (By Rogers): Where did you hold your first conference with Mr. Darrow after your arrest?

Answer (By Franklin): In the Higgins building.

Q: What was said?

A: I don't remember anything at this time.

Q: Will you later?

A: I don't remember at this time.

Q: Where was your next conference?

A: I don't remember.

Q: Perhaps you remember the third conference?

A: Now see here Mr. Rogers, I don't remember any particular conference after the first one—so you might as well remember it. I saw Mr. Darrow after my arrest, almost every day.

Q: After your arrest?

A: Yes, certainly.

Q: I would like you to relate the conversations you had with Darrow.

A: Darrow said to me "'Bert, if you plead guilty and get a fine, we will give you $3,000 for your family."

Q: Did you ever have other conversations with Darrow about your defense in higher court or any aspect of your case?

A: That's a difficult question to answer, Mr. Rogers, in the way you put it. I have—I don't want to tell of a certain conversation pertaining to such—unless you want it.

Q: Tell everything.

Objection (By Prosecution): Now your honor we object to the method of such procedure; the answer your honor —

Objection (By Rogers): I object to the prosecution's counsel putting the answer in the witness' mouth. Now this is unfair to us.

By the Court: Well, let the witness examine the transcript of his previous testimony.

Answer (By Franklin): I don't need it. I will answer it this way. I asked Mr. Darrow if the rumors about the $4,000 being placed by the district attorney in the safety deposit vault, marking it beforehand, were true. Darrow told me: "This is not true for it came direct from Sam Gompers."

Question (By Rogers): Well, that was the conversation you did not wish to tell?

A: No.

Q: Well, shoot over the other one.

A: Alright, I asked Darrow if there was not a record kept at the safe deposit vault of Harriman's visit there. Darrow told me: "Don't worry about that. Harriman took $500 of the sum to pay off a mortgage and in that way to cover up his visit."

Q: Well, it was solitude for Mr. Darrow that induced you to keep the Gompers matter and the the Harriman matter quiet, was it?

A: Well I would not have told it had you not made me.

Q: What other things were said by Mr. Darrow in that conversation?

A: One day he asked me how large the cells were at San Quentin and Folsom. I remember this because I was thinking seriously of it at the time myself.

Q: You were, eh? Did you not say to Fred Harshburger in the Waldorf saloon on the day after you were fined: "I wasn't worrying a damn about my case. I knew I would not have to go up?"

At this point objections were voiced by both Fredericks and Ford, contending that the trial on hand was not the proper moment for attacking the witness' veracity in that manner. The objections were overruled.

Answer: I deny making that remark to Harshburger. I never said anything that he could infer such from.

Q: Well which is true—you do or don't deny it?

A: Both.

Q: Now did you have any such conversation with Mr. Davis?

A: Now your honor, have I got to tell conversations with my attorney? Davis was my attorney then.

By Rogers: According to the appellate and supreme court decisions, your honor, the witness must tell all. I have authority to prove it.

By Judge Hutton: The objection is not allowed. The question must be answered.

A: The first conversation that I had with Davis was while I was in the county jail. Davis said not to be impatient; that they would get me into court directly. I told him I wanted a cash bond. He said he believed that it could be attended to—then he left. The next conversation was in the courthouse after my arraignment. He told me to keep my mouth shut, especially to strangers and reporters. When I saw him again he told me to plead guilty to attempting to bribe George Lockwood and that the penalty would be a fine of $5,000, one year in the penitentiary, or both. Davis said that he thought he could get me off with a fine and that they would give me $1,000 for my family.

Q: Did Davis tell you that Lockwood had been trying you out?

A: I told Davis that Lockwood had come to my office to solicit a bribe. I told him this after my arrest.

Q: Where was this conversation held?

A: In the office of Gage and Foley.

Q: Who did you tell Davis was there when Lockwood called?

A: My wife and my daughter.

Q: Did you ever tell Davis where you got the money?

A: He never asked me. Davis was acting between Darrow and myself

Q: Now see here, I will get -

A: You see here, I want to finish.

Q: Then go ahead and finish.

A: Davis was acting between Mr. Darrow and myself and he never asked me, I think.

Q: Did you ever tell Davis that a Chicago man gave you the money?

A: No; Davis told me to say that

Q: That's what I want to know.

A: You have it there.

Q: Where was it he told you?

A: In his office, I believe.

Q: Did you tell Davis or others that Mr. Darrow did not give you one five-cent piece for a dishonest purpose?

A: No, Mr. Rogers, I never told anyone on God's footstool that. At that time I was telling everyone that I was innocent.

Q: Did you not say to Messrs. Timmons, Parsons, White, Dunn, newspaper men, that you had never given Lockwood a damn cent and that Mr. Darrow is the most honest man I ever knew?

Vehement objections were made by the prosecution and overruled by the court.

Answer: Do you want the question answered yes or no?

Question: Yes.

A: No!

Q: Did you tell Mr. Nicholson of the *Examiner* that Mr. Darrow did not ever give you any money to bribe jurors?

A: Certainly not.

Q: Do you remember telling John Drain, Frank Dominguez and F.E. Nichol after inviting them into the Belasco theater saloon for a drink, "I never received a dishonest dollar from Darrow." He never gave me a dollar for a corrupt purpose in the world. He was the most kind-hearted and best man I ever worked for?

A: Part of that is true, and I say that now—he treated me splendidly.

During further cross-examination by Rogers, Franklin testified that his confession to the bribery charges was executed in the offices of attorney Oscar Lawler, a special federal prosecutor of various alleged dynamite conspirators. Franklin also testified that prior to his connection with the McNamara defense case, he had sought a position from Assistant District Attorney Joseph Ford. Rogers also questioned Franklin concerning his meetings and friendships with members of the Merchants and Manufacturers Association. Rogers was able to ascertain that just before leaving the employ of the United States Marshals office, Franklin had sought to obtain a position with the District Attorney's office. Rogers was hopeful of leaving the impression that Franklin had been used as a "plant" to try and set up Darrow. Franklin was friendly with members of the hard-line anti-union Merchant and Manufacturers Association, and he had sought employment at the District Attorney's office; yet, somehow, he wound up employed by the McNamara defense team. Was this part of a plot to frame Clarence Darrow and destroy a man closely associated with the American labor movement? Franklin admitted that he had met with friends on various occasions at the Merchants and Manufacturers offices.

> Question (By Rogers): How does it come you went on the McNamara defense?
>
> Answer (By Franklin): It was business, just as you were induced to defend Mr. Darrow.

At this point an objection by the prosecution was made to which Rogers responded as follows:

> Your honor, this is a unique situation. Picture this witness being a personal friend of such men who are fighting Mr. Darrow—have always fought the men whose champion he has been; who fought the McNamara case—and working for the McNamara defense. The situation, I say, is most unique—a most peculiar coincidence.

D.A. Fredericks responded:

> Counsel here is trying to show that because the Merchants and Manufacturers were interested in the McMamara case they are interested in the Darrow prosecution. There is not one scintilla of evidence proving this. There is no connection between the Merchants and Manufacturers Association and their strike breaking committee and this case.

> Question (By Rogers): Were you seeking comfort and aid when you went there?
>
> Answer (By Franklin): No, Sir.
>
> Q: Did you not know that those men were friendly to the state?
>
> A: I did not know whom I was going to meet, therefore I could not know whether they were friendly to the prosecution.
>
> Q: Before you pleaded guilty and got that so-called fine—was it before that date that you talked with the district attorney?
>
> A: It was after I had made a sworn statement of my case to the district attorney.

Statement by Rogers: Now, your honor, I make request that we be furnished with a copy of that statement.

Statement by District Attorney Fredericks: We object and charge counsel with misconduct for asking such a question.

The Court: Request denied.

Question (By Rogers): When did you make that signed statement to the District Attorney?

Answer (By Franklin): On January 25th, I think, subsequent to making this statement to the District Attorney.

Q: (Rogers reading from Franklin's diary): Is this Lawler, Oscar Lawler, special federal prosecutor of the dynamite cases?

A: Yes.

Q: And that signed statement was made in Mr. Lawler's office?

A: Yes.

Q: Did Ford request you to go to Lawler?

A: Yes.

Q: You have not seen Mr. Lawler since January 25th, when you made out the statement?

A: No.

Q: Did you see him often before that time?

A: Yes, regularly, for months.

One of the jurors, F.E. Golding, asked Judge Hutton if he could question Mr. Franklin. The Court granted permission and the juror asked of Franklin:

"After you left the elevator in the Higgins building, did you carry the money for the Lockwood bribe in your hand?"

"Yes, sir," Franklin politely answered.

There were some additional questions asked of Franklin by juror M. E. Williams concerning the total amount of money Franklin had received from the McNamara defense and the various uses of those monies. These questions by the jurors led to endless speculation as to what led to the inquiries.

Rogers' co-counsel, Horace Appel, asked some questions of Franklin on cross-examination.

Question (By Appel): Did you not make a statement before the grand jury implicating Mr. Darrow before talking to Mr. Dominguez and before the indictment was returned?

Answer (By Franklin): I don't remember the date when I appeared before the grand jury.

Q: Now, if I told you that the date of your appearance before the grand jury was a date that was before the date that you have testified as to your having spoken to Mr. Dominguez, would that alter your opinion?

A: No, not considering that you are the source of the information.

At this point counsel on both sides jumped excitedly to their feet. Appel stared in the direction of Franklin but was restrained by Earl Rogers.

Rogers addressed the Court, "See here your honor, this is an absolute reflection on the defense counsel."

D.A. Fredericks stated, "The witness has every right to make such a remark."

Rogers exclaimed, "I have the floor!"

Judge Hutton interjected, "Gentlemen, sit down. Clearly and firmly this is a matter for the court. Mr. Franklin, I admonish you not to speak so disrespectfully of counsel in the future."

Franklin responded, "I meant no harm."

Earl Rogers said, "I suppose we desire the truth from this witness. I suppose in the interests of truth and justice we have a right to show that he accused Mr. Darrow in private, but not in public. In an effort to frighten us on this feature he pulled a memorandum book on us. We have tried to get the contents of that book into evidence here. That's all we want— the truth and no subterfuge from this kind of witness."

Fredericks countered, "We object to counsel in referring to this witness as 'this kind of witness.' This witness has borne the brunt of cross-examination of the defense counsel for a week and the way his testimony has stood up under test should protect him from such references from defense counsel. This witness is not dodging questions."

The Court: "The objection is overruled. Mr. Franklin, will you refer to your memorandum books and see whether this Dominguez conversation occurred before your appearance at the grand jury chamber?"

> By Franklin: No, sir. It is my private book.
>
> By Rogers: We ask the court to order the witness to refer to this book.
>
> By the Court: The witness is so ordered.

Franklin complied with the court's directive, looked in his books and stated that he had appeared before the grand jury prior to the date of the conversation.

> Question (By Rogers): If you had made a confession to Ford and had implicated Darrow before the grand jury, why did you then later tell a different story to Dominguez about Mr. Darrow?
>
> Answer (By Franklin): I hoped against hope that Darrow would clear himself before the matter became public.
>
> Q: But you told the grand jury and Ford that Darrow had given you the money and you still hoped to keep it from becoming public?
>
> A: Yes.

On June 14, 1912, the prosecution won a major evidentiary victory when the court admitted into evidence certain checks which they contended were the source of the money provided by Darrow to Franklin for purpose of juror bribery. A check in the amount of $10,000 went into evidence which was bore the names of Frank Morrison, Clarence Darrow, and Olaf Tveitmoe. Morrison was the secretary of the American Federation of Labor. The check was made out by Morrison to Darrow, and was subsequently endorsed and cashed by Tveitmoe at the Paris and London Anglo National Bank of San Francisco. It was made out by Morrison on August 21 st and cashed by Tveitmoe and Darrow on September 2nd. The foundation for the admission of the checks was laid by the testimony of Henry Flather, the cashier of the Riggs National Bank of

Washington, D.C. and custodian of the McNamara defense fund.

The court admitted over $200,000 of checks into evidence, including the one alleged to have financed the Lockwood bribery. All of the checks passed through local banks except the alleged bribery check, that one check was cashed in San Francisco. The prosecution alleged in their opening statement of the case that Darrow had cashed the check himself in San Francisco and had brought the Lockwood bribery money to Los Angeles himself.

The prosecution called John Harrington to the witness stand. Harrington had worked as an investigator on the McNamara case from the time Darrow was first retained in April of 1911 until the day the McNamaras pleaded guilty on December 5, 1911. Harrington was a key witness for the prosecution because testimony implicating Darrow with the bribery was needed from someone who was not a co-conspirator in the underlying crime. Harrington testified that Darrow had shown him a wad of $10,000 in cash and told him that the money could be used to bribe jurors. Darrow allegedly had told him that he had received the money from a check cashed at Olaf Tvietmoe's bank in San Francisco and that the money could not be traced to any bank in Los Angeles. He testified that Darrow had informed him of Bert Franklin's arrest for bribery and that Darrow told him: "My God, if he speaks I am ruined."

On cross-examination, Rogers inquired in great depth and repetition concerning any immunity agreement that Harrington had with the prosecution; all of which Harrington denied. Rogers inquired in detail about numerous alleged prior statements Harrington had made to the effect that Darrow had nothing to do with the bribery of any jurors. During his cross-examination, Harrington refused to look at Rogers or Darrow and constantly focused his gaze on the jury. Rogers kept changing his location during his examination of Harrington; but to no avail, he could never get Harrington to look at him.

To draw attention of this fact to the jury, Rogers engaged in an argument with District Attorney John Fredericks in which the jury heard Rogers state that Harrington could not and would not look him in the eye during his cross-examination. Fredericks blundered when he stated to the court that Harrington did not want to look Darrow in the eye for fear that Darrow would cast him under an hypnotic spell; which drew derisive laughter from spectators as well as from the jury.

At one point Rogers' co-counsel Horace Appel was so successful in goading the D.A. that Fredericks attempted to throw an inkwell at him during an argument. Rogers stuck his hand out to prevent the inkwell from hitting Appel and received a gash on his hand as a result.

A key theme in the defense of Darrow set forth by Earl Rogers was that no motive existed for the bribing of any juror or prospective juror. Rogers set forth to prove that Darrow was in the process of negotiating a plea bargain on behalf of the McNamara brothers in return for their guilty pleas at the very time that Franklin was to have allegedly been offering Lockwood a bribe. Why spend money to bribe a juror when you are in the process of pleading your client guilty? In addition, what if Bert Franklin had made some over-zealous and unauthorized effort to improperly influence a jury member in the McNamara case without the prior knowledge or consent of Darrow? Would Franklin's testimony under these circumstances, coupled with his escape from a prison sentence by virtue of his immunity agreement, cause a juror to doubt the credibility of his testimony?

Famed magazine writer Lincoln Steffens took the witness stand at one point during the Darrow trial. Steffens testified that he had assisted Darrow in facilitating in the negotiations which led to the guilty pleas of the McNamara brothers. He explained his actions in assisting in the negotiations, that he knew the McNamara's were guilty of the crimes charged and that he felt Darrow needed his assistance.

> Question (By Rogers): When you, Mr. Older and Mr. Darrow conferred about the McNamara case settlement was there not an agreement to prevent the matter becoming public?
>
> Answer (By Steffens): Yes.

Rogers was intent on proving that the matter of strategy regarding the plea bargain of the McNamara brothers was already established before Franklin allegedly bribed Lockwood; thus no motive existed. Assistant D.A. Ford put Steffens through a rigorous cross-examination.

> Question (By Ford): Now Mr. Steffens, it is a fact that Darrow told you that if they had delayed the matter it would become public and the matter would be all off?
>
> Answer (By Steffens): Yes.
>
> Q: Did you at any time say to Mr. Chandler (son-in-law of *Los Angeles Times* owner General Harrison Gray Otis) or others that there was a chance of J.J. McNamara pleading guilty?
>
> A: No, I think not except to Mr. Chandler.
>
> Q: Well, up to the night of November 29th, with the exception of Chandler, you had not told any of the business committee that J.J. would plead guilty?
>
> A: Well, on November 29th, I talked frankly to Chandler and admitted J.J. would plead guilty if necessary.
>
> Q: When did you learn that J.J. McNamara was guilty?
>
> A: After I got here.
>
> Q: You learned it from J.J. McNamara?
>
> A: Indirectly, yes.
>
> Q: Do you think it is right to try to get a guilty man off?
>
> A: Anyone trying to get a man free who is guilty of the commission of the individual crime does wrong—but the McNamaras' crime was a social crime.
>
> Q: You believe you were justified in going to any length to save such men?

A: No, not as far as murder. I believe no crimes are justifiable. The cause is what should be first considered, however, not the punishment. A social crime is different from an individual crime.

Q: You believe it would be right to go as far as bribing a jury to save them?

A: No. My feeling about bribery is the same as about murder—they are not justifiable, but are understandable. The wrong lies in the fact that we don't understand them and treat them from an understandable basis. Our system of punishment, our legal machinery, is not proper to solve the labor or social problem; the sending of the McNamaras to jail does not solve the problem. When the state has a victim down it does not solve the social problem by sending society's individuals to jail for a crime that's a part of society.

Q: You tried to save J.J. McNamara?

A: Yes, I tried hard.

Q: After knowing he was guilty?

A: Yes, I tried hard.

Q: Was it because that J.J. McNamara would suffer that you tried to get him off?

A: No, that labor would. The danger was that this community would suffer because they would be led to believe that satisfaction was gained by them just because a man was to be punished.

Q: On the night that you spoke to Mr. Chandler about the fact that McNamara was going to plead guilty; on this same night did you say to Mr. Chandler, "Now let us get Fredericks to agree to drop any prosecution of Darrow and Franklin."

A: Yes—but I was acting for myself—Steffens—against the wish of Darrow. You see, the arrest of Franklin came like a thunderclap. So Darrow came to me and said: "Now, I am in favor of settling the McNamara cases. Don't let any fear of my connection with Franklin stand in the way of the settlement. Don't bother with me—don't consider me in the negotiations at all."

Q: Do you consider Franklin's crime as a social one?

A: No, but it was a part of the McNamara case and I wanted the whole thing cleared up.

Earl Rogers then announced that the defense would call Clarence Darrow to the witness stand, which caused a flood of spectators to show up at the courtroom on July 28, 1912. For hours before the barrier was dropped by Deputy Sheriff Ficketts, the would-be spectators stood in line, hoping with great anticipation to gain admittance. The proceeding began with the announcement that Juror L.A. Leavitt of El Monte was discharged from further duty due to illness and that alternate juror A.M. Blakes would take his place. To the disappointment of the crowd, Darrow did not take the witness stand that day due to the consumption of time by other matters; first and foremost being Rogers' attempt to secure the grand jury testimony of Olaf Tveitmoe. Rogers requested that the Court issue an order which would allow him to have access to the transcript of the testimony of the San Francisco resident, stating that it would be an "injustice" for the defense to be denied the transcript. Rogers told the court that the Penal Code supported his position, and that while the court considered the matter he would put on several witnesses.

J.J. Petermichael, a court reporter who transcribed the testimony of Tveitmoe when he appeared before the grand jury took the stand.

> Question (By Rogers): You transcribed Tveitmoe's testimony taken before the grand jury in this case?
> Answer (By Petermichael): Yes.
> Q: Where is it?
> A: Here.
> Q: Give it to me.

At this point A.D.A. Ford objected, stating that the transcript of grand jury testimony was "sacred." Rogers argued that it was only right that the defense should have access to Tveitmoe's testimony. He argued that Tveitmoe's testimony was directly related to the Darrow case and that under applicable rules of law, all such testimony must be placed at the disposal of the defense.

District Attorney Fredericks' response was that the defense

had the opportunity to put Tveitmoe on the witness stand and to learn in that fashion what his testimony had been before the grand jury. Fredericks argued that in objecting to the request of Rogers to obtain the transcript of the grand jury testimony that the prosecution was not attempting to suppress Tveitmoe's testimony. The resolution of the issue was deferred.

On July 29, 1912, the excitement began when Earl Rogers called Clarence Darrow to the witness stand to testify in his own defense against the charges that he was guilty of the bribery of George Lockwood.

Darrow's demeanor during his testimony was frank and open and this impression seemed to sink into the minds of those who were present. Darrow adamantly denied that he had ever given Franklin any money to bribe jurors, or for any other improper purpose. He admitted that he had given Franklin, who was his chief of detectives on the McNamara case, money in the amounts of two hundred to one thousand dollars at a time for his office expenses. Darrow flatly denied each and every aspect of Franklin's testimony regarding every allegation concerning bribery of jurors and/or prospective jurors. Darrow testified that every conversation that he ever had with Franklin during his employment with the McNamara defense was for legitimate purposes regarding the case. Darrow testified:

> I did not know Lockwood at all. Franklin did not receive any money from me to bribe Lockwood -besides, I never had $4,000 in cash among any of my accounts here. I believe $4,000 was the sum taken by Franklin at the time he was arrested.

Question (By Rogers): Did you give Bert Franklin a check for $1,000 on October 6th.

Answer (By Clarence Darrow): I gave him a check for $1,000 on October 4th.

Q: Why did you give him this check?

A: To pay office expenses —just like I had given him other checks.

Q: The check was not given Franklin to pay a bribe?

A: No, certainly not; he got it to pay expenses.

Q: Do you recollect the conversation you had with Franklin on October 4th concerning this check?

A: Yes.

Q: Well, tell us about. Also all other conversations you had.

A: All our lawyers—the defense lawyers—and Franklin were present when we discussed jurors. Mr. Bain was one of the first jurors chosen. Franklin said he knew Bain and that he had been a laboring man all of his life. Now you know in a fight where labor and capital are involved we try to get men whose sympathies are with the laboring class. Franklin said Bain had helped to form the first carpenters' union in this city.

At this point in time Ford broke in and lodged an objection, which in turn caused Rogers to interject during the middle of Ford's objection to state:

"Your honor, this is only a pure attempt to break in upon the witness' story and prevent him from properly defending himself. It is rotten, and I stand here ready to defend my words."

D.A. Fredericks responded, "Your honor, this objection is neither wrong nor rotten. We have a right to object to this witness making a speech from the witness chair. A speech is not wanted or necessary here—let's get his story devoid of oratorical frills."

Co-counsel Appel objected to everything said by both Fredericks and Ford and charged that a fraud had been perpetrated on the court by the prosecutors by raising such objections.

Question (By Rogers): You may state why you kept Mr. Bain on the jury; please state everything.

Answer (By Darrow): When I examined Bain he said he never had trouble with the unions and that at one time he had been a union man. Bain was an old man and I have found that old men are more kindly disposed and more charitable.

Q: Did Franklin ever report to you of visiting or giving money to Bain or his wife?

A: No, Franklin said he knew Bain; but that was all.

Q: Did you ever hear or know of money being offered to venireman Krueger by Frank Fowler?

A: No sir. I never remember of meeting Fowler until this case was presented in court. Fowler said I met him once during the McNamara case but I don't remember it. I met so many people here and forgot scores of them.

Q: Did you ever know of Franklin offering Krueger money?

A: I never had any talk with Franklin about Krueger let alone giving him money for Krueger.

Q: Tell us what occurred at the Alexandria hotel when Franklin and Lincoln Steffens were there.

A: When a venire was drawn during the case the lawyers waited until we got a list. In that list we always found a name or two about whom we had no report. These men then we turned over to Franklin to report upon at once. On the morning of November 25th, there was such a venire drawn. On that list there were ten about whom we had no reports. I did not give that list to Franklin because I believed the case would be settled and that we did not need it. That afternoon he called me up and asked why he had not been given the list. I said I would be at the Alexandria that night with the list. Krueger's name was on that list. When Franklin called at the Alexendria I gave him the list. We did not discuss the list. I did not comment on the names. He said 'I better get busy.' Of course I could not tip him about the probable settlement of the case and for that reason I agreed that he better get busy on the reports.

Q: Did you ever know about Franklin paying money to Juror Lockwood?

A: No; all I know about that is what Franklin said here. I did not know Lockwood and even did not remember him. I know nothing about the matter—nothing.

Q: Would you narrate the events of the morning in which you were informed of Franklin's arrest?

A: I arrived about 9:30 at my office the morning of Franklin's arrest. With me was Frank Wolfe. I received a phone call to go to socialist headquarters on Main Street. I started to go there right away. I reached a point near Third and Main streets when I saw Franklin with a man I did not know. Later when I came up to the Hall of

Records building I saw Franklin, Detective Browne and others. I asked Browne what it meant. He said Franklin had been arrested for jury bribing, and that was all that was said between us.

Q: Did you have $4,000 in cash which could have been used by Franklin in the jury bribery?

A: I had plenty of money but not cash. I had three accounts.

Q: Did you ever get the $ 10,000. 00 from O.A. Tveitmoe in San Francisco?

A: No sir, but I want to explain. When I first came to California I met Tveitmoe. He told me that many union labor officials had suffered financially as a result of the *Times* grand jury inquiries and the effort of the Burns men and he asked for $10,000 to reimburse these men. I gave him a check for $10,000 - the one I received from Secretary Frank Morrison of the American Federation of Labor.

Q: Who had charge of the defense fund in San Francisco?

A: Tveitmoe.

Q: Did you ever tell John Harrington that you had $10,000 for some purpose?

A: No sir. I never showed Harrington a roll or had such a conversation.

Darrow also testified that approximately $2,000,000 was promised from organized labor and outside interests for the defense of the McNamaras. He testified that Joseph Scott, a former aid of his in the McNamara case, was told of the intent to have the McNamaras plead guilty on Thanksgiving day. On cross-examination, A.D.A. Ford asked Darrow if he had sent a wire to Leo Rappaport in a secret code informing him that the McNamaras were going to plead guilty. Darrow testified that this was a fact.

Question (By Rogers): Harrington was a guest at your home—ate at your table and slept at your home from December 18th to January 1st, isn't that true?

Answer:(By Darrow) Yes.

Q: What did Harrington tell you while staying at your home—the time when he was going before the grand jury?

A: Harrington told me that he told Oscar Lawler that I knew nothing about the bribery of jurors, and that if necessary he would help me try my case. He also said that I should let the case run on two years (the McNamara case) so that we could get more money out of it. After I paid him for his services in the McNamara case and afterward he came and said he wanted $1,000 more for traveling expenses and I refused to pay it.

Q: Did you ever say to George Behm. in reference to his efforts to 'break McManigal,' "God, you've got to make him come across."

A: No sir, I could not have said it if I tried.

Q: Did you ever say to Behm, when he told you he had refused to let McManigal's boy see him, "Good. That's it. Tease him?"

A: No sir, never.

Q: Did you ever have money in your possession to bribe jurors—did you plan to bribe jurors or anything of that nature, or did you ever talk of such to Franklin or anyone else?

A: No, never.

Q: Did you ever learn from anyone that Franklin was talking too much; that someone had said that Franklin had remarked that Juror Bain was all right?

A: I may have had. I heard lots of stuff. Now right here I want to ask a question. I want to know if it is universally understood that it is customary for both defense and state to investigate jurors before they are sworn.

Q: Oh, everyone knows that it is custom for lawyers to have prospective jurors investigated. There is nothing novel in that. Now, Mr. Darrow, if you paid $5,000.00 per juror with nineteen indictments to try, how long

Question (Cont'd): do you suppose your fund would have lasted?

A: Not long.

At this point some of the jurors requested to ask questions of Darrow.

Question (By Juror Golding): How much money was promised the McNamara defense fund by the affiliated unions?

Answer (By Darrow): Approximately $2,000,000.

Q: What stand did Joseph Scott take on the compromise of the McNamara case?

A: Scott was employed as a lawyer. He did not know of the compromise until Thanksgiving day. Scott was with us at the Thanksgiving day conference with the McNamara boys in the county jail. As soon as we talked the matter over with Scott he agreed that it was best.

Question on Cross-examination (By Ford): On the day that the McNamaras pleaded guilty you sent a code wire to Mr. Rappaport?

Answer (By Darrow): Yes, I sent such a wire—it may have been in code.

Q: Throughout the trial you were sending wires or inquiries about J.B. McNamara or 'Brice'—these were also in code?

A: Yes, I made many inquiries.

Q: You learned that dynamite was found in the vault under the American Bank building, in Indianapolis, where the offices of the International Association of Structural Ironworkers are located?

A: Yes.

Q: And that vault was the property of J.J. McNamara?

A: I heard it was.

Q: And also dynamite was found in a barn near Indianapolis by Burns and police officers?

A: I did not learn that the dynamite was found by police.

Q: You learned that some dynamite was stored in a barn at Ohio, at Ortie McManigal's father's home?

A: No; I don't remember that.

Q: Did you learn from Mr. Rappaport that the officers did not enter J.J. McNamara's vault until a search warrant was produced?

A: No. I don't recall.

Q: Did you send a wire to Guy Biddinger in San Francisco and sign the name Johnson?

A: Yes. I sent the wire, but don't remember the name.

Under further cross-examination Darrow testified that the American Federation of Labor had assumed charge of the raising of all funds in connection with the defense of the McNamara brothers. Darrow was on the stand for several full days of direct and cross-examination and began to appear tired and weary. However, he came across as an intelligent, honest, straightforward and sympathetic man. During all of the arguments and outbursts which took place between the prosecutors and the other defense attorneys, Darrow maintained a composed and respected demeanor. Once Darrow's testimony had concluded, all that remained of the trial were some rebuttal witnesses, and then the closing arguments. It had been previously agreed that after Earl Rogers would deliver a portion of the defense's closing argument, Darrow would then be permitted to directly address the jury by concluding the closing argument for the defense team.

When Earl Rogers entered the jam-packed courtroom on August 12, 1912, to deliver his closing argument to help save Clarence Darrow from a trip to San Quentin, he was attired in a Prince Albert coat and a Lord Byron tie. His waistcoat was spotless white. He carried his lorgnette. On the next day when Rogers concluded his argument he was clad in a long black frock coat and wore a black stock. Some of the female spectators at the courthouse stated that Rogers' appearance resembled portraits of Patrick Henry.

Rogers came to court armed with a large chart to be utilized while he made his points during his closing arguments. It extended from the judge's bench to a courtroom wall. Every one of the thirty-eight prosecution witness' names appeared on that chart. Rogers explained to the jury that Darrow had only been charged with the bribery of one person, George Lockwood, and that a careful examination of the chart would reveal that only two of the thirty-eight names implicated Darrow in the alleged crime.

During his closing argument, Rogers portrayed Darrow as a great man who had fought and struggled for the masses. Rogers asserted that Franklin and Harrington were perjurers whose testimony should not be trusted. Rogers stated:

Gentlemen, you will be instructed that if you have a reasonable doubt based on the circumstances and facts of the case, you must acquit this man and, considering the kind of evidence produced here, in view of the type of witnesses the state has produced here, there is nothing for you to do but acquit him. Who did organized labor send to arbitrate the great coal strike? Clarence S. Darrow. And so well did he handle the affairs of his clients that there has been no coal strike since then. Go back to the coal mines of Pennsylvania where the men with the head lamps work, and ask them how they got to be educated. The worker will say that at the time the court of arbitration convened he was a young breaker boy, and was working in the great black hole sixteen hours a day. Since the great historic arbitration court convened, however, this boy's hours of labor were shortened and thus he was given an opportunity for education. Who was it that arbitrated the trouble with the great stores in Chicago? Who forced the employers to provide seats for you when you go up to a counter? Clarence Darrow. Did Clarence Darrow taint these men? Did he bribe President Roosevelt's arbitration court, an institution as historic as the United States Supreme Court? No. Yet they charge he tainted all with whom he came in contact.

What would you do, gentlemen, if your starving baby cried for food? I would tear the front off the First National Bank with my finger nails if my baby cried for food. For we know that all the while there are other people who are living on humming birds' tongues. And yet they term this anarchy! Believe me, I am a firm believer in law and order and the punishment of crime. But they do a great wrong when they refuse to look at Darrow as a man who is reaching out trying to better our condition. There have got to be pioneers. And one thing is certain. Darrow has been at work trying to solve this great question of the masses which is more than can be said of various men here.

The McNamara case was virtually settled. Do you believe that Darrow, a man who has financial peculiarities, would let go of $4,000? It is a physical, mental and moral impossibility. Witnesses testified that Darrow is the stingiest man in the world. And I believe it fully. I know whereof I speak. Mr. Darrow is exceedingly careful in money matters. Darrow would not pay $4,000 for a juror whom he would never have use for.

> You are called upon to convict the greatest figure at the American Bar, Clarence S. Darrow, upon the evidence of perjurers, and informers who have testified under the cloak of immunity.

Rogers concluded his masterful performance which was described by a reporter as having had moved the audience from tears to laughter at will. Clarence Darrow then gave his portion of the closing argument which lasted for two days of emotions including the tears of Darrow himself. He concluded his argument:

> Gentlemen, I came to this city as a stranger. Misfortune has beset me, but I never saw a place in my life with greater warmth and kindness and love than Los Angeles. Here to a stranger have come hands to help me, hearts to beat with mine, words of sympathy to encourage and cheer, and though a stranger to you twelve men and a stranger to this city, I am willing to leave my case with you. I know my life, I know what I have done. My life has not been perfect. It has been human, too human. I have felt the heartbeats of every man who lived. I have tried to be the friend of every man who lived. I have tried to help the world. I have not had malice in my heart. I have had love for my fellowman. I have done the best I could. There are some people who know it. There are some who do not believe it. There are some who regard my name as a byword and a reproach, more for the good I have done than for the evil.
>
> There are people who would destroy me. There are people who would lift up their hands to crush me down. I have enemies powerful and strong. There are honest men who misunderstand me and doubt me, and still I have lived a long time on earth, and I have friends—I have friends in my old home who have gathered around to tell you as best they could of the life I have lived. I have friends who have come to me here to help me in my sore distress. I have friends throughout the length and breadth of the land, and these are the poor and the weak and the helpless, to whose cause I have given voice. If you should convict me, there will be people to applaud the act. But if in your judgment and your wisdom and your humanity, you believe me innocent, and return a verdict of not guilty

in this case, I know that from thousands and tens of thousands and yea, perhaps of the weak and the poor and the helpless throughout the world, will come thanks to this jury for saving my liberty and my name."

District Attorney John Fredericks concluded the case for the prosecution by delivering a forceful rebuttal argument. He implored the jury to find Clarence Darrow guilty. He stated, in part:

> Don't let this snaky monster of jury bribery creep within our courtrooms and into our jury boxes. Don't let the statue of justice be torn down and the head of a serpent erected instead. Go and obey your consciences. Why punish the humble instrument and let the master go free? Vote this man guilty as the evidence shows. Do not let sympathy or sentiment come into this matter. If the defendant is old and feeble, let the court deal with him as kindness and mercy would dictate. That is not your task. Be men and take it home to your hearts and to God.
>
> I don't care what they had agreed to about the McNamaras, they had to play out the Lockwood string. Of course, you can well imagine an ordinary man would wonder why the defense was trying to compromise on the one hand and to reach jurors on the other, but it was all a part of the plan to free the two McNamaras. Franklin didn't get his bribe money when it was promised him because of the uncertainty, but he finally did get it and was caught right in the open, as the evidence shows.

Both sides concluded their closing arguments, Judge Hutton instructed the jury, and they then began to deliberate. On August 16, 1912, after deliberating for only 35 minutes and taking only one ballot, a verdict of not guilty was reached by the jury who had spent months listening as the case had been presented to them. As jury Foreman M.R. Williams read the verdict, Darrow jumped to his feet and embraced his wife Ruby. Darrow rushed to the jury box where he was greeted by the jurors with open arms. Several of the jurors had tears streaming down their cheeks. Men and women rushed Earl Rogers as he stood at the head of the counsel table with his wife. He was slapped on the shoulders and the back until he was forced to stand against the courtroom wall.

The jurors had filed out of the courtroom after being instructed by Judge Hutton at 9:20 a.m. At 9:50 a.m., the buzzer from the jury room announced that a verdict had been reached. At first it was assumed by some that the jurors simply wanted to ask some questions or have some testimony read back to them. Shortly after Judge Hutton took his place on the bench and amid total silence he turned to the jurors and was informed by the foreman that a verdict had been reached. Foreman Williams then announced the not guilty verdict. The trial consumed three months and two days and cost the county of Los Angeles $25,000 to try.

The D.A.'s office later decided to charge Darrow with the bribery of juror Robert F. Bain. At that trial, Darrow, indeed ever the miser where his wallet was concerned, elected to save himself the cost of paying the legal fees of Earl Rogers and thus defended himself. The jury at the conclusion of that case was hopelessly hung; eight votes for conviction and four votes for acquittal. The District Attorney's office struck a deal with Darrow. It agreed not to retry the case, and Clarence Darrow agreed never to practice law in the State of California again.

Earl Rogers had saved the great defender from a stay in San Quentin and the loss of his license to practice law. Thanks to Rogers, Darrow went on to win some of his greatest legal victories after the bribery cases. In 1924, he defended Nathan Leopold and Richard Loeb, saving them from execution, if not from prison sentences. He defended anti-war protesters after World War I. In 1925, he would ensure his name's inclusion in history books by defending schoolteacher John T. Scopes in what became known as the "Scopes Monkey Trial." The case took place in Tennessee and involved the educator's teaching of Darwin's theory of evolution to his students in violation of state law. Darrow would later be portrayed in the movie *Inherit The Wind* by actor Spencer Tracy.

In 1926, Darrow secured the acquittal of Henry Sweet, a black doctor who had been forced to use violence to defend his family from being forced out of their home in a white Detroit neighborhood. Darrow passed away in Chicago in 1938.

Had it not been for Earl Rogers' masterful defense in the Lockwood case, the most famous cases and victories that made Clarence Darrow a household name might never have materialized.

CHAPTER ELEVEN

The Case of the Deadly Knockout Punch

THE PARTICIPANTS

DEFENDANT:	Jess Willard
PROSECUTOR:	Joseph Ford, Assistant D.A.
DEFENSE ATTORNEYS:	Earl Rogers, Chief Trial Counsel
	H.L. "Jerry" Giesler, Co-Counsel
CHARGE:	Second Degree Murder,
	Illegal Prizefight

Jess Willard was the six-foot, seven-inch giant, the great white hope who beat Jack Johnson to become the heavyweight champion of the world. However, the journey which eventually brought Willard's boxing career to the pinnacle of the heavyweight title was a long winding road, with some interesting twists and turns which brought him into contact with Earl Rogers.

On August 22, 1913, Willard was matched to fight John "Bull" Young in a scheduled twenty round bout in the Vernon Arena which was put on by the Pacific Athletic Club. Willard easily won the first seven rounds of the bout, but during the eighth round, Young seemed to be making a comeback as he got the best of Willard. In the ninth round of the contest, Willard came back and delivered a crushing blow to

Young's head which sent him to the canvass—for good. Young died after undergoing brain surgery after the fight.

The District Attorney's office ultimately charged Willard with second degree murder, in connection with the unlawful killing of John "Bull" Young in what was characterized as a "prize fight." Apparently a distinction was to be drawn by the District Attorney's office between a boxing match, which was legal, and a prizefight, which was not. This distinction did not appear to revolve over the issue of a winner's purse, or even whether or not the fighters were to be paid. In a "boxing match," the event was to conclude when one of the fighters achieved superiority over the other. According to this logic, the Willard/Jones bout should most likely have been stopped during the third round, since at that point it was certain that Willard had achieved superiority over Young in the bout.

The objective in a boxing match, it was argued, was not to achieve a knockout over the opponent, but merely to achieve superiority; at which time the bout should have been terminated. The prosecution contended that when the boxing match was not terminated, that Willard then resorted to efforts to end the fight by means of a knockout punch rather than simply achieving superiority over his opponent in the ring. The effort thus made by Willard resulted in the fatal blow to Young. At that juncture, it was contended that the event's character had changed from a boxing match to a "prizefight;" an illegal event in the State of California at that time. Since the death of Young resulted from the illegal act, the prosecutor charged that Jess Willard had committed murder in the second degree. And if you lived in Los Angeles in this era, and were charged with murder, you did what Jess Willard did—hire Earl Rogers to defend you.

On October 14, 1913, the D.A.'s office sent deputy sheriffs to the Vernon Arena where Young was killed to watch the boxing contest between Joe Azevedo and Johnny Dundee, with

specific orders that if the deputies decided that the boxing contest had escalated to a prizefight that they were to step in and
stop the fight.

Initially Rogers sought to use his expertise in medical matters to prove that the death of Young was not caused by
Willard's punch, but by the medical malpractice of the surgeon who operated on Young after the knockout punch. The
District Attorney did not call the autopsy surgeon to the stand
during the trial; so Rogers put him on as a defense witness.
Dr. Maisch testified:

> I found the brain where the instrument which opened the
> skull penetrated had been reduced to a jelly-like substance.
> This to me, indicates that damage had been done in a man-
> ner other than by a blow.

This testimony meshed perfectly with Rogers' argument
that Young's brain was not injured at all before the skull was
opened, and that the fatal injuries to Young resulted from a
cause other than the blow which Willard delivered. Dr. R.B.
Griffith, one of the surgeons who attended John "Bull" Young
from the time he was injured in the Vernon arena until his
death took the witness stand.

> Question (By Rogers): Dr. Griffith, what was Young's condition
> immediately after the blow was struck?
>
> Answer (By Dr. Griffith): He was as limp as a rag. We took him to
> the hospital and gave him a hypodermic injection of strychnine
> and nitroglycerin.
>
> Q: (By Rogers): What symptoms did you observe?
>
> A: (By Dr. Griffith): In addition to the pulse, respiration and gen-
> eral apparent condition, we found a slight swelling on the back
> of the skull. We chose at that point to open the skull.
>
> Q: Did you cut the skull open all by yourself?
>
> A: No, I did about 35 percent of the cutting.

On January 7, 1914, Thomas J. McCarey, the man who promoted the fight, was placed upon the witness stand to describe

what happened during the bout. He testified that from the beginning of the fight through the seventh round, Willard had everything his own way. He was winning the match easily, and spectators began to view the fight as a farce. He testified that Young suddenly found strength during the seventh round of the fight. Young began to make a showing for himself until he was knocked out by Willard in the ninth round. The prosecution contended that this description of the event should be classified as a prize fight under the penal code. Earl Rogers contended that this description was that of a boxing contest for points within the meaning of the penal code.

McCarey testified that both fighters were given a medical examination before the scheduled twenty-round fight. Regarding the blow which sent Young down, he testified:

> The movement of Willard's fist was not more than eight inches and the blow was not severe. Physicians were in attendance and the rounds were of the length always followed in California.

Prosecutor Ford then argued:

> The law requires medical examination. This was given. The law says that when one of the contestants shows a marked advantage over his opponent the contest must close. McCarey says during the first seven rounds the fight was a farce, Willard winning easily. The contest, to be legal, should have stopped then.

Earl Rogers argued in reply:

> The fight was scheduled to go twenty rounds and a fight of this duration is permitted by the penal code. The blow that ended Young's life was not a severe one but one which is administered in every boxing contest of any kind.

Willard's manager took the witness stand and admitted that in preparing Willard for the fight he informed his fighter that Young had a weak jaw, which is where the knockout punch was delivered. There was also testimony that during the first round Willard missed some punches and Young said, "Better be a little quicker, old man, because I really can't wait for you," and that this banter was kept up until the knockout round.

The case went to the jury and on January 13, 1914, after taking five ballots, the jurors concluded that Jess Willard had participated in a legal boxing match and he was found not guilty of the charges that had been brought against him.

Willard, who went on to become the heavyweight champion of the world, retained Earl Rogers on other occasions to resolve many of Willard's contractual and other legal problems associated with his fighting career. Rogers was successful in resolving Willard's problems. On one matter alone, Rogers went on the road for an entire month's time on Willard's behalf. On October 16, 1916, Earl Rogers filed suit against Jess Willard to collect $25,000 "for reasonable legal services that remained unpaid." Rogers asserted that much of the champ's reputed fortune was due to Rogers' efforts in straightening out matters concerning the pugilist's many contracts, to ensure that Willard would be paid the sums which they promised.

The case of the deadly punch was but a footnote to Earl Rogers' remarkable career. However, for sports fans, the case would prove to be very significant. Even though the distinction in the Penal Code between boxing contest and prizefight was as murky as ever, after Willard's acquittal the District Attorney would cease to pursue putting a stop to professional boxing, which allowed boxing to continue in California and to grow in popularity and prestige.

CHAPTER TWELVE

The Case of the Police Chief's Secret Sex Den

THE PARTICIPANTS

DEFENDANTS:	Charles Sebastian, Co-Defendant
	Lillian Pratt, Co-Defendant
PROSEUCTORS:	Thomas Woolwine,
	District Attorney
	Asa Keyes, Assistant D.A.
	Assistant D.A. McCartney
DEFENSE ATTORNEYS	Earl Rogers, Chief Trial Counsel
	H.L. Giesler, Co-Counsel
	W. Joseph Ford, Co-Counsel
CHARGE:	Contributing to the Delinquency
	of a Minor

In 1915, handsome Charles Sebastian was Chief of Police in Los Angeles. Sebastian was born on a farm in Missouri. He moved to California with his widowed mother, who bought a small grocery store. He eventually entered the police department, worked as a patrolman and was subsequently given the rough assignment at that time of working Chinatown. Mayor Alexander was responsible for Sebastian becoming the Chief of Police. Sebastian later announced that he was going to run for Mayor of Los Angeles and attracted a number of backers.

After announcing his plans to run for mayor, allegations surfaced that Mr. Sebastian had participated in certain criminal conduct involving a seventeen-year-old minor girl named Edith Serkin. The investigation centered around rumors that Chief Sebastian had participated in lovemaking trysts with Serkin's guardian and sister, Lillian Pratt. Pratt was married, as was Sebastian, and the rumors circulating were to the effect that Sebastian and Pratt would participate in secret lovemaking sessions in a boarding house room when the minor Serkin was present. Rumor also had it that Serkin may have done more than just watch Sebastian and Serkin's older sister Lillian, and she had actually participated in the sexual shenanigans. The grand jury began to subpena witnesses in connection with their investigation of whether or not Chief of Police Charles Sebastian and his alleged paramour, Lillian Pratt, had contributed to the delinquency of Miss Edith Serkin. At the same time, the grand jury was investigating several other possible instances of alleged misconduct between the Chief and other minor females.

Sebastian retained Earl Rogers to represent him in connection with the criminal investigation that was being conducted by the grand jury. Rogers helped the Chief draft a letter to the grand jury foreman requesting a fair investigation, and alleging that the charges against Sebastian were part of a political frame-up by his political foes. The letter was sent out on the Chiefs letterhead.

On April 5, 1915, Charles Sebastian and Earl Rogers were both indicted by the county grand jury on charges of having attempted to corruptly intimidate and influence the grand jurors in their investigations of the allegations of misconduct involving the Chief and a minor female. The charges constituted felony crimes. It was claimed that the letter contained entreaties and persuasions in an attempt to influence the grand jury.

Bench warrants for the arrest of Rogers and Sebastian were issued and the two appeared before the Presiding Superior Court Judge, and posted the appropriate bail to secure their release pending trial. After the arraignment Rogers stated: "This is a forty-two centimeter joke. Any juror who thinks that letter is intimidation is crazy."

April 5th, 1915, was not a particularly good day for Earl Rogers. Not only was he indicted for allegedly participating in a felony crime, after posting bail for that charge Rogers would find himself appearing before Judge Monroe in connection with a dispute he was having with his ex-wife, Belle Green Rogers. Mrs. Rogers had filed an Order to Show Cause alleging that her ex-husband was delinquent on alimony payments of $300 a month, and child expense payments of $50 a month, for March and April of that year. Rogers explained to the judge that he had been paying $350 per month for thirteen months but had recently discovered that the cost of the baby nurse was only $30 per month and not the $50 per month he had been paying; he wanted a credit. The judge ordered that Rogers only had to pay his ex-wife the exact amount which she paid the nurse, and then promptly found that Rogers was in contempt for not making the March, 1915, alimony payment to his ex-wife. The judge continued the matter until the following morning so that Rogers could make arrangements to make immediate payment that day to Mrs. Rogers.

On April 6, 1915, Chief of Police Charles Sebastian and Mrs. Lillian Pratt were indicted by the county grand jury on the charge of having contributed to the delinquency (dependency) of Miss Edith Serkin, the seventeen-year-old sister and ward of Mrs. Pratt. Both of Serkin's parents were deceased, and her sister, Mrs. Pratt, had previously been awarded custody, care and control of her sister. Both Pratt and Sebastian posted bail and were arraigned before Judge Wood.

Chief Sebastian wrote a letter to the Mayor which stated:

> I request my suspension from duty for the reason that I do
> not desire to override the established custom in departmen-
> tal affairs nor to take any unfair advantage over those in a sub-
> ordinate position. I sincerely trust that the charge against me
> will be disposed of shortly and that I shall be restored to duty.

As a result of the suspension, the Chief s assistant, Captain Flarnmer, was appointed as "acting chief of police." The
indictment against Sebastian was over 1,000 words in length
and stated in part:

> That the said defendants, Charles Sebastian and Lillian
> Part, on or about the 20th day of December, 1914, and for a
> period of six months prior thereto, at and in the county of Los
> Angeles, State of California, did willfully and unlawfully
> encourage, cause and contribute to the dependency of the said
> Edith Serkin, a female person, as aforesaid.

It was alleged by the District Attorney's office that the Chief
and Mrs. Pratt, along with Miss Serkin, often visited a private room in an apartment house adjoining the Police Station at First and Hill Streets where illicit conduct was
participated in between Sebastian and Pratt, within view and
hearing of Miss Serkin, and that illicit conduct was participated in between Sebastian and Miss Serkin.

Thomas Lee Woolwine was now the District Attorney of
Los Angeles, having replaced John Fredericks, Rogers' nemesis in more than one murder trial, who had been recently
elected to Congress. Woolwine was well-connected, married
to a woman from one of Los Angeles' wealthy families, and
was politically ambitious. He issued this statement after the
Chief s indictment was handed down and made public:

> It is a grave and solemn duty to be called upon to prose-
> cute any human being. I cannot look upon it in any other light.
> The persons charged in this indictment have been treated with
> unusual fairness by the grand jury and the District Attorney's
> office in an effort to arrive at the real truth of the matter. The
> people should remember at all times that I am but a servant

Thomas Lee Woolwine,
District Attorney
"Courtesy of University of South-
ern California, on
behalf of the USC Library
Department of Special
Collections."

of all the people, and I cannot find it in my heart to swerve
from my duty, even though persons in high places be involved.

When Miss Serkin appeared before the grand jury she was
accompanied by a probation officer. She was dressed in a styl-
ish dark red dress trimmed with fur and wore a heavy veil.
After her testimony she met for over an hour with District
Attorney Woolwine. She was then taken to her home by a
detective from Woolwine's office, who ensured that she remain
isolated and under armed guard.

The alleged trysts were to have taken place in room number 17 at the rooming house which adjoined the police station. The grand jury also examined Mrs. Florence M. Wilbur,
the landlady of the rooming house, Police Sergeant Matuskiwiz, a tenant in the building, and Mrs. Martha Oliveras who
was another sister of Miss Serkin.

Prior to the commencement of trial an interesting series of twists took place in the Sebastian investigation. Two other under aged girls were alleged to have participated in illicit conduct with Sebastian. Apparently they had both already testified before the grand jury regarding the alleged improper conduct. One of the girls was named Victoria Desparte. On April 9, 1915, Miss Desparte appeared before Superior Court Judge Taft and confessed that her prior testimony to the grand jury was false, that she had been paid for her perjury, and that it was all part of an effort to "frame" Chief Sebastian. In fact, her entire testimony was a lie paid for by the Chief's enemies. Miss Desparte then went before the grand jury and repeated to them what she had just told Judge Taft.

After giving her new grand jury testimony, Miss Desparte was placed in the charge of an officer and taken to the County Jail. Judge Taft had participated in an extensive interview with Miss Desparte to make sure her story was reliable. Judge Taft stated:

> I cross-examined Miss Desparte and she stuck to her story that she had never been out with Chief Sebastian and had never seen him until she appeared before the grand jury.

The day before she met with Judge Taft, Miss Desparte had told a Miss Gould, who was a nurse at the Juvenile Hall, that she had something on her mind and wanted to talk about it. She then made her confession, repudiating her previous testimony regarding Chief Sebastian. She was promptly taken to Judge Taft's chambers by Dr. Harriet Probasco, the Juvenile Court physician and the juvenile hall nurse. Prior to telling her revised story, Judge Taft had the oath administered to Miss Desparte. While in his chambers, Miss Desparte told the following to Judge Taft:

> Sullivan came to me first and afterward Sullivan and Ellsworth came and asked me if I had not been out with Chief Sebastian. I said 'No, I don't know Sebastian.' Then they

showed me a picture and asked if he was the man I had been out with. I said 'no.' Then they asked me, 'Are you sure that is not the man? I want to know for sure whether that is the man or not.' Then they described the Chief, and I said, 'I have never seen Chief Sebastian.' But from the picture and their description I was able to pick him out in the grand jury room. I did it from the picture and from what they said. But it wasn't true. They told me I was to say it was Sebastian and that I would not be expected to do it for nothing.

It came as a surprise when Chief Sebastian was indicted on April 10, 1915, on the charge of contributing to the delinquency of two additional under-aged girls; Victoria Desparte and Cecile Livingtson, both wards of the juvenile court. On the same day, Miss Desparte was indicted on charges of perjury. Miss Desparte originally testified before the grand jury implicating Sebastian for improper conduct. After recanting under oath before Judge Taft, she was taken before the grand jury by District Attorney Woolwine where she again recanted her original testimony.

But Woolwine then took Miss Desparte before the grand jury a third time in which she recanted her statements before Judge Taft and recanted her most recent grand jury testimony. She told the grand jury that her allegations regarding her participation in an attempt with others to frame Sebastian were not true and she testified that she had been offered a large reward if she would deny her story and say the Chief was innocent. It was alleged that Desparte had been approached by agents of the defense in connection with her change of story action. Desparte was taken to county jail pending her trial on perjury charges.

District Attorney Woolwine publicly condemned the alleged defense tactics and announced that he had placed guards armed with shotguns to protect many witnesses from potential intimidation. He issued a public statement which stated in part:

The time has come when the people should know what a public servant in my position has had to bear in the performance of his sworn duty. This office had been hampered and interfered with in a manner that should arouse the indignation of every fairminded citizen. In the discharge of a plain duty, I have had to contend with a band of legalized bandits. The police department of the city of Los Angeles has been largely turned over to the defense of a man who stands charged by a grand jury with serious offenses against the laws of the commonwealth. Witnesses have been falsely imprisoned and other witnesses have been hounded to the point of distraction by officers of the law whose duty it is to protect them. If I could at this time disclose the means by which Miss Victoria Desparte was brought to perjure herself, such methods would arouse public sentiment that could not be stemmed. For the purposes of protecting witnesses from intimidation or being spirited away, it has become necessary to place them with guards armed with shot guns. If persons in high places are to be granted immunity and the friendless and lonely prosecuted, it will mean the doom of law and order.

Chief Sebastian then issued the following response to the allegations made by Mr. Woolwine:

All the charges contained in the District Attorney's statement are absurd and ridiculous in the extreme and but a palpable attempt on his part to gain public favor in an endeavor to offset the effect of the voluntary confession in open court by Victoria Desparte. I challenge Mr. Woolwine to point to a single instance where any witness who has been subpoenaed before the grand jury has been questioned or interfered with by any member of the police department. It is a fact that Mr. Woolwine has surrounded his witnesses by paid detectives and has given us no opportunity, even if we desired, to question them. Mr. Woolwine's charge that he has been dealing with legalized bandits is particularly ridiculous in view of the conduct of his own officers. Apparently, the complete and expensive detective force of Los Angeles county is being directed in a systematized effort to discredit my candidacy and to impugn the integrity of the members of the police department. I have been followed and have been under constant espionage;

my wife has been hounded; every sort of devilish character of intimidation has been indulged in. The motive is to get me, to assassinate my character and to force me to abandon my candidacy for Mayor.

On April 21, 1915, the testimony finally began in the prosecution's case against Chief Sebastian and Mrs. Lillian Pratt for contribution to the delinquency of Mrs. Pratt's sister, Miss Edith Serkin. Nearly 1,000 men and women jammed the corridor on the third floor of the courthouse outside the courtroom, which only had seating capacity for slightly less than 100 people. Five deputies were needed to keep the crowd in line. There were several fist fights which erupted between curiosity seekers. The participants were escorted from the building by deputies.

Edith Serkin, described as a rosy cheeked, dark-eyed girl of seventeen years, and the principal accuser against Chief of Police Sebastian and her sister, Mrs. Lillian Pratt, took the witness stand as the first witness called by the prosecution.

On direct examination, Edith Serkin told of Chief Sebastian's caresses of her, hugging and kissing her, pinching her breasts and sexually arousing her, and of making love to her sister, Lillian Pratt, in and/or near her presence in room number 17 in the Arizona lodging house at First and Hill Streets. She told of automobile rides and of presents given to her by the Chief. Her testimony was given in such a low voice that virtually every answer had to be repeated. As she gave her testimony the jurors leaned forward in their chairs so as not to miss a word. She was on direct examination for four hours her first day on the stand and Judge Wood adjourned court until the next morning at 10:00 a.m.

After the first session of Miss Serkin's testimony Chief Sebastian stated that:

> She did not tell the truth and I don't think there is one person in Los Angeles who will believe her story. A blind man

could see that she has been coached by older persons. All I ask is that the people of Los Angeles wait until my side is told before judging me or Mrs. Pratt."

Joseph Ford, the former Assistant District Attorney and former nemesis of Earl Rogers, was now sitting at the defense counsels' table, as Rogers' co-counsel, along with Jerry Giesler, in the defense of Chief Sebastian. At the close of the first day's session of Miss Serkin's testimony, Mr. Ford complained about the court order that the witness was in the constant care of prosecution detectives and her other sister, Mrs. Oliveras, who harbored great animosity towards Lillian Pratt. Mr. Ford suggested that the young Miss Serkin be placed under the control of neutral persons. Judge Wood spoke privately with Miss Serkin and ordered that she remain under her current guard but instructed Mr. Woolwine to locate other quarters for Mrs. Oliveras.

As Miss Serkin left the courtroom, more than five hundred men and women were waiting in the corridors to get a glimpse of her. They were somewhat disappointed because of the heavy black veil which completely hid her face . She was escorted through the crowd by two detectives to a waiting automobile and spirited away.

The defense made and won a motion during the first day that Miss Serkin's was on the witness stand that she had to provide specific dates as to when the alleged immoral acts of Chief Sebastian took place, or her testimony would be stricken. District Attorney Woolwine took her through direct examination:

Question (By Woolwine): Do you know Charles Sebastian, one of the defendants in this case?

Answer (By Miss Serkin): I do.

Q: When did you first meet him?

A: In the Temple Block about two years ago.

Q: Did you ever meet Mrs. Pratt and Chief Sebastian in a lodging house at First and Hill Streets?

A: Yes sir, many times.

Q: How often?

A: About twice a week for many months.

Q: What was the number of the room?

A: Room 17.

Q: When were you the rooming-house last?

A: Christmas eve.

Q: What happened between you and your sister and Mr. Sebastian during the visit on Christmas eve?

A: Mr. Sebastian hugged and kissed me. We were all lying on the bed.

Q: How long were you on the bed together?

A: About an hour.

Q: What else did he do?

A: He pinched my breasts. They were sore for several days.

Q: What was the effect of his pinching your breasts?

A: It excited and aroused me.

The jury was taken to dinner by Deputy Sheriffs Woods and Henry and taken to their rooms at the Trenton Hotel where they were sequestered for the evening.

On further direct examination Miss Serkin admitted that about a month prior to trial she had told two probation officers at the home of her guardian sister, Mrs. Pratt, that she had never seen the Chief or Mrs. Pratt in a room together. But she testified that Mrs. Pratt had asked her to sign a written statement to that effect and she refused to do so. Miss Serkin went on to testify as to other instances when the Chief would hug and kiss her, and of lovemaking sessions in room 17 in the Arizona lodging-house. She told of a pink silk bathrobe and a necklace given to Mrs. Pratt by the Chief; and of an automobile ride to Downey with the Chief and a man who she remembered was referred to as the "Colonel." She testified that Mr. Pratt had voiced suspicion and jealousy towards the Chief when he accused Mrs. Pratt of having a relationship with him, all of which she heard Mrs. Pratt deny.

She testified that she had seen a framed photograph of the Chief on the piano in the parlor of the Pratt residence. She said that the Chief gave her $5 on her birthday on April 4, 1914, and smaller sums at other times.

Question (By Woolwine): When was the first time you visited the Arizona rooming-house?

Answer (By Miss Serkin): In June, 1913.

Q: Who was present?

A: Mr. Sebastian.

Q: What time did you get there?

A: A quarter to eight.

Q: How long did you remain?

A: All night.

Q: Who was present during the entire night?

A: I was in room 17 and Mrs. Pratt and the Chief were in Room 18,

Q: Whose room is 18?

A: Billy Matuskiwiz.

Q: What happened between you, Mrs. Pratt and Mr. Sebastian?

A: We kissed and hugged.

Q: Chief Sebastian hugged and kissed you while you lay on the bed with him?

A: Yes.

Q: What did he do to Mrs. Pratt?

At this point vigorous objections were made by the defense; however Miss Serkin answered in such a way that it was clear that she observed and heard lovemaking between the Chief and Mrs. Pratt.

Question: Did either the Chief or Mrs. Pratt give you anything to drink that night?

A: Yes, they gave me some apricot brandy

On April 23, 1915, Miss Serkin was cross-examined by Earl Rogers.

Question (By Rogers): When did you first meet Chief Sebastian?

Answer (By Miss Serkin): June 19, 1913.

Q: Are you sure of that?

A: Yes.

Q: How do you know?

A: That was the night Bundy killed a boy.

Q: How do you know?

A: They told me the next morning.

Q: Do you remember whether it was in the summertime or winter time?

A: It was summertime.

She had fallen into Earl Rogers' trap. At this point Rogers produced some legal documents. He advanced towards the witness reading from the official paperwork in which Bundy was accused of having committed murder on December 19, 1913. The Court then inquired of the prosecution as to whether they conceded that the murder committed by Bundy occurred on that date and Assistant District Attorney Keyes conceded the date.

Question (By Rogers): Did Mr. Sebastian ever tell you not to tell of what had occurred?

Answer (By Miss Serkin) Yes.

Q: Now begin at noon and tell me on the day before Christmas and tell me what happened.

A: I went shopping during the day.

Q: Did you go to the room that night?

A: Yes sir, around 6:45,

Q: When did you meet Mrs. Pratt?

A: After being in the room; it was about 7:15.

Q: Where did you meet her?

A: At Second and Hill Streets.

Q: Were they waiting for you?

A: Yes sir. The driver Cecil Lewis and Mr. Pratt were in the machine. My sister and I walked up and met them.

Q: Then you got into the car and were driven to a department store?

A: Yes sir.

Q: Then let me show you your testimony of the other day where you said: I went to see Chief Sebastian and then I went shopping, and then I met Mrs. Pratt at the Hollenbeck Hotel," did you so testify?

A: Not exactly.

Q: Point out the difference.

A: Well, it wasn't exactly like that.

Q: Were you in the Hollenbeck Hotel that night?

A: Yes.

Q: When?

A: After I met my sister and went to telephone at Second and Hill Streets.

Q: When you said you went to Second and Hill streets with Mrs. Pratt is that true? Then why did you say that you met her at the Hollenbeck Hotel?

A: I met her at Second and Hill streets and went to the Hollenbeck with her. It was this way. We went down to Second and Hill. Mr. Pratt wasn't there, so we went to the Hollenbeck Hotel and then came back and found them.

Miss Serkin went on to testify that her sister Mrs. Oliveras hated her other sister Lillian Pratt, and that Mrs. Oliveras had several conversations with her regarding the criminal case. She had first complained about the conduct of the Chief and Mrs. Pratt to her sister Oliveras. She denied ever telling a probation officer that she had ever been intimate with the Chief. She testified that Mrs. Pratt and Mrs. Oliveras had been involved in a legal dispute over her custody in which Mrs. Pratt prevailed the previous March 10th.

Serkin testified that Mr. Sebastian gave her a watch on June 19, 1914, and that she remembered the exact date because it was Mrs. Pratt's birthday. She testified that she and Mrs. Pratt visited room 17 on June 18, 1914.

A driver by the name of Cecil Lewis took the witness stand and corroborated many aspects of the testimony of Miss Serkin. He also testified that he obtained a letter of introduction for a job interview signed by the Chief and obtained at the request of Mrs. Pratt. The mystery over the man who had been referred to as the "Colonel" was cleared up when Earl Rogers presented Colonel Emil Bloch in the courtroom and he was identified by Miss Serkin as the person whom she had met and whom the Chief had referred to as the "Colonel." Colonel Bloch was a lieutenant in the citizens' police.

The sister of Lillian Pratt, Martha Oliveras, took the witness stand on April 27, 1915, and testified that she overheard Mrs. Pratt tell her husband, Mr. Pratt, that "he would spend the rest of his life in a dungeon if he informed Mrs. Sebastian of the Chief's alleged relations with Mrs. Pratt." The defense claimed that Mrs. Oliveras was upset that she had lost a battle over the custody of Miss Serkin and that she had framed the Chief and Mrs. Pratt, in part to obtain custody of Miss Serkin. The defense claimed that Mrs. Oliveras wanted to get control of Miss Serkin so that they could place her in a house of prostitution in El Paso, Texas. Mrs. Oliveras also testified that on one occasion Mrs. Pratt told her that Chief Sebastian was "in love" with her and had knelt down and kissed her hands and told her how much he loved her. She testified that the Chief had given Sgt. Matuskiwiz a $25 a month pay raise in appreciation for his having allowed his apartment to be used by the Chief and Mrs. Pratt for their secret trysts.

On cross-examination Earl Rogers obtained an admission from Mrs. Oliveras regarding her nine-year-old daughter Tootsie. She admitted that after she was told of Mrs. Pratt's immoral conduct as it related to Miss Serkin, she had entrusted her daughter's care on several extended occasions with Mrs. Pratt.

Having presented the testimony of Edith Serkin which gave details of immoral conduct of Chief Sebastian and Mrs Pratt, along with specific dates, places and times, and with additional testimony which corroborated many of these facts, the prosecution rested and Earl Rogers and his co-counsel put on their defense.

There were two particular dates which the prosecution had placed great reliance on June 19, 1914, and December 19, 1914. Miss Serkin had previously testified that she and Mrs. Pratt had spent those dates with the Chief and that hugging, kissing, lovemaking and breast pinching had occurred. The testimony of the Chief, and other credible and respected witnesses, provided accounts for his whereabouts for every moment on those two dates. Ex-Police Commissioner Morgan testified that he visited the Chief on December 19, 1914, and that the Chief was sick in his bed. A neighbor of the Pratt's testified that she saw Mr. and Mrs. Pratt drive away from their home in their car at about 6:30 in the evening on that date. Serkin had testified that she, Pratt and Sebastian were all together in room 17 on that date.

In his opening statement before putting on the testimony of the defense, Rogers told the jury:

> The Chief will prove an alibi for every specific night in the testimony of the Serkin girl as to dates of meetings in room seventeen. We will show you gentlemen that on the day of June 19, 1914, Chief Sebastian was not in room seventeen, as Miss Serkin has told you, but was in fact in San Francisco with Mrs. Sebastian and could not have been here. On December 19, 1914, mentioned by Miss Serkin we will show you that he was out helping a friend of his to find his wife. On June 19, 1914, when he was charged with being in room seventeen we will show you that he was with General Royer and Police Commissioner Owen on a trip. We propose to show you that the Chief never had any immoral relations with Mrs. Pratt. We propose to show you that Chief Sebastian never mistreated Edith Serkin. Miss Serkin had testified on direct examination that she, Mr. Sebastian and the "Colonel" had ridden together in Sebastian's car to Downey. Colonel Emil Bloch took the witness stand and declared that he had never been in an automobile trip to Downey as alleged. He testified that he didn't know where Downey was and doubted that he could find the place on a map. He testified that the Chief had introduced him one day to Mrs. Pratt and Miss Serkin outside of their residence.

General Royer took the stand and gave testimony which created a detailed alibi for the Chief for June 19, 1914, another date when the Chief was to have been with Mrs. Pratt and Miss Serkin. This was a particularly important date because Miss Serkin stated that it was Mrs. Pratt's birthday and she gave specific details as to gifts given, etc. More testimony, documents, and official reports were offered into evidence providing detailed alibis for the Chief. For every date and time that Miss Serkin had testified that she was with the Chief, the defense lawyers provided witnesses and supporting documents to prove otherwise.

On the evening of May 3, 1915, two bullets were fired through a window of the Sebastian home, coming close to striking the Chief. Neighbors saw a tall man carrying a handbag rush away from a vacant lot beside the Chief's house right after the shots were fired. The Chief had just answered the telephone when a stranger who identified himself by the name of Mr. Conklin was on the other end of the phone. It was then that the shots rang out with the bullets shattering the window of Sebastian's home. General Royer was present and ran outside the home armed with his revolver to see if he could ascertain who had fired the shots. One bullet that entered the Chief's home struck a dictionary; it was a .32 caliber.

That next day the Chief took the witness stand and during his testimony he shouted: "I hope God may strike me dead if I ever mistreated Edith Serkin."

The Chief denied that he ever met Mrs. Pratt or Miss Serkin in room seventeen in the Arizona lodging house; that he ever met them in any other place; that he ever gave Mrs. Pratt his photograph; that he ever gave her a pink bathrobe; that he gave her a necklace; that he ever went riding with Mrs. Pratt and Miss Serkin in a police car; that he took Serkin on a ride to Downey with Col. Emil Block; that he ever gave Miss Serkin a gold watch, that he ever stayed away from his home all night during the past three years except when he was out of town.

The Chief testified to his background beginning as a grocery store clerk and street car conductor—and up to his becoming Chief of Police of Los Angeles. Sebastian came to California when he was six years old. He worked on a ranch in Santa Rosa when he was nineteen, moving to Los Angeles when he was twenty-one years old and marrying Miss Elsie Babcock. He resided at Artesia for a short time and returned to Los Angeles where he secured a position as conductor on one of the old cable car lines. He worked that job for three years and became an inspector in the city street department. He was employed as a conductor for three years and was then employed by the police force as a patrolman. He was promoted to sergeant in January of 1907 and in May of that year was placed in command of the Chinatown squad to suppress gambling and vice. He was advanced to lieutenant in September of 1910 and Mayor Alexander appointed him Chief of Police on December 24, 1910.

> Question (By Rogers): Did you ever meet Mrs. Pratt and Miss Serkin in room seventeen?
>
> Answer (By Sebastian): I hope God may strike me dead right now if I ever did!
>
> Q: Did you ever enter any rooming house with Mrs. Pratt and Edith Serkin?
>
> A: Never in all my life!
>
> Q: Have you ever been away from your home all night long in the past three years except when you were out of town?
>
> A: No, sir.
>
> Q: Did you ever give Mrs. Pratt a picture of yourself?
>
> A: I never did.
>
> Q: Did you ever give Miss Serkin a gold watch?
>
> A: No, sir.
>
> Q: Did you ever pinch Miss Serkin's breast?
>
> A: I hope God may strike me dead if I ever did.

The Chief gave testimony on direct which accounted for

all of his time, with the names of corroborating witnesses, on each and every date and instance which Miss Serkin had testified that he was with her and Mrs. Pratt in room 17 of the boarding house. The Chief did say that he was frequently in the Arizona boarding house to visit his friend Sgt. Matuskiwiz which he testified was a "hang out" for many of his friends. He testified that he visited Matuskiwiz's room on occasion with Judge Morrison and Judge White.

On May 6, 1915, Earl Rogers sent a letter to the Governor and Attorney General requesting that they investigate the attempt to kill Sebastian at his home. In his letter, Rogers wrote:

> I ask your intervention in order that justice may be done and in order that the evidence of a most damnable attempt to assassinate a prominent citizen may be investigated and prosecuted without the preconceived opinion of the prosecuting officer, which shields attempting murderers.

On that same day all hell broke loose in the courtroom when District Attorney Woolwine made a comment that the assassination attempt on Sebastian was a "fake." The rancor became so bad, that Judge Wood had to order a recess so that tempers could cool down. Rogers stated: "That statement is the most damnable stigma on jurisprudence in the history of California."

Chief Sebastian's wife took the witness stand. Mrs. Sebastian testified that her husband was never away from home all night since they have been married, except when he was out of the city. B.A. Davis, a humane officer testified that Edith Serkin had told him: "There is nothing to the charges at all" (in reference to the charges against Sebastian and Pratt). Reverend Charles Locke, former governor Henry T. Gage, Judge Rives and Judge Reeve all testified to the good character of the Chief.

When the testimony for prosecution and defense was all in, the net result was that Chief Sebastian, through the testimony of various witnesses and through various documents, had provided alibis as to each and every date and time that Miss Serkin had testified that the Chief was with her and Mrs. Pratt. It was now time for closing arguments.

The prosecution asserted in their closing arguments that "the story of this little schoolgirl of 17 years has been uncontradicted except by friends of Chief Sebastian."

Earl Rogers gave his closing argument and stated in part:

> This is too serious a matter for words. A man's honor is at stake and also the name of a woman. I feel that it is my duty now to prove that not only is Sebastian not guilty of the charge made but that there never was any foundation for the charge or even a suspicion against him. It's as old as Adam and as gray as Noah. There is no older thing than a case of this kind. It is an old saying that when you want to get a man in a high place, put him behind a closed door with a woman. Why was this case brought at the time it was brought? Sebastian was the biggest man in sight. And furthermore, he was the man who cleaned up the town for Mayor Alexander and was going to keep it cleaned up. So they attacked him in their typical way. Never could they find anything against him. His record was straight and honest. They tried this. Whether it is to succeed is in your hands. The District Attorney will no doubt try to induce you to forget this mountain of evidence. But look at it and don't forget it. The prosecution's witnesses are a mass of contradictions.

Closing arguments were concluded and jury instructions given by the Judge on May 14, 1915. The jury deliberated for approximately three hours and delivered their verdict of "not guilty." District Attorney Woolwine stated that "I have done my duty and I bow to the will of the jury." The courtroom broke into celebration among spectators, the defendants and the attorneys. On May 17, 1915, Judge Wood dismissed the indictment charging Chief Sebastian and Earl Rogers with attempting to corruptly intimidate the county grand jury. District Attorney Woolwine also moved that the indictment charging the Chief with contributing to the delinquency of Victoria Desparte be dismissed and the Court granted the motion and the charges were all dismissed. Also dismissed were the perjury charges pending against Miss Desparte and she was ordered released from the countyjail.

During the course of the Sebastian trial, Rogers found time to marry the new love of his life, Miss Edna Landers to whom he had become engaged during the prior year. Charles Sebastian was elected Mayor of Los Angeles, and later resigned. He spent his last years in ill health with the loyal companionship of his devoted lover—Lillian Pratt.

At left: Percy Tugwell
Above: Mrs. Percy Tugwell
Below: Mrs. Phillip Kennedy
"Courtesy of University of
Southern California, on
behalf of the USC Library
Department of Special Col-
lections."

CHAPTER THIRTEEN

The Case of the Dead Woman's Diamonds

PARTICIPANTS

DEFENDANT:	Percy A. Tugwell
PROSECUTOR:	William C. Doran; Deputy District Attorney
DEFENSE ATTORNEYS:	Earl Rogers, Chief Trial Counsel Frank Dominguez, Co-Counsel
CHARGE:	Murder

Young Percy Tugwell had already been convicted of first degree murder and sentenced to life in prison for the killing of Mrs. Maude Kennedy. During his trial the prosecution put on evidence that the young man was in need of money due to his impending marriage. Tugwell was friends with Mrs. Kennedy's son, and as a result of that relationship was also friendly with Mrs. Kennedy. The prosecution convinced the jury that Tugwell, in need of funds, had killed Mrs. Kennedy for the purpose of stealing her expensive diamond rings. Also placed into evidence was a confession that Tugwell had given while he was in police custody. During questioning, Tugwell stated that he had choked Mrs. Kennedy to death with chloroform and stole her diamond rings. Moments after giving the jailhouse confession, Tugwell retracted it and said that he was not Mrs. Kennedy's killer. During Tugwell's trial, only

Tugwell's confession was brought before the jury; his retraction was conveniently excluded. Therefore, the jury was never informed that Tugwell had recanted.

On May 25, 1915, Tugwell's life sentence almost became moot when he appeared to have been mortally wounded in a knife attack by a fellow prisoner, H.W. Cecil, in the county jail. Cecil had been arrested earlier on Temple Street where he had been standing on the street corner making faces, swearing at and making threats to passers by. He appeared to be drunk. Thinking that Cecil had sobered up, he was being taken from his cell for release and while in the tank he began yelling and screaming, waving a large knife around in the air. Cecil slashed Tugwell across his abdomen and then plunged the knife into Tugwell's chest just under the heart. It did not appear, at first, that young Percy would survive the injury. Tugwell was taken the County Hospital where medical treatment was administered and his life was saved.

Tugwell's wife was pregnant at the time of his murder conviction and she gave birth to a baby boy in June. On July 7, 1915, Tugwell received the gift of seeing his newborn son. His family also gave him another gift—just as priceless as the sight of his child, if not more—the retention of Earl Rogers to attempt to obtain a new trial.

Rogers agreed to represent Tugwell and successfully argued before the district court of appeal that the retraction of Tugwell's confession, made only moments after the confession was given, should have been admitted. Tugwell's conviction of first degree murder was set aside and he was granted a new trial.

On March 19, 1915, the prosecution caused a sensation at the commencement of trial when they announced to the judge that the state's star witness, sixteen-year-old Llewellyn Gorsuch, had mysteriously disappeared. Gorsuch was one of the strongest circumstantial links in the prosecution's case against Tugwell. It was his testimony that he had sold the defendant chloroform on the day before the murder. The medical experts in the first trial testified that the slain woman had been chloroformed. Deputy D.A. William Doran informed the judge that he had sent out a detail of detectives to attempt to locate his missing witness.

Gorsuch had disappeared without even taking his hat, coat, or $55 due him from his father. All circumstances seemed to indicate a hasty departure. The district attorney told the court: "I believe he was spirited away by someone interested in the case who did not want to see him testify against Tugwell."

When trial began after selection of the jury, Llewellyn Gorsuch was still nowhere to be found and Earl Rogers issued the following statement:

> The defense knows nothing of his disappearance outside of the fact that Mr. Gorsuch, the boy's father, we understand did not want his son mixed up in this trial. We understand also that it was at the father's suggestion that the boy disappeared.

The first witness called to testify for the prosecution was the slain woman's son, Phil Kennedy. He testified that his mother and Tugwell were friends, that Tugwell was soon to be married, and that he needed money. He accused Tugwell of murdering his mother.

Question (By D.A. Doran): When did you last see your mother alive?

Answer (By Kennedy): August 31, 1914, at night.

Q: Did your mother go out that night?

A: Yes, I saw her go. I don't know where she went.

Q: Did you have any telephone calls that night?

A: Yes, there were two calls; my mother answered one and my wife answered the other.

Q: How long after the call did your mother leave the house?

A: About forty-five minutes.

Q: Did your mother own any jewelry?

A: Yes, she wore five diamond rings.

Q: When did you next see your mother?

A: At the morgue.

Q: Do you know Percy Tugwell?

A: Yes, I've known him about five years.

Q: Did he know your mother?

A: Yes, they were very friendly.

Q: Did he ever call to see your mother?

A: Yes, about a week before the murder. They talked for about fifteen minutes.

Q: Where were you on the night of the murder?

A: I was at home with my wife. The next day some newspapermen came and told me about the murder.

Q: Did Tugwell visit you again?

A: Yes, that very morning. I knew he intended to get married and I asked him when it was going to happen. He said he didn't know because he didn't have the money. He walked through the house and was gone. The inside of the house was being painted. I didn't know my mother was dead when he first called.

Q: Did he call again?

A: Yes. About a week later. He came and told me a fellow named Cyclone Thompson had been out to his house. He saw a man coming down the street and said, "I'd better be going. Here comes a dick.'"

Rogers than cross-examined the witness:

Question (By Rogers): Now Mr. Kennedy, I must ask this question although it will be very disagreeable to bring it up. Isn't it a fact, that Mrs. Tugwell, Percy's mother, ordered your mother and a man named Cyclone Thompson from the Tugwell house? Isn't it true that your mother gained the consent of Mrs. Tugwell to meet a man there and when Mrs. Tugwell came back to the house she found your mother and this Thompson locked in a room?

Answer (By Kennedy): I think something like that happened.

A sensation was caused during the trial on March 22, 1916, when Walter Gorsuch appeared in court. He was the father of the missing boy who had testified in the first trial that he had sold Percy Tugwell chloroform on the day before the murder of Mrs. Kennedy. Mr. Gorsuch had been on the witness stand and had testified for the state on direct examination that:

> Answer (By Gorsuch): My son disappeared mysteriously May of last year and I don't know where he is right now. The police have been looking for him.

Rogers took his turn cross-examining Gorsuch:

> Question (By Rogers): Did you tell Mr. John Tugwell, the father of this defendant, that you had ditched your son?
>
> Answer (By Gorsuch): I did not; I told him they had him locked up.
>
> Q: Who do you mean by they?
>
> A: I meant you!

Rogers then addressed the Court:

> (By Rogers): You remember your honor I went to you about this matter when I first learned that the young Mr. Gorsuch was gone?
>
> A: (By Gorsuch): You know where my boy is better than I do!

At this point Mr. Gorsuch got off the witness stand as Rogers continued his statement to the Court:

> (By Rogers): I don't know where his boy is. I haven't the slightest idea. I want him in court. I want to cross-examine him!

At this point, the witness, who was standing in the aisle of the court room, yelled out at Rogers: "Then why don't you bring him here!"

Gorsuch then proceeded to the courtroom door, turned around and yelled out at Rogers, "I'll knock your brains out. I want my boy back!"

At this point Rogers turned and started quickly towards the door where Mr. Gorsuch was and stated, "I think I'll step outside and see if he will!"

A startled and angry Judge Houser had lost his patience at this point and ordered the court bailiff to bring Mr. Gorsuch to the court railing.

(By the Court): Did you make that remark Mr. Gorsuch?

A: (By Gorsuch): I did your honor, I lost my temper. I did not even realize what I said. Please excuse me. All I want is my boy back again. I thought they knew where he was. Please excuse me.

(By the Court): I hold you in contempt of court and reserve sentence until after this trial has been completed. Meanwhile, we'll see if you can hold your temper.

Judge Houser then left the bench and got onto the witness stand at the request of Rogers. He testified as to the fact that Rogers had informed the court previously as to his knowledge of young Gorsuch's disappearance and offer of any efforts to help locate the boy.

The prosecution then put on a witness named Henry Keller who had been at a picture show on the evening of August 31, 1914. He testified that he crossed a vacant lot near his house and saw a man and a woman walking there together and then saw them appear to struggle somewhat. He testified that he heard a "gurgling" sound. He saw the man leaving the area appearing to be dragging something heavy. It was very dark and the witness testified that he could not see what the man was dragging and that he could not see what the man looked like. He placed the time at about 9:00 p.m.

At the first trial the prosecution called Henry Strauk as a witness who testified that Percy Tugwell had come to him the day before the murder looking for a loan. He was called by the prosecution to testify in the second trial and surprised them when he altered his testimony. He testified that Tugwell had approached him for a loan but that he had been previously confused as to the date that the request was made. Strauk stated:

> At the first trial I testified that Tugwell had asked for money on August 3 1 st. I was wrong. I had my days mixed. Perry came to me on August 16th, two weeks before the murder, and asked for money. It was not on the date of the murder that he asked me for money. On the night of August 31st,

when Mrs. Kennedy was killed, I met Percy on the street. It
was about eight o'clock. He told me he was going to San Francisco the next day to get married and for me to say goodbye
to all the boys. He was with me until eight fifteen that night.

The prosecution's theory was that Tugwell was with Mrs.
Kennedy on the night of her murder from 7:00 p.m. until the
time of her death at around 9:00 p.m.

Strauk also testified that he was taken into custody by the
police, handcuffed, had a pistol pointed at him, and was com-
pelled to state that Tugwell had asked him for the money on
the day of the murder. Even more sensational was when
another of the prosecution witnesses, Raymond L. Aaron, testified that the same detectives handcuffed him, threatened him,
and held him in jail over night. Aaron testified that the detectives threatened that if he did not testify they would reveal
his relations with a young girl in the neighborhood. Mr. Aaron
did go on to testify, however, that Tugwell, several months
before the murder, had suggested that they rob Mrs. Kennedy
of her diamonds.

Joe Ford, former deputy district attorney, took the stand and
testified as to the confession made by Tugwell after he was
taken into custody. According to Ford, Tugwell explained during his confession that he pulled out the bottle of chloroform
and told Mrs. Kennedy that he wanted her to smell some new
perfume and that he then proceeded to grab Mrs. Kennedy's
head and pour the chloroform down her throat.

A second witness who did not testify at the first trial was
put on to testify. Mrs. Aletha Gilbert testified that she went
to Tugwell's cell and that Tugwell had placed his head in his
arms and had stated that he didn't know why he had done
"it." She testified that Tugwell told her that he had strangled
Mrs. Kennedy with chloroform, and that the only reason he
could have done it was to get money so that he could get married.

With the two witnesses relating the confessions of Tug-well, the prosecution rested their case.

Mrs. Florence Cheney, an intimate friend of the slain woman, took the stand for the defense. Her testimony brought to light a married man who had become Mrs. Kennedy's lover. Several days before the killing, Mrs. Kennedy had told her that this lover was being sued for divorce and that she was going to be named as a co-respondent in the case. Mrs. Cheney testified:

> Mrs. Kennedy told me that this man had pressed a revolver against her and said it was time to finish it all for both of them. She showed me the bruises she received when she tried to stop this man and her son from fighting. Mrs. Kennedy was to have left her home to come to live with me on the night that she met her death. She never mentioned Percy Tugwell's name in any conversation that she had with me.

The defense was also floating out the idea that Mrs. Kennedy's death might have been suicide. George Silver, a real estate dealer testified that shortly before her death Mrs. Kennedy was very despondent because of financial reasons. Silver stated from the witness stand: "she came to me and asked me to lend her some money. She said that some man had taken one of her diamonds from her."

Minnie Appel testified that Mrs. Kennedy told her how despondent she was and that she had spoken with the dece-dent on the day she was slain.

Sam Cohn, a pawnbroker, testified that Mrs. Kennedy, sev-eral days before her death, gave him a number of diamonds as security for a loan. This testimony was considered to be of great importance by the defense because it undercut the pros-ecution's theory as to the motive for the killing. If Mrs. Kennedy had already pawned her diamonds, then no motive existed for Tugwell to kill her. Mr. Cohn was later re-called to the witness stand, at which time he produced a pawn ticket which showed that Mrs. Kennedy had put up several diamond rings as security for a loan shortly before her death.

Additional witnesses testified in order to establish Tugwell's alibi defense. Various witnesses testified and established that they were with Tugwell from about 7:00 p.m. until just about 9:00 p.m., at which time the testimony established that Tugwell was at his home with his parents. The defense then put on T.B. Tegarden, a street car inspector, who testified that it took at least forty-seven minutes to get from the Tugwell home to the scene of the murder.

The defense wanted to call Mrs. A. H. Matthews to the stand but she was unable to attend court due to being severely ill. On March 30, 1916, Judge Houser ordered the defense and prosecution attorneys and the defendant to be present at Mrs. Matthews home so that her deposition could be taken under oath to be subsequently read to the jurors. Mrs. Matthews was a former neighbor of Mrs. Kennedy and testified from her bedside that the slain woman had previously told her of threats that some man had made to kill her. She testified further that Mrs. Kennedy was despondent and had threatened that she would take her own life.

On April 3, 1916, closing arguments began. The prosecutor asked the judge to send Tugwell to the gallows for the woman's slaying. Earl Rogers gave a passionate argument, going over all of the evidence showing that Tugwell had an alibi; that no financial motive existed for Tugwell to have murdered the woman since she had already pawned her jewelry, that evidence had been introduced that Mrs. Kennedy had been threatened with death by some other man; and that her mental condition was such that she might have voluntarily consumed the chloroform and committed suicide.

At first it appeared that the jury was hopelessly deadlocked and that there would be a hung jury. But on April 6, 1916, the jury brought back a guilty verdict; not for first degree murder, but for manslaughter, in a compromise verdict. The only evidence of criminal conduct on the part of Tugwell that was produced during the trial was that of an intentional killing for financial gain; yet the jury convicted Tugwell of manslaughter in order to avoid a hung jury. Instead of facing life in prison, or execution, Tugwell was sentenced to seven years in prison. Tugwell survived being stabbed near the heart, and had escaped from his appointment with the hangman by a hair's breadth. Due to the gift of Earl Roger's retention, Percy Tugwell, his young son, and his devoted wife—whom newspaper accounts portrayed through the two trials as always present in court, steadfastly believing in her husband's innocence—would one day be reunited.

CHAPTER FOURTEEN

The Decline and a Few More Murder Cases

Earl's alcoholism began to severely impact his career during the time period 1915-1919. It was said by many people that a "drunk" Earl Rogers could provide a better defense than most any lawyer around who was sober. He began to take on less cases as his drinking became more and more persistent. At one point he entered a private sanitarium at the insistence of his family members in an attempt to clean himself up.

He was brilliant in court, notwithstanding that he might have been drunk just the day before; however the impact of his alcoholism made him less productive and less reliable. In earlier years his ability to recover from a drinking binge was quite remarkable. In her father's biography, *"Final Verdict,"* Adela recounts the many occasions when a visit to the Turkish baths and a little rest was all that was needed to ready Earl for his next court appearance and trial.

During the famous San Francisco Graft cases which have already been discussed in great detail in this book, Rogers' evenings of drunken debauchery in the Bay Area's famous Barbary Coast, with his close friend, author Jack London, were legendary. While Earl was in San Francisco during those famous graft cases, he was even arrested when he punched out a police officer who attempted to give him a speeding ticket. But during these later years, Earl was not able to recover from his drunken binges as quickly and easily as he had during earlier times. In his waning couple of years as the volume of his cases began to dwindle, and before he stopped representing clients altogether, Earl still tried some high publicity murder cases, including the defense of Gabrielle Dardley for the murder of her boyfriend, the murder of A.B. Shaw by R.E. Lomax, and the grotesque tale involving the gruesome murder of Mrs. Benton Barrett and her son, by Benton Barrett.

Gabrielle Dardley was a beautiful twenty-year-old woman who had fallen in love with Leonard Tropp while she was working as a teenager in the sporting houses of Arizona. The couple moved to Los Angeles, and Gabrielle turned all of her earnings over to her boyfriend, who was to purchase a wedding ring for her in connection with their intended marriage. When she learned that her no-good-for-nothing boyfriend had used the money to purchase a ring for another woman, Gabrielle shot and killed Leonard in a jealous rage. Rogers made an emotional appeal to the jury and secured Gabrielle's acquittal. Earl's daughter later wrote a story about the trial called "The Red Kimono" which was subsequently made into a movie.

A jeweler named R.E. Lomax was charged with the first degree murder of A.B. Shaw. Rogers put on the defense that Lomax had shot in self-defense and that Shaw was attempting to obtain money from Lomax in a blackmail scheme. Rogers appeared in court to deliver his closing argument, still the Beau Brurnmel of Los Angeles legal circles, dressed in a perfectly fitting costume which was set off by a two-tone velvet waistcoat from which flashed a row of amethyst buttons, touched with gold. The big crowd in the courtroom leaned forward in breathless silence to watch Rogers as he delivered his oratorical eloquence in his closing argument to attempt to save Lomax from a death sentence. Lomax avoided conviction for first degree murder, but was convicted of second degree murder and sentenced to prison for twelve years by Superior Court Judge Gavin Craig. Lomax thanked the Judge and the jury for affording him a fair trial. The widow of the murdered man, Mrs. Shaw, made this statement:

> I have to pay for Lomax's crime with a life sentence. Can any number of years that he serves in prison atone for my wrecked home and happiness?
> Lomax will be behind bars but a few years. But I shall taste the sorrow all through the years of my youth and on into the days of my old age—if I can live that long without my husband. I must find work, hard work, to support myself and my children.

A most bizarre case involved the murder of a woman and her son who were killed, chopped up, and burned by the woman's jealous husband. Benton Barrett was a retired farmer from Indiana who lived with his wife and stepson in Santa Monica. Mr. Barrett was sixty-four years old; his wife was approximately thirty-five years old and the stepson was sixteen. In October of 1916 the boy and Mrs. Barrett mysteriously disappeared.

One day Barrett was in his attorney's office and stated that he had killed his wife and stepson, burned up their bodies in a bonfire, and then buried their remains. Barrett's memory was not clear on any of the other details and he could not recall where he had buried the bodies. District Attorney Woolwine promptly charged Barrett with the first degree murder of his wife and stepson.

Santa Monica Police Chief Ferguson was convinced that the killings had not taken place in the manner described by Barrett in his confession. He stated on October 23, 1916, that Barrett had either shot or chopped the two people to death with an ax, dismembered their bodies in a stall in his barn and disposed of them in some manner after he had tried unsuccessfully to burn up small portions of their bodies. He indicated that substantial evidence existed to show that the two bodies were dragged about considerably before they were disposed of.

Sand samples from the barn were sent for analysis to Dr. C.C. Shipman, of Santa Monica, to determine if dark stains in the sand were human blood. A bloodhound pack was used to sniff out the buildings at the residence to help discover where Barrett had buried the dismembered bodies of his wife and stepson. Blood stains were also found on an ax and on Barrett's shirt collar. There were no metal clasps, shoe nails, buttons or large bones found in the bonfire where Barrett claimed to have burned the bodies.

Crematory experts employed by the district attorney's office concluded that no human body could be completely consumed in any such fire as Barrett maintained in his back lot and that in such a case, large bones would have remained. Barrett also told investigators that he had killed his wife and stepson in self-defense following a quarrel with his wife over a neighbor, with whom he suspected his wife was having an affair.

The prosecution began to build their case against Barrett. They located bloodstains where Barrett asserted he killed the two victims. They found Mrs. Barrett's two hairpins near the same spot. Articles carried in the stepson's pockets were located. Also found were love letters which had been written by Mrs. Barrett to her lover, this infidelity being seen as the motive for Barrett's actions. One puzzle was the absence of the smell of a burning body in the vicinity of where Barrett claimed he burned the remains.

On October 23, 1906, charred bones, crushed and splintered, and several heavy iron bars were discovered in the pit of an outhouse on Barrett's property. In his original confession Barrett stated that he killed his wife and stepson in a yard and burned their bodies in a bonfire. The evidence found by police investigators indicated that the two were murdered in a horse stall in the barn. Based upon the evidence found, investigators were now of the belief that Barrett may have had an accomplice in the murders.

Who in the world was better suited than Earl Rogers to help prove that Barrett was insane? Barrett did retain Earl Rogers to defend him. Jerry Giesler, Ona Morton and Lewis Collins acted as co-counsel to Rogers, who, as always, was chief defense counsel in the case. The prosecution was handled by Thomas Woolwine, the district attorney. Rogers immediately arranged to have the defendant examined to help determine if he was insane. The defense began to develop an insanity defense that asserted that the aged Barrett was insane at the time of the killings. Two of Barrett's children from a prior marriage provided Rogers with evidence that Barrett's mind had broken down under the strain of constant quarreling with his wife.

Intrigue, love, adultery, plots, counter plots, marriage, divorce, and trickery were all elements involved in the case of the double murder allegedly committed by Benton Barrett. The prosecution contended that love was the keynote of the Barrett case; that his love and jealousy of his adulterous wife provided the motive for first degree murder. Barrett was making comments outside the courtroom that he still loved his wife. He continued to wear a ring on his little finger which was given to him by Mrs. Barrett on the day that they were married.

A witness in the case, Miss Lillian La Franiere, testified as to the quarrels which had taken place between the couple. She also testified that Mrs. Barrett was concerned that she might lose custody of her son due to allegations of her poor moral character and the fact that her prior marriage might not have been legally terminated. Miss La Franiere testified that she was told by Mrs. Barrett that it was her intention to take her boy out of the state if any attempt were made to take custody of him away from her. The defense contended that this statement was made the day before the woman and her son disappeared. They claimed that Barrett's insanity might have led him to believe that he had killed the two; when in fact they simply might have left him without giving him notice as to their whereabouts.

Barrett began praying on an hourly basis and stated that guilty or innocent, he believed in God and believed that God would take care of him. He believed that his mind was deranged when he committed the murders, that he was not acting of his own volition, and that God would take all of this into account on judgment day.

S.L. Kirby, a Los Angeles police detective, testified that when he first questioned Barrett about his wife he was told by Barrett that "I don't think I'll ever see her again." Barrett also told Kirby that two men had obtained evidence of infidelity on the part of Mrs. Barrett, and that when faced with this evidence, she had deeded back property to him. He said that Barrett had forgiven her for the one indiscretion, but when he found letters showing further evidence of adultery, he became very angry.

Shortly after the murders had taken place a group of neighbors had met with Barrett and held detailed conversations with him about the whereabouts of his wife and stepson. The defense claimed that Barrett was suffering from hypnotism and auto hypnosis; that he had no actual memory of having done anything to his wife and stepson absent the suggestive information that had been planted in his mind when questioned by his neighbors. There were rumors and published reports during the trial of sightings in different states of Mrs. Barrett and her son. Barrett was found insane and was committed to a mental institution. The case was officially listed as an unsolved crime.

The last case that Rogers was known to try was during 1919

in defense of a young man who was charged with evading the draft in violation of federal law. He was charged along with a doctor and a nurse as part of a conspiracy. Each defendant had their own counsel, the boy's family retaining Rogers, whose alcoholism by that point in time was so severe that he was rendered virtually incapable of the further practice of law. With great effort Rogers was able to give one more passionate closing argument. His client was acquitted while the nurse and the doctor were convicted.

Rogers later had scrapes of his own with the law. A warrant had been sworn out for his arrest by his son, to try and have him committed to a sanitarium in connection with his abusive drinking problems. When he was approached by a police officer in 1920 in connection with the warrant, Rogers pulled out a gun and tried to shoot the officer. Fortunately for both the officer and for Rogers, the policeman had successfully placed his hand on the gun as Earl tried to shoot. In so doing the police officer's thumb was placed between the hammer and the bullet on Rogers' pistol, thus preventing the bullet's discharge. Had the officer not reacted as quickly as he had, Rogers may have been charged with murder. Of course, Rogers managed to have the attempted murder charges which were filed against him subsequently dropped.

Earl's daughter, Adela, in a last ditch effort to save her father, appeared in court to testify in order to have him committed to help deal with his alcoholism. According to Adela's account in *Final Verdict*, Earl approached her while she was on the witness stand to begin cross-examination. He walked up to Adela, kissed her on the check, and asked her if she really wanted to lock him up. Rogers then assisted his sobbing daughter off the witness stand and the judge dismissed the proceeding.

Earl Rogers won over seventy murder trials. He had achieved acquittal in some of the most celebrated cases of his day. He earned a king's ransom in legal fees, making the equivalent in today's dollars of millions of dollars per year in fees. In his era he was a bigger star and was better known than any stage or film actor. After the untimely death of his second wife in 1919, Earl lived in a drunken stupor and his health steadily declined until he died, penniless, in a Los Angeles boarding house in 1922 at the age of 52.

Epilogue

When Earl Rogers passed away while living in a Los Angeles flophouse, he was a broken-down, impoverished and hopeless alcoholic. However, he did leave behind a legacy as one of the greatest trial lawyers in the United States during the first half of the 20th Century.

During his downward spiral near the time of his death Earl had a conversation with his daughter Adela. A biography about Earl Rogers was published in 1934 entitled *"Take The Witness,"* which was written by Alfred Cohn and Joe Chisholm. In the Foreword to that book, Adela recounted the words told to her by her dad:

> It will not be long and you must let me go and hide away and live out these days as best I can. It is easier for me when I am alone for then sometimes I can forget. Forget what I have been, what I should be—and what I am.
>
> And when I am gone, which I pray may be soon, I don't want you to grieve, because all that is best of me will remain with you. The blessed gift of memory will keep me close to you. You will remember the times we have spent together; and your love for me, which has survived so much else, will survive death. You will lose nothing but this broken down, burned out shadow which has become a burden to us both.

Regarding her father's death, Adela wrote:

> So he prepared me for death as he prepared me for everything else in life. That very day standing shoulder to shoulder with him, his hand in mine to comfort me, I suffered the real pangs of parting and when at last his heart failed beneath the strain he had willfully put upon it, my grief had grown

strong in the conviction that I would never loose him. I never have.

Earl Rogers was a great and brilliant trial lawyer; a man who achieved great fame with scores of courtroom triumphs. Thousands and thousands of words had been written about his exploits and his courtroom activities were to become legendary among members of the bar for many years after he died in 1922. After his death, Adela wrote these words about her father:

> He had a touch of genius. And though perhaps we could not love him without pain, we could and did love him without reservation. Someone may question his preeminence as a lawyer. But no one can ever question that as a Dad he was supreme.

And so Earl Rogers left behind the greatest legacy a man could ever leave; the love and respect of a child. Is there really anything in life more precious?

CAST OF KEY CHARACTERS

William Alford: Charged with the first degree murder of Los
Angeles lawyer and socialite Jay E. Hunter. Mr. Hunter was
killed in 1899.

Horace Appel: A well-regarded Los Angeles trial lawyer, he
acted as co-counsel with Rogers in several cases including
the defense of Clarence Darrow.

Alfred Boyd: A twenty-year-old who was charged with the
first degree murder of W.A. Yeager after a card game at the
Metropole Hotel on Catalina Island.

William Broome: He was shot to death in Acton, California
after having a dispute with Norman M. Melrose.

Luther Brown: Brown for a good period of time was Rogers'
law partner and was co-counsel with Rogers on numerous
cases. Brown was known to be an excellent jury investigator. During the San Francisco Graft trials, he was indicted
in San Francisco for the alleged kidnapping of newspaper
editor Freemont Older. He was tried and acquitted of the
kidnapping charges in San Francisco.

Morris Buck: He was charged with the first degree murder
of Mrs. Charles Canfield who was shot to death on January 27, 1906. Earl Rogers acted as a special prosecutor in
the case; an unusual role for Rogers.

Paul Burke: He was an attorney and acted as co-counsel with
Rogers in the Alford murder case.

Patrick Calhoun: The grandson of John Calhoun, Patrick was
the president of United Railroad Company and was charged
with bribing San Francisco officials in connection with
obtaining the overhead trolley franchise. His trial took place
in 1909.

Mrs. Charles Canfield: She was a popular Los Angeles socialite, and the wife of wealthy businessman Charles Canfield, who was business partners with Edward L. Doheny. She was murdered by a former employee on January 27, 1906, when she declined the man's request to borrow money.

Joseph Choisser: A sixty-year-old businessman from the Midwest who was shot to death in his Los Angeles hotel room in 1903 by officers with the LAPD.

Louis Choisser: The son of Joseph Choisser, Louis was shot to death in his Los Angeles hotel in 1903 by officers with the LAPD.

Bert Cohen: A member of the Los Angeles police force who was charged with manslaughter in connection with the deaths in 1903 of Joseph and Louis Choisser.

Clarence Darrow: Considered to be the most famous and prominent attorney in the United States during the first half of this century, Darrow was retained to defend J.J. McNamara and his brother James McNamara in connection with the murder of twenty people who were in the *Los Angeles Times* building when it exploded and burned on October 1, 1910. The McNamaras were charged with planting sixteen sticks of dynamite in the alley behind the building with a timing devise which caused the explosion. During the McNamara trial, Darrow's chief investigator, Bert Franklin, was indicted for bribery of a juror and prospective juror in the McNamara case. Before Franklin's case went to trial, Darrow negotiated a plea bargain on behalf of the McNamara brothers. The Los Angeles District Attorney's office then indicted Darrow for juror bribery on January 28, 1912, and he was tried in connection with that indictment.

LeCompte Davis: Mr. Davis was a well-respected trial lawyer who acted as co-counsel with Earl Rogers on several cases. He also represented, for a short time, Bert Franklin, on charges of bribery of a juror(s).

Frank Dominguez: A well-regarded trial lawyer, he acted as Rogers' co-counsel in numerous cases, including the defense of Percy Tugwell for murder.

Joseph Ford: He was an excellent trial lawyer who opposed Earl Rogers in many trials when he was an assistant district attorney. When he quit the D.A.'s office he acted as Rogers' co-counsel in the defense of Police Chief Charles Sebastian.

Tiery Ford: Ford was the general counsel for United Railroad Company and was charged with bribery of San Francisco city officials in connection with the overhead trolley franchise. He was tried three times. His third trial ended on May 2, 1908.

Bert Franklin: Mr. Franklin was the chief investigator for Darrow's defense team in the McNamara case and was charged with the bribery of George Lockwood.

John Fredericks: He became the district attorney in the early 1900s and held that position until his election to Congress. He appeared as the prosecutor in numerous trials against Earl Rogers, including the Melrose murder trial and the bribery case against Clarence Darrow.

Henry T. Gage: A former California Governor and known as one of California's best trial lawyers, he acted as co-counsel with Rogers in the prosecution of Morris Buck, Mrs. Canfield's murderer; he was the special prosecutor of Griffith J. Griffith on the charge of the attempted murder of Mrs. Griffith, and he was retained by Clarence Darrow to defend Bert Franklin when Franklin was initially indicted.

H.L. "Jerry" Giesler: Starting off as a bag boy for Rogers, he went on to become a celebrated Los Angeles trial lawyer in his own right, defending many movie stars. He attended almost every trial Rogers was involved in from the San Francisco Graft cases to the defense of Clarence Darrow.

Colonel Griffith J. Griffith: Los Angeles land baron who acquired Rancho Los Feliz in the late 1800s, he donated land to the city which is now Griffith Park. He married wealthy Mary Agnes Christina Mesmer; known to her friends as Tina. The Colonel was charged with the attempted murder of his wife in connection with his shooting of her in 1903 in Santa Monica at the Arcadia Hotel.

W.A. Harris: He was an attorney and acted as co-counsel with Rogers in the Alford murder case.

James J. Hawley: A member of the Los Angeles police force, he was charged with manslaughter in connection with the deaths in 1903 of Joseph and Louis Choisser.

Francis Heney: He was the special prosecutor who was friendly with President Teddy Roosevelt. He successfully prosecuted grafters in the Oregon timberland, then came to San Francisco and prosecuted grafters there. He won the convictions of San Francisco Mayor Eugene Schmitz, political boss Abe Ruef, and Pacific States Telephone and Telegraph Chief, Louis Glass. He was responsible for negotiating immunity agreements with most members of the San Francisco Board of Supervisors in return for their testimony in the graft trials. During the second trial of political boss Abe Ruef, Heney was shot in head November 13, 1908 by Morris Haas. The shooting took place in the courtroom and Heney, by a miracle, survived the shooting. Morris Haas was found dead in his jail cell the next morning with a bullet wound in his head.

Jay E. Hunter: Mr. Hunter was killed during a dispute with William Alford in 1899 at the age of 34.

William P. James: The assistant district attorney, he prosecuted the case against policemen Bert Cohen, James J. Hawley, and J.W. Murphy in early 1904.

Bill Jory: He was Earl's trusted investigator who would often have the task of "sobering" Earl up just before a big trial.

Mrs. Maude Kennedy: She was murdered on August 31, 1914, allegedly by Percy Tugwell. Her son and Tugwell were friends and th e alleged motive for the murder was to get Mrs. Kennedy's diamonds.

H.A. Landon: He was killed during a fight with D.E. Mellus on a railroad car.

Oscar Lawler: He became the Assistant Attorney General of the United States. Prior to that he acted as co-counsel with Rogers in the Boyd murder trial, and was a federal prosecutor in connection with many cases including various dynamiting cases.

George Lockwood: He was the prospective juror who Darrow was charged with having bribed.

Billy McComas: McComas was charged with the first degree shooting murder of his mistress, Charlotte Noyes.

C.C. McComas: Mr. McComas was a Civil War veteran and an experienced and colorful trial lawyer for the district attorney's office. He opposed Rogers in numerous cases including the Mootry murder case, the Boyd murder case, and the Melrose murder case. He was also brought out of retirement by the D.A. to assist in the Darrow bribery case.

Congressman James McLachlan: He appeared as co-counsel with Rogers in the Melrose murder trial, but was largely window dressing.

D.E. Mellus: He was initially convicted of the murder of H.A. Landon and was represented by Earl Rogers during the retrial.

Norman M. Melrose: He was charged with the first degree murder of William Broome at Acton, California. He became a bodyguard and investigator for Earl Rogers and assisted him during the San Francisco Graft trials of Tiery Ford and Patrick Calhoun.

Mary Agnes Christina Mesmer: Known as Tina to her friends, she was the daughter of wealthy Louis Mesmer, owner of the United States Hotel in Los Angeles. She married Griffith J. Griffith on January 27, 1887, and was said to have holdings worth over $1,000,000 at the time of the wedding. She and Griffith had a son, Vandell, born August 29, 1888. She was shot in the face at close range by her husband at the Arcadia Hotel on September 3, 1903, and was permanently disfigured.

Charles Mootry: He was charged with first degree murder in connection with the shooting death of his wife Martha on September 15, 1899. He was called a "slimy pimp" by Earl Rogers after the trial was completed.

Martha Mootry: She was the wife of Charles Mootry and died on September 15, 1899, of a gunshot wound that was inflicted under peculiar circumstances.

J.W. Murphy: He was a member of the Los Angeles police force who was charged with manslaughter in connection with the deaths in 1903 of Joseph and Louis Choisser.

Charlotte Noyes: She was shot to death by her boyfriend Billy McComas in 1908. McComas claimed that she had just thrown sulfuric acid in his face prior to the shooting.

Lillian Pratt: Lillian Pratt was a married woman who had custody of her sister, Edith Serkin. She was indicted along with Charles Sebastian for contributing to the delinquency of a minor, her sister Edith Serkin.

James Rives: Mr. Rives was the district attorney in Los Angeles during the early 1900s and appeared opposite Earl Rogers on numerous trials including the Boyd murder trial.

Charles Sebastian: Sebastian was chief of police and was elected to be Mayor of Los Angeles. He was indicted for contributing to the delinquency of a minor; Miss Edith Serkin. He was accused of making love to his mistress in the minor's presence and of improper sexual relations with the minor herself.

Edith Serkin: An orphan, she had several sisters who wanted custody of her; and her sister Lillian Pratt was awarded legal custody. Miss Serkin alleged that Chief of Police Charles

Sebastian was having an affair with her sister Mrs. Pratt, and that the lovemaking sessions took place in a boarding house adjacent to the police station while she was present. She also alleged that the Chief had illegal sexual relations with her.

Percy Tugwell: Tugwell was convicted of the first degree murder of Mrs. Maude Kennedy and was almost killed when he was stabbed in the county jail by another inmate on May 25, 1915. He retained Earl Rogers to represent him in the re-trial of his case in 1916.

Stephen M. White: A former United States Senator, he was regarded as the best trial attorney in Los Angeles at the turn of the century. Earl Rogers was a student in his law offices when he studied to become a lawyer. White acted as the Special Prosecutor in the murder case against William Alford and lost at the hands of his former student, Earl Rogers. White was afflicted with alcoholism and died before he turned fifty years old.

Jess Willard: A six foot, seven inch tall boxer who became heavyweight champion of the world. He was charged with second degree murder in connection with his knockout of John "Bull" Young is a Los Angeles boxing match.

Thomas Woolwine: He succeeded John Fredericks as district attorney when was elected to the Congress. Mr. Woolwine was politically ambitious and was the prosecutor in the case against Police Chief Sebastian for contributing to the delinquency of a minor. He opposed Earl Rogers in this case in 1915.

W. A. Yeager, a.k.a. the "Louisville Sport": Mr. Yeager was a cardsharp who was killed at the Metropole Hotel on Catalina Island with two shots fired into his head.

John "Bull" Young: He was the unfortunate boxer who was killed in the ring in Vernon, California in 1913, after being hit with an uppercut thrown by Jess Willard in the ninth round of a bout scheduled for twenty rounds.

Index